Beyond Test Scores

Beyond Test Scores

A Better Way to Measure School Quality

JACK SCHNEIDER

Harvard University Press

Cambridge, Massachusetts, and London, England   2017

First printing

Library of Congress Cataloging-in-Publication Data

Names: Schneider, Jack (Writer on education), author.
Title: Beyond test scores : a better way to measure school quality /
Jack Schneider.
Description: Cambridge, Massachusetts : Harvard University Press,
[2017] | Includes bibliographical references and index.
Identifiers: LCCN 2017003844 | ISBN 9780674976399 (cloth)
Subjects: LCSH: Education—Aims and objectives—United States. |
Educational accountability—United States. | Educational tests and
measurements—United States. | Education and state—United States.
Classification: LCC LA217.2 .S34 2017 | DDC 370.11—dc23
LC record available at https://lccn.loc.gov/2017003844

FOR KATIE AND ANNABELLE

AND FOR DAVID TYACK

Contents

Beyond Test Scores

Introduction

THE IDEA that I would have to move was ridiculous, but that's what the numbers kept suggesting.

In the spring of 2013, the *Boston Globe* created an online tool called the Dreamtown Finder, which proposed to help people choose a place to live. The tool prompted users to rank values in six categories, and then produced a customized list of Massachusetts cities and towns— ostensibly ordered by fit. Naturally, one of the categories was schools.

Like many people, I rated the "schools" category as very important. I did the same for "fun," "location," and "housing cost." I enjoy living in a diverse neighborhood, so I toggled the "people like me" bar down. I was neutral on the remaining variable—"hipster."

The site told me to pack up my family and move—a quarter-mile west, into Cambridge. I clicked the "back" button, determined to stay in Somerville, where I currently reside and am quite happy. I altered my rankings, and resubmitted, but I couldn't make it work. That is, not until I dropped my concern with school quality down to zero.

The Somerville schools certainly aren't perfect. Parents, teachers, and principals all have wish lists and complaints. However, if you spend enough time in any school district in America, you will learn that every community has its own set of priorities and concerns. People care enough about education to want more from it.

Yet few people in Somerville seemed unhappy with the schools. Like Americans in general, residents of the city tend to express relatively high levels of confidence in the schools their children attend—a surprising fact given the doom-and-gloom rhetoric that dominates headlines about the nation's educational woes.[1] From what I could see, their general satisfaction seemed warranted. Still a relative newcomer to the city, I had yet to visit every school, but I did know several of them, and I had already begun to work closely with the school across the street from our house—a K–8 elementary school that my daughter now attends. We were also, at the time, preparing to enroll our daughter in the district's early childhood center—a diverse school with what seemed to us a solid mix of traits. The faculty was warm and caring, children seemed happy, the building was well kept and decorated with student artwork, and students appeared engaged in activity as we walked through on a tour.

Of course, judging a school from the outside is incredibly difficult. In lieu of decent information, parents often rely on imperfect measures of quality—a new computer lab, for instance, an array of impressive-sounding classes, or a list of prestigious colleges attended by graduates. No one knows this better than the leaders of private schools, which must sell their clients on the idea that education—free to all children in the United States—should actually come with a hefty price tag. Go on a private school tour, and you will see lots of bells and whistles, but you will learn less than you imagine about what your child's actual experience at that school will be.

My wife is a teacher and the daughter of a retired administrator. I am a former high school teacher who left the classroom to become a professor of education; much of my research is in school quality. As such, we thought of ourselves as relatively savvy. Still, we wondered: Why would anyone think the Somerville schools are bad?

There were a few reasons.

Most obviously, the district's raw standardized test scores were relatively low.[2] That, certainly, could be explained. The district serves a very diverse range of students who come from a wide variety of economic, racial, and ethnic backgrounds—many from low-income and minority families. As an extensive body of research indicates, there is a strong connection between family background and standardized test scores, so it made sense that anyone who saw test scores as an indicator of school quality might be misled about the quality of Somerville's schools.[3]

Many parents also tend to use race as a proxy for school quality. Knowing that students of color have long been denied equal educational opportunities, middle-class white parents often shy away from schools with large concentrations of black and brown students.[4] In so doing, they exacerbate segregation, take their high levels of capital elsewhere, and ensure that people like them continue to avoid schools with large populations of color.

I hoped that the *Globe* wasn't using raw test scores to measure school quality, and though I was relatively certain they weren't using race as a variable, I was curious enough that I dug into the methodology.

As it turned out, schools were being ranked by SAT scores and teacher-student ratios. The former, as research has borne out, is more strongly correlated with socioeconomic status than it is with college performance.[5] In response, some colleges are dropping the requirement that prospective students sit for the test.[6] The latter measure, beyond being generally misleading—it counts the number of adults in the building rather than the average class size—is often not meaningfully different across schools. Consequently, it can lead to perceived differences where there may be none.

These were bad measures of school quality. But I wasn't particularly surprised. Most available measures of school quality are weak, and user-friendly data interpreted by third parties tend to be even weaker.

I wasn't in a position to offer much more than criticism. Nevertheless, I began using my newly minted Twitter account to go after the *Globe*. "Tools like this," I tweeted, "could be powerful if the methodology weren't so simplistic." I included the link to the *Globe* website.

It wasn't much in terms of public engagement. But to my surprise, it led to several interesting conversations, and eventually produced a response from the designer of the tool, who contacted me directly. His question, in essence, was a challenge: Do you think you can do better?

Two weeks later we were sitting in my office at the College of the Holy Cross, a small liberal arts college forty miles west of Boston. I suggested a few measures I thought were better gauges of school quality, as well as some ways of adjusting for the different kinds of populations various schools work with. We looked at the statewide data available to us, and though they were limited, we agreed that we could certainly do better than what had been included in the Dreamtown Finder.

Using educational research to inform our decisions, we picked several measures that captured more about school quality. And recognizing the fact that rating schools is an inherently subjective enterprise, we designed a model that allowed parents to customize rankings based on personal values—values that, in our version of the tool, included academic growth, school resources, college readiness, school culture, and diversity. Rather than assume a single vision of a good school, our tool asked users to distribute an allotment of one hundred points, in five-point increments, according to their own personal values. Thus, a parent who values the diversity of the student population and also wants to assure that his child will be college-ready at the end of high school could weight these two variables more heavily than the others. Alternatively, a parent concerned first and foremost about academic growth could allocate all of her points to that category.

The tool had some strengths, perhaps chief among them its user-friendliness. We labeled variables using accessible terminology and offered brief descriptions of our measures. Although in several cases we used aggregate variables to simplify user interpretation, each variable was accompanied by a brief description of its importance and the methodology for measurement. For those interested, a much longer rationale, including research citations, was provided on a separate linked page. In short, if people wanted to use the page to learn about educational data, they could. We were proud of that.

The second great strength of our tool was its multivariate nature. Though still new in education, balanced scorecards are commonplace in the field of performance management.[7] And for good reason. In any complex enterprise, goals will be multiple and will not always overlap; and education is an extremely complex enterprise. States and districts have increasingly come to recognize this fact over the past few years, and in the future the balanced scorecard will be standard in education as well. However, it seemed important to us to send a message, loudly and clearly, that there are many ways to measure school quality.

Our tool's third strength was that it allowed users to personalize their weightings—and hence their rankings—thereby avoiding a single, rank-ordered list of schools and any commensurate stigmatization. To put it another way, because you might rate some aspects more highly than I do, your list of "top schools" will look different from my list. That's a good thing, first, because it disrupts the message that there is a clear hierarchy of schools, and second, because a "good" school is often good for a particular family with a particular set of values. Being able to tailor measures of school quality to those values is important in challenging the notion that there is one single model of a successful school. As I continue to believe, supporting this diversity of values and needs is an essential asset of any school system interested in serving a broad and diverse constituency.

In sum, our tool, which the *Globe* called the Dreamschool Finder, sent several important messages: that a lot goes into creating a good school, that test scores reflect only a fraction of what we want schools to do, and that not all people want the very same things in the very same amounts. It also opened the door to the possibility that we could celebrate schools for their different strengths—allowing users to view schools through the lens of "fit" rather than through a mono-modal lens of "one best school." Our tool also provided more easy-to-digest information that, we hoped, would drive high-quality decision making—among parents, community members, and educators.

Still, it was far from perfect.

First, we were severely limited by the data available. Relying on the state for our measures, we were forced to use imperfect proxies for a number of categories. Thus, despite our focus on moving *beyond* standardized test scores, we still relied heavily on scores from the Massachusetts state standardized test—the MCAS—for indicators of learning. Additionally, for dozens of important variables there were simply no data, and we lacked the resources to collect those data ourselves. We had to pretend that factors such as how safe students feel, or how strong student-teacher relationships are, didn't matter, even though we knew that they did.

Second, our data were produced from measures implemented *at most* twice yearly. Student attitudes, knowledge, and behavior change daily. Teachers have good days and bad days, and schools themselves transform over time. Yet current data collection procedures capture only single moments in time. In an ideal world, we would want to figure out how to capture multiple snapshots across the school year—in order to produce more accurate data, as well as to produce a picture of change over time.

Third, our categories for school quality were educated guesses at best. To produce a truly effective measure of school quality, we would have needed to determine the full range of outcomes valued by parents, educators, and the public. Lacking the necessary time and resources to do that, we relied on our existing knowledge. If we were to do the job really well, we would not only want to study polling data but also to conduct some of our own research—through polling, surveying, and focus groups.

Imperfect though the tool was, however, it did generate some interesting conversations.

First, it challenged conventional thinking about school quality. If you placed equal weights on all of the variables for high schools in Massachusetts, for instance, Somerville High came in at number fifteen. To some people, this was a shock. When the *Globe* released the results of the 2013 MCAS test, Somerville High ranked 271st out of 354 schools in English and 262nd in math. But that, of course, was based on raw test scores—unadjusted for any student background variables—which often reflect more about family income and parental education than they do about school quality. Suddenly people were forced to confront the possibility that schools they knew to be "bad" might turn out to be otherwise. Alternatively, many schools assumed to be "good" because of their high test scores might actually have some things to work on.

Second, it led to conversations about how to improve the tool. I readily acknowledged the limits of the Dreamschool Finder and was content to have tinkered around the margins. What I didn't expect, however, was that I would be asked repeatedly how to make it better.

Although I initially brushed that question aside, I found myself thinking more and more about it. What if we could collect data on anything? What would we go after?

Those conversations eventually led to meetings with Somerville mayor Joe Curtatone and then-superintendent Tony Pierantozzi. Joe had just started his sixth term as mayor of what the *Boston Globe Magazine* called the best-run city in Massachusetts. He had already secured several new subway stops for the city, brokered some smart development projects, established Somerville as a home to the arts, and strengthened an already very livable city; but he wanted to do more to support education than just increase the size of the budget. Tony was approaching what would be his last full year as superintendent, having managed the city's schools for nearly a decade. Both were willing to experiment, as was Tony's successor, Mary Skipper. All felt that the schools were on the verge of something special, and all of them felt that existing test scores failed to capture the real quality of education in the city. As Tony put it, "We're better than the data."

The idea was to collect more information about the performance of Somerville public schools, but it soon became clear to all of us that a better data system would do more than collect and disseminate new information. It would be a challenge to the existing test-based accountability system.

For years, parents and educators have been pushing back against the singular focus on standardized test scores in measuring school quality. Each time, however, they have been met by the same reply: "What do you propose to do instead?" After all, stakeholders in public education are desperate for information. How can policy leaders govern—in an already massive and complex system—if they don't have measures of success in their tool kits? How can parents advocate for their children? How can communities and their allies advocate for the vulnerable? As Tony Pierantozzi observed, the emphasis on data collection, problematic though it may be, was a response to a "pretty miserable track-record of dealing with poor students, minority students, and English language learners . . . it was embarrassing."

Efforts to measure schools, in short, were not going to go away, but it seemed undeniable that test-based measurement was having a troubling impact on schools. Consider, for instance, how states use test scores to hold schools accountable. In most states, schools are responsible for raising the test scores of all students across a variety of demographic subgroups. If they do not, the state intervenes by imposing sanctions, penalties, and eventually school shutdowns. Yet, because students from low-income and minority families are likely to score lower on standardized tests, their schools are far more likely to be stigmatized by state intervention, or closed down, regardless of almost every other aspect of school performance. Such stigmas and penalties create churn in school staff, as teachers flee or are fired. They drive away parents with options. And they send a message to students that they are on a dead-end track.[8]

State accountability measures also have a second problematic impact. Because schools are held accountable for a narrow set of scores— generally on math and reading tests in grades three through eight, as well as one year of high school—school leaders have responded rationally: by narrowing the curriculum. Arts, history, science, health, and other aspects of a diverse curriculum have been cut back dramatically. Emphasis on test-aligned math and English instruction has been ratcheted up. Furthermore, even teachers outside those content areas have been asked to focus on them as much as possible. As a result, teachers are increasingly unhappy with their profession, and many are deciding to leave. Responding to a 2012 MetLife survey, only 39 percent of teachers indicated that they were "very satisfied" with their jobs.[9]

Students are unhappy, too. They are bombarded with benchmark tests, practice tests, diagnostic tests, and the high-stakes tests themselves—and all for what? For many, school feels increasingly ir-relevant and uninspiring. New evidence also suggests that upswings in test scores, though they may be associated with greater acquisition of content knowledge, may not be associated with cognitive growth.[10]

To be fair, states have tried to improve the way they measure school quality. Prompted by the Every Student Succeeds Act—the successor to the much-reviled No Child Left Behind law—many states have incorporated measures of "nonacademic factors" into their account-ability systems. In Massachusetts, for instance, the Department of El-ementary and Secondary Education (ESE) generated a list of several dozen indicators "suggested by external stakeholders and ESE staff" that might help round out the state's picture of K–12 schools.[11] Nev-ertheless, test scores remain the coin of the realm for the state. By extension, test scores continue to play an outsized role in how parents and the public think about schools.

All of this means that districts—and particularly urban districts like Somerville, which often have lower raw standardized test scores because of their demographic makeup—should be seeking to build better measures that more fairly capture academic performance, and more fully reflect the range of qualities that characterize good schools.

Our project, consequently, had the potential not merely to overhaul how schools are measured in Somerville but also to stand as a model for other districts. It might be a response to the question "What do you propose to do instead?"

In the intervening months, I began thinking more about the project, and particularly about who might help us tackle the first step—building a new framework for evaluating school quality. One person who jumped to mind was Rebecca Jacobsen, a professor at Michigan State University and an expert on how the public values ed-ucation. Along with Richard Rothstein and Tamara Wilder, she had written a book about what better measures of school quality might look like—*Grading Education: Getting Accountability Right*—and had conducted research into how data on school quality are presented to parents. Rebecca expressed a strong interest in the project, and we soon began reviewing polling data on what Americans want their schools to do.

I also began looking for a survey design expert. After all, if we were going to build a new framework for measuring school quality, we would also need to build new *measures* of school quality. Once we reviewed the available data in Massachusetts, Rebecca and I discovered that data on most of what we needed to know were not currently being collected. In fact, we reviewed the available data across all fifty states and found that no state was gathering the full range of information we wanted. Even if we chose to draw on existing survey scales, we would want someone to thoughtfully guide us through that process. Hunter Gehlbach—a survey design expert then at Harvard University, who had recently accepted a position at Panorama Education—indicated an interest in helping.[12]

As the project took life, I wondered if Somerville was still the right place for it. The city obviously appealed to me because it's where I live and where my daughter goes to school. We also had strong civic support there—support that might have been difficult to generate elsewhere, given how untested our work was.[13] But perhaps we were making the convenient choice rather than the best choice.

Nevertheless, Somerville remained highly appealing as a research site. Perhaps the chief argument in its favor was its diversity. Somerville is one of the most diverse cities in the United States, with more than fifty languages spoken in the public schools. Forty percent of students are Hispanic, 35 percent white, 11 percent African American, and 9 percent Asian.[14] Half of the students in the city are from non-English-speaking homes. Sixty-seven percent are designated as low-income. Twenty-one percent have disabilities. These figures more or less match the demography of our nation's schools. Nationwide, roughly 50 percent of students are low-income and 12 percent are classified as Special Education students. Half are white, a quarter are Hispanic, 15 percent are African American, and 5 percent are Asian—figures that, according to projections, will grow to look more like Somerville over the next decade. According to the National Center for Education Statistics, by 2023, 45 percent of public school students will be white, 30 percent Hispanic, 15 percent African American, and 5 percent Asian.[15] In short, the city seemed like a highly reasonable test case.[16]

The second reason Somerville stood out was because of its size. Despite being the densest city in New England and one of the twenty most densely populated cities in the United States, Somerville is also quite small. There are only 75,000 residents, eleven schools, and 5,000 students in the city. That would make it possible to pilot our project across the entire district despite our being a small team. We would also be able to get major stakeholder involvement because the district's size would allow us to cultivate face-to-face relationships.[17]

Three years into this work, we have erected what I believe to be a formidable challenge to the test-based accountability system that dominates public education. Our model measures school quality far more holistically than any state system currently does, collecting roughly three dozen separate measurements, including a performance assessment of student knowledge and skills. We have developed a data visualization tool that offers more useful information and a more accurate picture of school quality than any existing state database. And, with support from the state legislature, we have assembled a group of districts—the Massachusetts Consortium for Innovative Education Assessment—that continues to push this work forward.

This book tells our story.

It is important to note, however, that this book is not merely a case study of one district. Rather, it uses my team's work in Somerville to tell a larger story about how we think about school quality in the United States. All of us have ideas about what constitutes a good school. All of us have taken standardized tests. All of us care about school quality. And all of us have something to learn by thinking more deeply about how to assess the work of schools. Consequently, while the book draws substantially upon on-the-ground research in Somerville, it is designed for a national audience—of parents, educators, policymakers, and the public—interested in thinking through our current approach to educational data.

One way this book can be read is as background for better decision making. If we could value schools for the many things they do, we might reject the notion that there is a single "best school" out there to compete over. We might give up the pursuit of policies that diminish the mission of schools. We might stop ignoring a range of factors that are critical to school success. We might provide some relief to our most vulnerable schools—from the attacks that have magnified their burdens over the past two decades.

A second way the book can be read is as a field guide for improving the way we measure school quality. For those interested in more fairly and more comprehensively gauging educational effectiveness, this book will offer relevant information, instruments, and methodologies—a tool kit for parents, teachers, administrators, and policy leaders seeking to take concrete action.

We don't have all the answers. Our project, in many ways, is in its infancy, and each day we learn more about how to do this work the right way.

But this is also a matter of great urgency. We have two decades of evidence that current approaches to educational measurement are insufficient and irresponsible. Each day that we fail to act, we ignore the fact that we can do so much better.

1

Wrong Answer: Standardized Tests and Their Limitations

IN 2014, 59 percent of students in Somerville public schools scored proficient or higher on the English Language Arts section of the Massachusetts Comprehensive Assessment System (MCAS).[1] Forty-eight percent were proficient or advanced on the math section.

Is that good or bad?

The numbers might be fine. But what about when we look at those numbers relative to the statewide average? Sixty-nine percent of students in Massachusetts scored proficient or higher on the English Language Arts section, and 60 percent scored at those levels on the Mathematics section.

Does that mean Somerville schools are academically underperforming? When Somerville's scores are compared with those for the state as a whole, that appears to be the case, so perhaps those numbers aren't as good as they seem at first glance.

What does proficiency measure, though? How was that cutoff point arrived at? Are students scoring below "proficient" unable to read and compute? Are they inches—or miles—behind their higher-scoring peers?

And how can the influence of school quality be separated out? After all, factors such as family income and parental educational attainment are strong predictors of standardized test scores.[2] That being the case, how much responsibility does the school bear for the test scores of its students?

The answer to this last question can be incredibly difficult to sort out. A school populated by students with well-educated and affluent parents will produce much higher test scores even if it does a mediocre job of educating them. Should the school get credit for the high test scores of students who entered with higher levels of academic preparedness?

And wouldn't that logic apply to schools working with students who enter school with *lower* scores? Should schools be punished for working with students who arrive with lower levels of preparedness but who receive an excellent education? This is not to say that we should accept unequal outcomes for students from less privileged backgrounds. It does, however, raise questions about what is realistic. It also raises questions about how much we can rely on test scores to gauge the quality of a school's educational program.

Two-thirds of students in Massachusetts are white; one-third of them are members of racial minorities. In Somerville, the reverse is true. Statewide, 18 percent of students speak a language other than English as their first language. In Somerville, that figure is nearly three times larger: 50 percent. And the rate of economic disadvantage in Somerville—36 percent—is ten points higher than it is in the rest of the state.

All of this means that, statistically speaking, we should expect to see much lower test scores in Somerville. Again, we should not establish lower expectations for low-income students, students of color, and nonnative speakers of English. But we should probably recognize that even if their scores are lower than those of their more privileged peers, their schools may be doing a good job. Blaming the schools, particularly when they may be the only social institution holding up their end of the bargain for these young people, seems counterproductive.

If we account for the student body, then, perhaps Somerville schools are doing incredibly well. Students who begin their academic careers at a disadvantage make up significant ground, at least insofar as academic ability is measured by those tests. Those who enter school with no significant disadvantages appear to do as well as students anywhere.

Of course, even if we look at the scores of various subgroups—across race, income, language, gender—we are still only looking at test scores. And what do those actually measure?

What the Tests Measure

Critics of testing sometimes make the case that standardized tests are not accurate measures of student learning. Although they aren't entirely wrong, this is an overstatement of the truth. Generally speaking, if a student scores below "proficient" on a measure of grade-level math or reading, that student is not thriving academically. This may not be the school's fault—the student may have arrived several grade levels behind his or her peers. Nevertheless, it is useful information for educators and policymakers as they seek to track student progress and allocate resources.[3]

Still, standardized tests are quite limited in what they can tell us about student ability. Consider a story from the educational psychologist Lee Shulman, recalling his own education:

> When I was an undergraduate at the University of Chicago in the
> late 1950s, I attempted to cram for the end-of-year comprehensive

examination in the history of western civilization—a nine-hour multiple-choice and essay test. I thought I had done quite well on the exam and was thus shocked to receive a "C" for the course. I asked to meet with a member of the Evaluation Office to learn why I had performed so poorly. We sat down and examined my performance, using Bloom's taxonomy as a template. I had "aced" the multiple-choice section, with its emphasis on recall; cramming can be a pretty good strategy for remembering facts and ideas, at least over the short term. But I had simply not studied well enough to integrate the ideas and to be able to synthesize new interpretations and arguments using the knowledge I had crammed into my head.[4]

If the evaluation of Lee Shulman's knowledge had been limited to what could be measured by a multiple-choice test, he would have appeared to be a highly accomplished student of history. What was revealed instead, however, was far more complex. He may have known the facts of history, but he hadn't learned to use them in the service of new ideas or to solve novel problems. Only something far more complex than a multiple-choice test—a series of essays, graded by human beings—could determine that.

Machine-scored multiple-choice questions are the main tool we use to measure learning in K–12 public schools. Why? Because they are cost-effective and easy to standardize. But they place far too much emphasis on memorization, and far too little on complex cognitive processes like problem solving. In fact, they tell us very little about what is going on inside students' minds.[5]

Consider a sample reading comprehension passage from the fourth-grade California English Language Arts test:

Long ago, when the world was new, Beaver had a long, thin tail. He loved to dive, but his long tail didn't help him get to the bottom of the pond fast enough. He couldn't use his tail to slap the mud into place when he built a dam. One day, Muskrat swam by. Beaver noticed Muskrat's broad, flat tail. He realized it would be perfect for diving and building dams. At the same time, Muskrat gazed enviously at Beaver's tail. Muskrat loved to swim fast, and his broad, flat tail dragged in the water and slowed him down. He thought it would be better to have Beaver's tail. So Muskrat said, "Beaver, I would do anything to have a tail like yours." "Is that so?" replied Beaver. "I was just admiring your tail. Why don't we trade?" Muskrat eagerly agreed, and they exchanged tails right then and there.

If a student cannot answer basic questions about the content of this passage, he or she is likely not a strong reader. Still, a student who answers comprehension questions correctly does not necessarily possess all of the skills and habits of mind we might wish to cultivate. What are the characteristics of a strong reader? Speed? The ability to pick up on tone and nuance? Attention to authorial style and word choice? None of this is measured by the test.[6] Instead, the answer bank presents four options:

What is the main event in "The Tail Trade"?
a) Beaver builds a dam with his tail.
b) Muskrat and Beaver exchange tails.
c) Muskrat and Beaver try out their new tails.
d) Beaver slaps his tail to warn of danger.

A student who cannot answer "b" is struggling, but beyond that, the question doesn't tell us much about the things that matter most—fluency, interpretive skills, analytical ability, or precision. Nor can the question help us to diagnose what a student needs in terms of instruction.

It is also worth noting here that even a question as seemingly straightforward as this one is not necessarily fair for all students. A student whose first language is not English, or who for some other reason has a limited vocabulary, may struggle to distinguish between "b" and "c" despite being a perfectly good reader. If he or she is unfamiliar with the word "exchange," that student will face a coin flip situation and have to guess.

Test questions, of course, can be much worse than those in this example. Several years ago in Massachusetts, a question on the state exam prompted elementary-level students to write a fictional story about a mysterious "trunk" they had stumbled upon. Naturally, as former Somerville superintendent Tony Pierantozzi recalled, "we had English language learners writing about elephants, cars, and swimsuits." The state's intention was for students to describe what would be in a box.

"That wasn't as bad as a question I remember from my own schooling experiences," Pierantozzi added. "It was an analogy: Caesar is to salad as yacht is to . . . what? The answer was boat. But I had no idea what a yacht was." Tony's experience was not exceptional. Research by scholars such as E. D. Hirsh makes a powerful case for the relationship between content knowledge and reading comprehension, and when it comes to reading passages on standardized tests, the inclusion of particular content can skew results dramatically. Largely, it is skewed in favor of white native English speakers from middle- and upper-income households.

Standardized tests favor culturally dominant students in other ways as well. The tests, for instance, are written in standard English, which is often not the English encountered by low-income and minority students at home. As a result, while some students may know how to read and write as well as their more privileged peers, they may be less familiar with particular phrasing. Or they may select phrasing that, though perfectly acceptable in their neighborhoods, reads as "wrong" on a test. Relatedly, test writers often assume that students are familiar with objects such as saucers or hampers that, though common in many homes, are not present in all of them, or that go by different names in different places. Or, perhaps even more unfortunately a student may respond with a right answer but still be marked wrong because it is not the *best* answer—the one the test publisher is looking for.[7]

Much of this, of course, is accidental—a product of test writers' crafting a product with a generic audience in mind. But some practices are glaringly problematic. When test items are measured for their psychometric properties—how well they measure what they are trying to assess—the items on which lower-scoring groups end up scoring higher are usually dropped from the test. In other words, if the kids who score worse—generally low-income kids and students of color—actually score *better* on a question, that question often gets cut from the test. The reason for this is that such outcomes do not align with results from the test as a whole. Consequently, those questions are viewed as aberrations in need of "smoothing." It is also worth mentioning here that many questions are never included in tests because too many students would answer them correctly. The test, after all, wouldn't be useful if everyone aced it. Yet this approach to design certainly distorts the picture of student achievement—sending a message that students know less than they actually do.[8]

Some problems with standardized tests don't have anything to do with the kinds of questions that get asked on them. For instance, we conduct examinations in a manner that requires students to sit for a prolonged period of time in silence—a format that squares more with the backgrounds and experiences of some students than others and has little in common with the world of work for which they are being prepared. While there may be some benefit to the skill of sitting quietly to focus on a test, that skill is separate from one's ability to read, write, and compute. Nevertheless, the ability to sit still does translate to higher test scores.[9]

Relatedly, cultural conceptions of young people, shaped by factors like race and class, can also affect test scores. A substantial body of research, for instance, indicates that students from minority backgrounds tend to experience "stereotype threat" when sitting for exams—fulfilling the high or low expectations that have been set for them. African American students, for instance, score lower when they feel that a test is a measure of their intelligence and when they worry that their performance will be viewed through the lens of racial stereotypes. Conversely, students who are stereotypically depicted as high achievers—particularly Asian American students—score higher in such situations. As surprising as it might sound, this phenomenon has been confirmed repeatedly by experts.[10]

Perhaps most significantly, there is the fact that tests often tell us more about student home lives than about schools. The two top predictors of student standardized test scores tend to be parental education and family income. Why? Not because higher-income families headed by college graduates can buy more books, which they certainly can, or afford tutors, though they can do that as well. Instead, the most significant impact of those factors seems to be an indirect one. From birth, families pass on to children a set of values and beliefs about the importance of school—signaling what is desirable and setting expectations about academic achievement. Parents with high levels of educational attainment and success communicate a particular worldview to their children, setting standards not only through their words but also through their actions.[11]

Especially before the start of formal schooling, families are also the primary teachers for children. In those early years, much of a child's cognitive development depends on the interactions he or she has with family members. Families from more privileged backgrounds, and who have resources at their disposal, tend to engage in more verbal interaction with children, provide more cognitive stimulation, promote particular kinds of learning strategies, and establish stimulating environments. Love, of course, matters a great deal, and no particular demographic group loves children more than any other. But when it comes to educational achievement, privilege matters tremendously. For quantitativeevidence of this fact, one need only count the words children hear in different settings. As one longitudinal study found, by age three, children from more privileged families hear thirty million more words than their less privileged peers.[12] No wonder that when it comes time to take standardized tests their scores are so much higher.

All of this makes testing problematic across racial, ethnic, linguistic, and cultural dimensions As a result, we have many reasons to question how much standardized test scores are telling us—especially when we recognize what the tests are *not* measuring.[13]

Take the case of Jones Elementary in Arkansas, which earned a D rating from the state for its student standardized test scores. This reflects the population of the school, where 98 percent of students are from low-income households and 80 percent are English language learners. Yet the school has been recognized by the U.S. Department of Education for academic growth, faculty collaboration, its school-based community health clinic, and, somewhat ironically, its effective use of data. The school has also initiated a home library program and a "parent university" program to help offset the effects of demography. In short, it is doing a tremendous amount to support the young people in its care.[14]

How, then, can we even pretend to determine a school's quality by looking only at its test scores?

Imagine that we have done a kind of calculus and concluded that, given the school's population, it is doing well according to the tests. Imagine that we have figured out what those tests tell us about the basic academic competencies of students, and imagine that we maintain a healthy skepticism about all of it. This would be quite an accomplishment. We would nevertheless have to ask: How complete is our picture of the school?

Remember: the tests used to measure school quality tend to assess only the domains of English Language Arts (or, as previous generations knew it, English) and Mathematics. Thus, while we have performance data for student work in those two subjects—limited data, at that—we lack such data for other areas. In addition, those tests tend to be given only in grades three through eight and once in high school—a highly incomplete picture, indeed.

One option, if we wanted to solve this problem, would be to expand testing.[15] Examining students in all subject areas, and at all grade levels, though, would take an inordinate amount of time—doubling or even tripling current commitments to testing. Imagine how exciting this prospect would be for the average student, who already may think school is a pencil-dulling drag. More disturbingly, consider the opportunity cost of testing: while testing is happening, no new learning can take place.

Additionally, there is the problem that not all school subjects are conducive to standardized testing. It is foolish to test a student's ability to think like a historian by asking multiple-choice questions. Historians, after all, don't sit around reciting facts; instead, they try to solve puzzles by weaving together fragments of evidence. For subjects such as art and music, the prospect of gauging ability through multiple-choice tests is even more absurd.

Yet even if we possessed student test score data for all subject areas, we still wouldn't have a complete picture of the schools.

We would have no data about how happy students are or how challenged they feel.

We would have no data indicating how safe they are in the hallways or how cared for they are by the adults in the school.

We would have no data on how creative they are or how hard they're working.

We would have no data on how healthy they are—physically, socially, or emotionally.

We would have no data on how many of them can play a musical instrument or program a computer or design an experiment.

In short, we would have no real picture of what life inside a particular school is like, and isn't that what we really care about?

The harshest critics are wrong that standardized tests are worthless. Tests tell us something basic about student achievement, and that information can be critical in advocating for additional resources and supports.

But critics of testing are right about a great deal else. Standardized tests are limited in what they reveal and are not entirely fair across racial, ethnic, and economic lines. They take up too much instructional time and overlook most of what we value in schools. Relying on test scores as a measure of school quality, it seems, is a fool's errand.

How Did We Get Here? A Brief History of Testing

If standardized tests are so limited, why do we use them?

As with many conventions in education—grouping children by age, closing school during the summer, assigning A–F letter grades for student work—history plays a significant role. We accept these things because they are standard, routine, familiar. Such features are so conventional as to go unremarked upon—noticed more when they are absent than when they are present.[16]

Standardized testing is cheaper than many alternatives. But we accept it because it has long been the norm. Sure, it may be odd to gauge student knowledge through a series of test-bubbles darkened by number two pencils. But testing is a fundamental part of education in the United States. It has been for generations.

All traditions have origins, though, and understanding those origins can help us cultivate a critical perspective toward what we might otherwise simply accept. This is no less true of standardized testing.[17]

At the end of the nineteenth century, educational policymakers sought to build stronger systems of governance as well as to make education more scientific—mimicking their colleagues in medicine. Having succeeded in creating a system of public schools during the previous generation, they were anxious to establish mechanisms that would give them more direct governance over those schools. In other words, it was not enough to have created statewide networks of schools that would be free and open to all children. They also wanted to control what was going on inside those schools.

State and municipal policy leaders in the period after the Civil War were particularly interested in asserting control over school principals, who had long operated with very high levels of autonomy and who tended to possess more power than administrators higher up in the system. To wrest this power from principals, experts and policymakers needed some mechanism for setting educational goals, tracking school progress, and casting judgment. Yet the bulk of their information about school progress came from these same principals. Standardized tests, then, promised to shift the balance of power—giving policy leaders a yardstick for measuring school performance and making centralized governance feasible. The practice quickly spread.[18]

The first standardized tests included short essays in the mix of questions. Over time, however, writing prompts were replaced by straightforward questions of fact. After all, it is far easier to measure whether a student knows who wrote the Gettysburg Address than to measure his or her ability to think critically about the speech. It is even easier to score questions that eliminate student writing entirely, and multiple-choice questions, developed in the early twentieth century, did just that. By asking students simply to circle correct answers, they eliminated the possibility of human subjectivity in scoring.

A great deal of excitement surrounded such advances in standardized tests. Even in the early years of testing, though, there were critics. A math department leader complained in 1927 that it was "quite possible to drill for an examination and to pass a large number of pupils with high ratings without giving any breadth of outlook or grasp of underlying principles."[19] And Henry Linville, the president of the New York teachers' union, in 1930 observed that the state's overemphasis on testing "indicates a frightful standardization of curriculum, of methods and of objectives."[20]

Perhaps the strongest pushback against standardized tests, at least prior to the twenty-first century, came in the late 1930s from the Educational Policies Commission (EPC). Formed by the National Education Association and the American Association of School Administrators, the EPC sought to pinpoint the features of American schools worth fighting for—in the wake of economic depression, and on the edge of another great war. In 1938 the EPC released *The Purposes of Education in American Democracy,* in which the group concluded that "most of the standardized testing instruments" used in schools had failed to address "the development of attitudes, interests, ideals, and habits." Instead, the tests focused "exclusively on the acquisition and retention of information." In the broader picture, that seemed to them "relatively unimportant."[21]

What the members of the commission wanted to see instead was a broader set of measurements that aligned with the facets of the American educational system valued by a democratic people. As they wrote:

Measuring the results of education must be increasingly concerned with such questions as these: Are the children growing in their ability to work together for a common end? Do they show greater skill in collecting and weighing evidence? Are they learning to be fair and tolerant in situations where conflicts arise? Are they sympathetic in the presence of suffering and indignant in the presence of injustice? Do they show greater concern about questions of civic, social, and economic importance? Are they using their spending money wisely? Are they becoming more skillful in doing some useful type of work? Are they more honest, more reliable, more temperate, more humane? Are they finding happiness in their present family life? Are they living in accordance with the rules of health? Are they acquiring skills in using all of the fundamental tools of learning? Are they curious about the natural world around them? Do they appreciate, each to the fullest degree possible, their rich inheritance in art, literature, and music? Do they balk at being led around by their prejudices?[22]

Without a doubt, these are all critical questions. But no tools existed to easily, inexpensively, and systematically address them. One can imagine policymakers nodding in agreement and then asking, frankly, "How on earth would you go about measuring these?" Projects like the Progressive Education Association's "Eight-Year Study" were designed to bring a degree of balance to assessment in American classrooms.[23] Ultimately, however, the ease and efficiency of standardized tests were too much to overcome, particularly in the late 1930s, when the first automatic test-scoring machines—including the one patented by IBM in 1937—became available.

Tests also served a variety of other purposes that made them seem indispensable. Perhaps chief among those purposes was structuring educational meritocracy.[24] Of course, American schooling has never been truly meritocratic; one need only examine the strong correlation between income and achievement to understand this fact. But unlike in other nations, where educational opportunity was limited to those of means, the American educational system was founded on the premise that it would serve as a "great equalizer." Open to most students and funded by tax dollars rather than by tuition, the schools would provide upward mobility to the poor and, in so doing, benefit those individuals and society as a whole.[25] Yet such a vision required a mechanism for reaching across schools and districts to identify top achievers. As one 1916 observer wrote, "Fairness in the award of honors, justice in determining failures and dismissals, and incitement of the student to better work can be attained only to the extent to which a common standard for the awarding of marks is understood, accepted, and acted upon."[26] How could such a common standard exist, though, without a common test?

Desperate for a fair way to identify the best and brightest students, many policymakers saw standardized testing as an important technology: a clear and seemingly unbiased way of comparing students against each other. As the author of a 1922 textbook wrote, "When such scores are represented by a simple graph, say with one line showing the given pupil's attainment in these tests and another line the attainment of the average American child of this age or grade who has taken these tests, then the pupil has his strong and weak points set before him in a manner that is perfectly definite and objective."[27] In short, standardized tests seemed to be an essential ingredient in creating a fair playing field. Of course, things wouldn't turn out that way. But there was a kind of hope, at least on the part of many, that testing would help identify and nurture raw talent.

As alluded to earlier, standardized tests also made governance easier. For decades, policy leaders had maintained little direct control over the schools, which operated with a significant level of autonomy with regard to curriculum, instruction, and assessment of learning. Consequently, it was impossible for policy elites to compare the work of teachers or students across schools. Their powers were largely limited to issuing recommendations.

Standardized tests changed this state of affairs by allowing policymakers and legislators to measure institutions from afar. Shortly after the development of the New York State Regents exam, for instance, policymakers began using the test to expand their direct control over the schools—primarily by tying funding to performance. "Successful" schools were rewarded with a funding carrot; their less successful counterparts received the stick. Still, not everyone took the Regents exams. As an investigator for the New York Board of Estimate and Apportionment put it in 1912: "The whole problem is one of lack of measurements and lack of definite tests . . . And as a result we go on year after year without looking for any positive checks on the results we obtain."[28] Even half a century later that would remain an issue. As a 1971 *New York Times* story reported, only by expanded testing could the state provide "an objective, uniform standard of attainment . . . from one locality to the next."[29] Only by conjuring a way to efficiently and uniformly "see" school performance—in this case, through test scores—could officials in central offices and state capitals establish enough systemic order to make governance possible.[30] Only then could they wield any real control.

Not surprisingly, the scores produced by such tests became increasingly important to policy and governance structures over time. As a 1954 *New York Times* story reported, the Regents tests, according to the state education department, were by that time being used "to measure pupil achievement, to serve as a basis for admission to college, and . . . [to] improv[e] the quality of instruction in the major secondary school subjects."[31] Because policy leaders were reliant on test scores to pursue those critical aims, they may have concluded that they simply couldn't do their jobs without standardized tests. Nor could they exert the kind of authority they had become accustomed to.

By midcentury, standardized test scores were a common currency in educational policy—the information underlying efforts to measure and control schools. This was disturbing to some, of course. As one critical scholar wrote in 1959: "It is regrettable that many schools appear to appraise teaching competence by making comparisons of groups of pupils on the results of standardized achievement tests. When teachers realize that their teaching effectiveness is being evaluated by this method, many of them find ways of teaching for the tests, thus reducing possible contributions the tests might make toward genuine program improvement."[32] Whatever their flaws, though, test scores represented the foundation of an increasing number of educational policy structures. And they remained an incredibly simple and straightforward tool for calculating school quality. As a 1970 report by the New York State Education Department put it, "The distributions of scores are processed by computer, and reports which summarize the results in conveniently interpretable form are returned to each school and central office."[33] Never mind their weaknesses. As a form of currency, they worked. They were easy to compile and easy to compare.

Standardized tests also won a foothold in American education because an entire corps of professionals arose around the standardized testing apparatus. The first wave of testing experts entered K–12 schools at the end of World War I. In the army, they had worked to develop and administer military intelligence tests used to sort and rank recruits—tests that scholars would later reveal to be highly problematic.[34] At the time, however, these military-trained testing specialists were presumed to possess a sophisticated set of skills, and they were returning to civilian life in search of work. In the eyes of many state and district leaders, the timing couldn't have been better. As one observer noted, "The fact that two or three hundred young men who have for several months been working in the psychology division of the Army are now about to be discharged offers an unusual opportunity for city schools to obtain the services of competent men as directors of departments of psychology and efficiency, for such purposes as measuring the results of teaching and establishing standards to be attained in the several school studies."[35] Soon every state office of education, as well as every large district, had its own staff of testing experts.

As the work of these experts grew more complex and specialized, they played an increasingly central role in testing. Given their positions, they were unlikely to focus on the fundamental limitations of standardized testing. Instead, they were far more likely to tout the incremental improvements being made—to the tests themselves, as well as to increasingly sophisticated analysis techniques for interpreting scores. Their science, as they understood it, was both highly precise and rapidly evolving.

Standardized tests were also highly profitable. And that meant that however many critics lamented the existence of such tests, entrepreneurs would work not just to meet demand but also to *manufacture* it—convincing schools and districts that testing was essential to progress. Already by 1920, plenty of individuals and organizations were making their livelihoods from the production and scoring of tests. They were scrambling to capture as much of the market for testing as they could in those early days.

Selected Tests from 1920 (listed alphabetically)
Baldwin's Public School Music Test
Barnard's Test in Roman History
Barr's Diagnostic Tests in United States History
Bell's First-Year Chemistry Test

Caldwell's Science Tests

Chapman's Physics Test in Electricity and Magnetism

Clemens's Grammar Test

Coleman's Scale for Testing Ability in Algebra

Courtis's Dictation Spelling Tests

Grier's Range of Information Test in Biology

Handschin's Foreign Language Tests

Harlan's Test of Information in American History

Henmon's French Tests

Hillegas's Scale for the Measurement of Quality in English
   Composition for Young People

Lohr's Latin Test

Manuel's Series of Tests for Studying Talent in Drawing

Minnick's Geometry Tests

Rogers's Mathematics Tests

Rugg's Tests for Historical Judgment

Starch's Tests for Measuring Grammatical Knowledge

Thorndike's Algebra Test

All told, roughly 250 tests were commercially available in the early 1920s, and that number continued to grow.[36] Providers multiplied until testing became truly big business—a business so lucrative that large organizations began to consume their smaller competitors.

By the 1950s testing had become a major industry—dominated by a handful of increasingly influential players. According to the National Board on Educational Testing and Public Policy, test sales to K–12 schools in 1955 were $7 million. Fewer than ten years later, that figure rose to $25 million.[37]

As the educational system grew larger, as students stayed in school longer, and as more schools and districts began tracking student performance via standardized tests, the market continued to expand. By the end of the twentieth century, standardized testing of elementary and high school students—to say nothing of college entrance examinations and the like—was a $300 million industry.

Industry growth was hardly at its apex. In 2013, Pearson, a British publishing company with wide reach in the U.S. market, posted revenues of roughly $10 billion, half of which came from the North American market, and much of which came from state and federal testing contracts. The company inked a five-year testing contract with New York worth more than $30 million. It won testing rights in Texas—a deal worth nearly half a billion dollars—and it secured contracts with roughly half the states for statewide testing. Pearson gets this business because it's big—it has purchased many smaller testing and publishing companies. But it also secures these contracts because it wields significant influence in Washington and in state capitals. Between 2004 and 2014, for instance, Pearson spent roughly $7 million lobbying at the federal level, and far more at the state level.[38]

Pearson is not alone. CTB / McGraw-Hill, a Pearson competitor, also has revenues in the billions, with major contracts in roughly two dozen states. And like Pearson, CTB / McGraw-Hill has also learned to wield its influence in the halls of government.

What about the public? Policy leaders, testing experts, and the testing industry had their reasons for continuing to support the use of standardized tests, but why did the public never demand an end to the testing regime?

One factor that kept opposition to testing relatively muted is that those best positioned to publicly decry the tests—leaders in government, business, and school systems—were often uncritical of them. This should not be surprising, as success in school frequently serves as a sorting mechanism for placing individuals in positions of influence. Naturally, as a result, many see their places at the top of the socioeconomic hierarchy as a product of their intelligence and hard work. After all, it is much harder to understand the inadequacy of tests if one has always succeeded on them. Rare are cases like that of the prominent American psychologist Robert J. Sternberg, who struggled with tests and still managed to achieve a position of influence—a position he then used to debunk our widely accepted notions about measuring intelligence.

Another key factor is time. Over decades of experience, the American public became accustomed to tests, to the numbers produced by tests, and to the narratives that arise around test results. By the 1920s, tests were already a routine part of life in school for teachers and students. As the *American School Board Journal* reported in 1922, "Measurements of achievement, through the use of educational tests, have come to be a common feature of the public schools."[39] Over time this situation only became more prevalent. A college-bound student in 1960, for instance, might take district- and state-mandated tests, diploma tests, Advanced Placement tests, and the SAT before arriving in college. The non-college-bound student might win a reprieve from a few of those, but after graduation from high school, there would likely be more standardized tests to face in the world of work: tests to become a licensed beautician, nurse, auto mechanic, or law clerk. Tests could not be avoided.

Ask almost anyone on the street, and they will acknowledge the importance of tests. They may not like them and may not be in favor of an overabundance of tests, but they accept them. As one Somerville community member observed: "I just don't want my kid getting tested all day instead of learning. But I do want him to do well on tests. I do want him to succeed." And as Somerville congressman Michael Capuano put it in a speech that was otherwise very critical of standardized testing: "Tests are just a part of life. You can't avoid tests."[40]

In short, constant exposure to tests over the years has led to general comfort with and acceptance of them. Culture is always evolving. And as each successive generation of Americans has come of age, they have done so in a world in which testing was increasingly natural—a part of normal life. One could certainly *dislike* testing, just as one can dislike sitting in traffic. But to imagine a world without testing is a different matter entirely.

Of course, it is also true that for most of the twentieth century, tests weren't as invasive as they are today. The standards and accountability movement, which culminated in the 2002 No Child Left Behind (NCLB) law, would change that.

A Nation at Risk and the Dawn of Test-Based Accountability

In the 1970s, schools using standardized tests to measure student achievement usually opted for exams like the Iowa Test of Basic Skills or the Stanford Achievement Test. Developed for a generic national audience, such tests were unrelated to any particular school curricula. Instead, they measured student knowledge of what was presumed to be basic or common content. Rather than weigh in on how many questions students should be able to answer correctly, test developers generally measured student performance relative to the scores of other students. Consequently, such tests tended to be used for diagnostic purposes rather than for accountability.

That would begin to change in the last decades of the twentieth century. In the 1970s, frustration with a perceived decline in educational quality led policymakers to seek a means of holding students accountable for their learning—via minimum competency testing and high school exit exams. Between 1972 and 1985, the number of state-level testing programs rose from one to thirty-four.[41]

Policy elites had long sought to pry open the classroom door to gain greater control over teaching. For generations they had been writing new curricula, setting new goals, providing more professional training, and pouring new resources into schools—all without much impact on the daily work of teachers, who could simply close their doors and ignore any reform efforts they deemed unsuitable for their classrooms. Sometimes this was prudent; teachers kept out ill-advised policy efforts. Sometimes, no doubt, this inhibited growth. But whatever the ultimate impact, policy elites were tremendously frustrated by the level of constancy in teacher practice across time.[42]

State-run testing offered a way of solving the problem of teacher autonomy. If the state were to create clear student learning standards and develop tests aligned with those standards, policy leaders might gain the power that had eluded them. They still might not be able to control what teachers were doing inside their classrooms, but if they could measure the degree to which the state-designed curriculum was being learned, they could light a fire under the feet of teachers and school administrators. This theory soon took on the moniker "standards-based accountability."[43]

Insofar as standards-based accountability would give policymakers new powers, it had a strong appeal. But it had a particular allure during the late 1970s and early 1980s, as rhetoric about a crisis in American public education escalated. Concerns about a deteriorating economy, the ongoing Cold War, the rise of foreign competitors like Japan, and declining SAT scores led to the assertion that schools were in trouble and that America's position in the world was in jeopardy. Perhaps most famously, *A Nation at Risk,* a report issued in 1983 by the National Commission on Excellence in Education, warned:

> Our once unchallenged preeminence in commerce, industry, science, and technological innovation is being overtaken by competitors

> throughout the world . . . We report to the American people that while we can take justifiable pride in what our schools and colleges have historically accomplished and contributed to the United States and the well-being of its people, the educational foundations of our society are presently being eroded by a rising tide of mediocrity that threatens our very future as a Nation and a people. What was unimaginable a generation ago has begun to occur—others are matching and surpassing our educational attainments.[44]

A slew of similar reports followed. Typical was that of the Committee for Economic Development—a group of 200 business executives and educators—which claimed in 1985 that "Japanese students study more and learn more. They spend more time in class than their American counterparts do; and by the time they graduate from high school, they have completed the equivalent of the second year at a good American college. In science and mathematics, Japanese test scores lead the world."[45] Standards-based accountability would give policymakers the tools to ratchet up their demands on schools to address this alleged crisis.

The first step toward a true standards and accountability movement was articulated by Tennessee governor Lamar Alexander in 1985. As he put it: "The Governors want to help establish clear goals and better report cards, ways to measure what students know and can do. Then, we're ready to give up a lot of state regulatory control—even to fight for changes in the law to make that happen—*if* schools and school districts will be accountable for the results."[46] Three years later, Republican presidential candidate George H. W. Bush made this idea the centerpiece of his educational policy agenda. Noting that he wanted to be "the Education President," Bush promised to lead a "renaissance of quality" by working with the nation's governors to devise more rigorous educational standards.[47]

Less than a year after his election, Bush and the National Governors Association co-organized the 1989 Charlottesville Education Summit. At the heart of the summit was the work done by a committee of governors, led by Arkansas governor Bill Clinton, who were seeking to exert more influence over education. In just two days, the committee hammered out a basic framework for educational standards.

Over the next several months, the Bush administration, along with Clinton and other members of the National Governors Association, crafted a piece of legislation—America 2000—that Bush proposed in his 1990 State of the Union address. The plan called for voluntary national standards and tests. Yet Congress, which had not participated in the Charlottesville summit, sank the bill. Not long afterward, Bush lost his bid for reelection.

Fortunately for backers of standards-based accountability, the candidate who defeated Bush was Bill Clinton, who swiftly resurrected America 2000, rechristened it Goals 2000, and shepherded it into law in 1994. Though Goals 2000 did not mandate testing or authorize consequences for low performance, it did establish a federal interest in standards and accountability. The goal for student achievement and citizenship, for instance, stated, "By the year 2000, all students will leave grades four, eight, and twelve having demonstrated competency over challenging subject matter including English, mathematics, science, foreign languages, civics and government, economics, arts, history, and geography, and every school in America will ensure that all students learn to use their minds well, so they may be prepared for responsible citizenship, further learning, and productive employment in our Nation's modern economy." The new law further specified goals for increases in academic performance and reductions in achievement gaps.[48]

Perhaps more importantly, the law also provided grants to help states develop content standards. By the time Clinton left office in January 2001, most states had established academic standards, and many had begun to assess students through statewide testing. A clear foundation had been laid for the architects of No Child Left Behind.

NCLB, ESSA, and the Era of High-Stakes Testing

No Child Left Behind was the first piece of legislation pursued by George W. Bush upon assuming the presidency in 2001. Continuing work initiated by his father a dozen years earlier, Bush also modeled the new law after his own work in Texas, where as governor he had strengthened the state's school accountability system. As a 1999 *New York Times* story put it: "The key to the Texas accountability system since it was instituted in 1991 has been relentless focus on testing. Every year, from third through eighth grade and once again in high school, virtually every Texas public school pupil takes a version of the Texas Assessment of Academic Skills . . . The results, along with school attendance figures, determine a school's rating in the state."[49]

NCLB had bipartisan appeal in that it advanced projects of previous Republican and Democratic administrations. And evidence from Texas seemed to support the model of standards-based accountability. Sure, there were those who complained about the focus on testing in Texas. As one mother observed: "In many years, all my daughters' teachers have done is drill them for [the test] instead of giving creative writing or interesting projects . . . The system may look good on paper, but I feel my daughters are getting ripped off."[50] Yet student achievement scores in Texas had gone up steadily under Bush's governorship. Of particular interest to lawmakers were the impressive scores of traditionally underrepresented minorities. Flanked by Democratic senator Ted Kennedy, Bush signed NCLB into law on January 8, 2002.

NCLB was the culmination of a federal legislative process that began a dozen years earlier in Charlottesville, Virginia, building on both America 2000 and Goals 2000. But NCLB was also erected on an even older foundation. Though technically a new law, NCLB was actually an updated version of a law passed several decades earlier—the Elementary and Secondary Education Act (ESEA). Signed by President Lyndon Johnson in 1965, the ESEA was conceived of as a part of the War on Poverty—a way of channeling federal funds to schools with relatively high rates of low-income students. The primary component of the law, Title I—"Financial Assistance to Local Educational Agencies for the Education of Children of Low-Income Families"— outlined a model in which federal funds would be distributed to state departments of education. States would then allocate resources to districts, and districts would provide funds to schools. Today, Title I funds reach roughly half of the nation's schools.

At the time of the original law's creation, when school funding formulas were even more inequitable than they are presently, these funds were particularly important. Even today, Title I funds are a critical source of revenue for schools with high percentages of students living in poverty. American schools rely heavily on local property taxes for their funding—nationally, 45 percent of funds come from local sources—meaning that high-poverty neighborhoods often struggle to adequately fund their schools. And though state funding, which on average accounts for another 45 percent of spending, can be structured to address the inequities in local funding, most states fail to achieve budget parity. Consequently, though the federal contribution is fairly small—accounting for roughly 10 percent of school budgets, on average—it is not insignificant. Some 50,000 K–12 schools count on those federal dollars to fund daily operations.[51]

The federal government has no direct constitutional authority over the schools. Instead, that power belongs to the states. In accepting federal funds, however, states agree to particular terms with regard to how that money will be used. In previous iterations of the ESEA, the federal government asked little in return for financial support. Schools could count on receiving federal dollars to alleviate the impact of poverty, and were responsible largely for showing that the money had been spent appropriately.

NCLB, however, would change that.

The key component of NCLB was test-based accountability. A reality for states like Texas prior to the law's passage, the new mandate was a shock for others. Specifically, the reauthorized law required states to conduct annual standards-based testing in math and English for all students in grades three through eight and one year in high school. States would control their own standards documents and define their own levels of "proficiency"—producing great disparity across states in defining academic competence—but all states would be required to bring 100 percent of students to a level of proficiency within twelve years of the law's passage.

Soon, all fifty states began testing students in math and English at a minimum of seven different grade levels. And those test scores carried significant consequences. Schools that did not meet targets— "Adequate Yearly Progress" in the language of NCLB—were to be sanctioned in accordance with the law's guidelines. A school that failed to meet targets for more than two years in a row, for instance, would be required to notify parents of its failures. A school failing to meet targets for over five years would be subject to closure. Never had standardized tests been so high-stakes for so many.

NCLB was the culmination of two decades of work. First, policymakers and the public had to be convinced that it was important to produce a quantitative picture of how the schools were doing. Then the states had to develop standards. Then states needed to develop tests aligned with those standards. Finally, once all of these pieces were in place, the muscle could be introduced—accountability for results. Still, as lawmakers would learn, it was far from a finished product.

The massive scale of testing, coupled with NCLB's reporting requirements, produced mountains of data—in many cases issued through school-level "report cards." Note, though, that those report cards were quite limited. As one nonpartisan group put it, "The metrics, weights, formula and report card do not reflect public values."[52] And, as one might expect, many of the data, from the outset, did not look good.

What surprised many lawmakers, though, was that scores did not seem to be improving much over time. The theory of action behind standards-based accountability, after all, was that educators would work harder to achieve the results expected of them, and that parents would exert more pressure on the system to improve. Whatever the initial levels of performance, the theory predicted widespread change.

Yet NCLB came with only a small increase in funding to improve outcomes, particularly given the new strings being tied to the federal revenue stream. It provided only weak supports for schools, such as a mandate to hire largely ineffective tutoring companies. And it came with little guidance about how to interpret data for parents.[53]

There were other obvious limitations to the new law. States could insist upon higher test scores, for instance, but they could not control any other aspect of school life, for which no data were available. In fact, they generally lacked data on anything other than math and English scores at seven grade levels. What was happening in the history classroom or the science classroom? What was going on in second grade? Or eleventh?

States also had no means for controlling the manner by which schools sought to raise test scores. It was obvious that some schools were narrowing the curriculum or emphasizing test preparation over other forms of instruction. Yet how could they be told not to when those were the only factors for which they were being held accountable? Many policymakers chose to put on blinders and assume that schools with high test scores were doing a good job. Others, however, worried that the new law was actually encouraging counterproductive practices.[54]

Some policy leaders at the state level also recognized early on that NCLB's accountability mechanisms offered little in the way of diagnosis. Low test scores on reading comprehension passages, for instance, can tell you that students are reading below grade level, but they are unable to tell you *why*. Insofar as that is the case, they aren't particularly good for actually helping schools improve. Many states, consequently, were faced with the task of taking a school district into receivership before actually determining what they needed to do to strengthen local capacity.[55] Others simply closed schools down; in New York City alone, roughly 150 schools were shuttered for low performance between 2002 and 2014.

Twelve years later, no state had succeeded in moving all students to levels of proficiency, as required by the law. Though many individual schools had met their targets, and though test scores on the whole were up modestly from a decade earlier, the vast majority of schools had not met their goals, and achievement gaps continued to persist. Facing a potential crisis, the U.S. Department of Education began issuing waivers to states in 2011, freeing them from NCLB's accountability mechanisms. In return for such a reprieve, states were asked to adopt new standards for college readiness—usually the Common Core State Standards—and to tie teacher evaluations to student achievement data.[56] The Department of Education also urged states to propose new accountability frameworks that included factors like test score growth and graduation rates. Bargains were ultimately struck with the vast majority of states.[57]

Thus, roughly a decade after its passage, NCLB—the most sweeping federal intervention ever into education—came to a quiet end. Rather than bringing all schools to proficiency, the law produced only minor gains in student achievement—some of which have been linked to cheating, and many of which have been linked to the phenomenon of teaching to the test. A consensus emerged, even among many of the law's initial supporters, that it had failed.[58]

But the phaseout of NCLB did not mark the end of the standards and accountability era. Criticisms were commonplace. Even many of the law's early supporters faulted NCLB's unrealistic expectations, its sticks-instead-of-carrots approach, and its harsh punishments for low performers. But it had become abundantly clear that, whatever the opposition to high-stakes tests, the practice of holding schools accountable for measureable outcomes wasn't going away. Not by a long shot.

In December 2015, President Barack Obama signed the Every School Succeeds Act (ESSA), reauthorizing the ESEA, and replacing NCLB. But though ESSA eased up on the punitive features of NCLB, it did not wipe the slate clean. As a U.S. Department of Education overview put it: "NCLB put in place measures that exposed achievement gaps among traditionally underserved students and their peers and spurred an important national dialogue on education improvement. This focus on accountability has been critical in ensuring a quality education for all children, yet also revealed challenges in the effective implementation of this goal. Parents, educators, and elected officials across the country recognized that a strong, updated law was necessary to expand opportunity to all students; [to] support schools, teachers, and principals; and to strengthen our education system and economy."[59] Though ESSA allowed more flexibility with regard to testing, it still required states to test students in grades three through eight, as well as once in high school, for both math and English. Consequently, testing still rules the day. By the time he or she finishes high school, the average American student has sat through roughly ten standardized tests a year for at least seven years.[60]

What about All Those Other Tests?

Of course, state-mandated exams are not alone in the testing eco-system. And though no other tests are used to, say, close a school down, the impact of an array of other exams can still be felt in policy discussions and parental decision making.

The oldest of these other tests is the SAT, developed in the 1920s by a consortium of prominent colleges and universities.[61] Although the test was not designed to measure school quality, SAT scores are often cited as evidence of student preparedness for college. By extension, SAT scores are commonly, if problematically, used to measure high school effectiveness, so it is perhaps worth briefly discussing the short-comings of the SAT.

The first problem with the SAT is the problem of new information. Much of what is covered on the SAT is learned in school. On the surface this seems fine; yet colleges and universities already know a great deal from transcripts and grades about what students learned in elementary and high school. Such overlap might seem harmless until we consider factors like test anxiety, poor test-taking skills, or a bad night's sleep—all of which can affect a single day of testing in a way they wouldn't affect a student's grade in a yearlong course. That isn't to say that grades are perfect; they aren't. But it should raise questions about high-stakes uses of a test like the SAT.

The second problem facing the SAT is cultural and class bias. SAT vocabulary words, for instance, are more likely to be in common use in some households than in others. Specifically, white students from higher-income families are more likely to have been exposed to some of the arcane language used on the test. Additionally, they are more likely to have been drilled by their parents on "SAT words."[62]

A related problem facing the SAT is that of coachability. Companies like Kaplan and Princeton Review have long staked their livelihoods on a guarantee—that your score will go up after a four- to ten-week-long test-prep course. And, generally, scores *do* go up. That's great if you've invested time and money in an SAT boot camp; but it should raise questions about the degree to which the test tells us anything about innate ability or school learning. Higher scores may, it seems, tell us very little about those things, and far more about how many test-taking tricks a student has learned or how many practice tests he or she has taken. More disturbingly, the cost of such courses—generally around $500—inherently disadvantages low-income students.[63]

Perhaps the clearest and most cogent criticism of the SAT as a measure of school quality comes from a report by the College Board itself—the corporate parent of the SAT. According to a 1985 College Board report: "Those who reject the SAT as a barometer of schooling are on firm ground. Students who take the test are a representative sample of neither high school seniors nor college-bound seniors. The SAT was never intended to represent all of the important areas of understanding, knowledge, or skill—not to mention constructive attitudes, values, or other noncognitive characteristics—in which schools aim to bring about student growth. Moreover, the scores are not affected only by formal schooling; they measure abilities that are developed both in and out of school."[64] Basically, SAT scores are inappropriate for measuring K–12 education.

The ACT, the SAT's biggest rival, is a somewhat different test. Rather than seeking to measure a student's reasoning ability, the ACT seeks to measure achievement in English, math, science, reading, and writing. Given this aim, the ACT does not suffer from some of the weaknesses of the SAT—a fact that has prompted the College Board to adapt its test and make it more like that of its rival. Still, ACT scores provide little new information to colleges, can be significantly influenced by studying, and correlate highly with both student race and family income.[65]

Three more tests are worth discussing here—one designed to goad high school students into working harder, and two designed to measure the quality of the nation's schools.

The first of those is the high school exit exam—a test predicated on the belief that high school students do not work as hard as they could because gaining a diploma is too easy. Acting on that belief, roughly half of the states now administer such tests, and many require passing scores for graduation. Because such exams suffer from the same problems as other state-run standardized testing programs, however, they tend to disadvantage particular students. The result, as research has revealed, is that exit exams significantly reduce the probability of completing high school, particularly for low-income students and students of color. Insofar as such tests appear to exacerbate inequality, many view them as misguided.[66]

Among the two tests used to measure the quality of American schools, the older, and exclusively domestic, test is the National Assessment of Educational Progress (NAEP). Created in the 1960s to serve as "the nation's report card," NAEP tests are given to sample populations in grades four, eight, and twelve. The tests assess a wide range of subjects and are issued every year. The long-term trend assessments are typically administered every four years.

There are a few advantages to NAEP over the state-run achievement tests mandated by federal law. First, not every student has to take the NAEP, meaning that the instructional time lost to testing is minimized. Statistically speaking, there's no need to test every student if a representative sample can be assembled—and that's exactly what NAEP does. Second, because schools and districts are not held accountable for NAEP scores, there is very little likelihood of anyone teaching to the test, and no pressure is directed at children to improve their NAEP scores. Third, NAEP tests a broader range of school subjects than high-stakes achievement tests do, meaning that even if

NAEP *were* used for accountability purposes, it would be less likely to narrow the curriculum.

Of course, NAEP has its limitations. NAEP is still a standardized achievement test that fails to account for prior knowledge and that relies on machine scoring. Additionally, because student academic achievement is the product of a student's out-of-school experiences even more than of his or her in-school experiences, NAEP scores ultimately may tell us more about factors like student poverty than they do about a school's quality. Finally, while NAEP may tell us something about academic achievement, it fails to tell us much else about schools.

The second test of national education outcomes is the Programme for International Student Assessment (PISA)—an exam created by the Organisation for Economic Cooperation and Development and given every three years to fifteen-year-olds from across the globe. PISA has many of the same advantages and disadvantages as NAEP. Given those disadvantages, it means that countries with lower levels of poverty, or stronger orientation toward test preparation, will outscore the United States. These score discrepancies have caused no small degree of hand-wringing. At the top of the annual heap are the usual suspects from East Asia: Singapore, Taiwan, South Korea, and three Chinese cities—Shanghai, Hong Kong, and Macao. The United States usually comes in somewhere in the middle of the pack, which usually elicits a reaction like that of a 2013 *New York Times* editorial: that America's students are falling "further and further behind."[67]

Even if we were to assume that PISA is a gold-standard measure, we might take heart in the fact that there is no statistically significant difference between the performance of American students and those in a place like Norway, which in 2015 was ranked by the United Nations as the best place in the world to live.

But tests like PISA should raise serious questions among observers. How can a test measure all of the different things that students learn across various national school systems? After all, comparative measures require a common denominator, and no such denominator currently exists. PISA's approach is to measure a set of "real-world" skills unrelated to national curricula. This may allow for comparison, but it creates an obvious problem: the test measures what many schools *do not teach*. It establishes a level playing field, but it does so by ignoring what each system is actually trying to accomplish. "This," as my colleague David Labaree put it, "is leveling the playing field with a bulldozer." These issues are further compounded by the fact that the validity of PISA test items is unsupported by research. All of these issues make the most common use of PISA—decrying the state of public education—at best inappropriate and at worst absurd.[68] Whatever the interpretations of journalists and policy leaders, none of these tests indicates much about the quality of American schools.

Caveat Emptor

Tests usually do measure something about what a student knows. And when implemented thoughtfully, feedback from testing can provide information to educators and policymakers that may help them engage in systemic planning. It can also help students understand how they are doing relative to their peers and relative to expectations, at least on the subject area being tested.

But tests are incomplete measures of school quality. In fact, they are incomplete measures of student academic achievement, and academic achievement constitutes only a single component of a good school. How else can we explain the research finding that high schools effective at improving test scores are not necessarily effective at reducing dropout rates? Or the research finding that schools can have a major impact on students' lives—leading to lower likelihoods of arrest and higher rates of college attendance—without raising test scores?[69]

Good schools do many things. They are places where children learn about the world and begin to imagine life beyond their neighborhoods. They are places where the arts are valued and pursued—where children learn to draw and dance and play the piano, as well as to understand a poem or a painting or a piece of music. They are places where ideas are sought and explored—for the purpose of expanding young people's notions of justice, broadening their visions of the possible, and welcoming them into ongoing cultural conversations. Our best schools are places where children gain confidence in themselves, build healthy relationships, and develop values congruent with their own self-interest. They are places of play and laughter and discovery.

Of course, good schools also promote student learning in core content areas, but measuring something as complicated as student learning, it turns out, is particularly hard when it has to be done in a uniform and cost-restricted way. It is particularly challenging given the fact that all students come to school with different prior levels of ability and preparation.

Tests have long been at the core of the American educational system. Consequently, most stakeholders view tests with less skepticism than they perhaps should. In one recent poll, for instance, more than two-thirds of respondents expressed support for federally required annual testing. Yet the public is increasingly bristling under the testing regime. Roughly two-thirds of respondents to the 2015 Phi Delta Kappa / Gallup poll expressed a concern that children are subject to too many tests, and they deemed test scores the least accurate of currently available measures of school effectiveness. There is, it seems, an increasing tension between Americans' historically rooted acceptance of testing and a rising uneasiness about the uses to which test scores are being put.[70]

Still, the public often lacks the tools to critique the testing regime. In a 2016 letter to The Ethicist column in the *New York Times Maga-*

zine, for example, a parent asked for advice about where to send his child. "State test scores came out recently," he wrote, "and our neighborhood public school, which is filled with some of the city's poorest kids, scored very low." Despite this parent's implicit recognition of the link between poverty and test scores, and despite the fact that he volunteers at the school and finds it "perfectly fine," he nevertheless concluded that there must be "something seriously wrong with how the school is educating kids."[71] That is certainly a possibility. In fact, it is a possibility at all schools, regardless of test scores. But what if the school, as this parent's intuition and experience tell him, is actually "perfectly fine"? What if the data available, in the form of standardized test scores, present a distorted picture of reality?

2

Through a Glass Darkly:
How Parents and Policymakers Gauge
School Quality

FOR OVER A DECADE, all K–12 public schools in the United States have been reporting student standardized test scores. Such data are now a part of life for teachers, school leaders, policymakers, and parents.

This does not mean that everyone looks at test scores in the same way. People differ in background knowledge, interest, and skepticism. They play different roles, are affected in different ways, and bear different levels of responsibility.

Yet, for most parties involved, test scores are a key driver in the educational enterprise. As the dominant measure of student learning and the primary output for which schools are held accountable, test scores are an inescapable fact of life.

The use of test scores as a measure of school quality has, of course, been challenged. Educators have pushed back against tests, which they see as distorting classroom instruction and misrepresenting the quality of their performance. Communities have fought to save schools slated for closure on account of low student standardized test scores. Parents, through a growing "opt out" movement, have asserted their right to excuse their children from federally and state-mandated testing programs. Despite mounting criticism, though, testing remains the primary mechanism for gauging school effectiveness.

The testing regime endures for many reasons, but the preference for tests persists because they reduce the complexity of education into something simple: a number. Parents, administrators, community members, and policymakers want information about how schools are doing. And although they want such information to capture reality, they also want it to be standard, concrete, and objective. Time constraints are the chief driver of those concerns; after all, to truly *know* a school can require weeks of careful observation. A number, on the other hand, can be quickly understood by everyone.

Standardized test scores cannot adequately capture the essence of a school; but they do provide a convenient shortcut. Consequently, test score data continue to function as a key source of evidence—from casual conversation to official policymaking.

How do policymakers use test scores, and how has a decade of resistance to test-based measures of school quality changed their work, if at all? How do parents and community members engage with test scores? What other sources of information do they tend to rely on, either in combination with or in lieu of test score data? And how accurate are perceptions of schools that are based on these numbers?

NCLB Waivers and the Every Student Succeeds Act— New Boss, Same as the Old Boss

In late 2011, the U.S. Department of Education announced that it would begin issuing waivers to No Child Left Behind. According to NCLB, all students needed to reach proficiency in every state by 2014, and it was clear that this was not going to happen. In fact, the majority of schools were headed for serious sanctions under the law. As former secretary of education Arne Duncan observed in 2011, "No Child Left Behind is broken and we need to fix it now." The law, he added, had "created a thousand ways for schools to fail and very few ways to help them succeed."[1] Consequently, Duncan began striking deals with states that would free them from NCLB's accountability mechanisms.

The Department of Education's waivers offered new forms of flexibility. Specifically, states could use more than just standardized test scores in their accountability structures. Even so, their options were limited. They could use attendance and graduation rates in their calculations. They could use test score growth rather than just proficiency rates—something that would treat diverse schools much more fairly. They could also set targets other than 100 percent proficiency, seemingly reflecting a greater degree of realism about what is attainable, as well as recognizing that such targets unfairly punish schools with large populations of traditionally underserved students. Consequently, as a product of these waiver agreements, a majority of states began reporting not only on standardized test performance but also on factors such as test score growth, graduation rates, and the degree to which schools are closing achievement gaps.[2] The waiver process, however, constituted only a minor adjustment to the system established by No Child Left Behind.

The Department of Education's waivers also came with strings attached. For one, states were required to tie teacher evaluations to student standardized test scores. That meant that teachers would no longer be evaluated by principal and administrator observations alone. Instead, their evaluations would be based in part on the test scores earned by their students. Additionally, the waiver process required states to adopt "college and career-ready" standards. In doing so, the Department of Education encouraged states to adopt the Common Core State Standards—a set of academic benchmarks for math and English designed to replace the fifty disparate standards documents then in use. Though many praised the standards for their rigor, the move incited resentment, particularly among advocates of local control.

Most states applied for and received waivers. Any relief from NCLB, even if it came at a cost, was a seemingly welcome addition. As a result, new measurement schemes generally held schools accountable for test scores, test score growth, graduation rates, and attendance. In Massachusetts, the state shifted from the NCLB goal of 100 percent proficiency to a new goal: cutting achievement gaps in half by the end of the 2016–17 school year. This would be measured by counting the number of students reaching the "proficiency" benchmark, by calculating annual student growth on standardized tests, and by including dropout and graduation rates.

Although NCLB technically expired in 2007, it took Congress eight more years to finally reauthorize the Elementary and Secondary Education Act. Despite agreeing on the need to fix the law, legislators were unable to agree about particular solutions. However, upon entering his last full year in office, Barack Obama, along with his outgoing secretary of education, Arne Duncan, marshaled the political will to act. The subsequent law, renamed the Every Student Succeeds Act (ESSA), was signed by Obama in December 2015.

ESSA addressed the most glaring flaws in NCLB, which Duncan and his office had tried to address through waivers. The new law, for instance, mandated the inclusion of not just test scores in accountability systems, but also some other academic factor—such as test score growth or graduation rates—as well as one factor to be determined by states. That final factor could be academic or nonacademic, opening the possibility of including measures such as student engagement or school climate. The law also provided the flexibility for up to seven states to test assessment methods other than standardized tests.

ESSA, which is both more flexible and less punishment-oriented than NCLB, does represent a modest improvement over its predecessor. But consider how heavily it still relies on standardized test scores as a measure of school quality. Schools are not being held accountable for providing access to the arts, or for helping children develop a strong work ethic, or for getting young people to see themselves as students. Those things, after all, are much harder to compile standard, objective, portable data on. Consequently, test scores still rule. As one Somerville school committee member observed: "We have great goals. But they remain abstract because we don't have real data for any of them. The only data available for any of our priorities is on standardized test performance." How, then, can a school board or a superintendent or a state secretary of education be expected to set clear expectations for schools?

Richer data are available in some places. In New York City, for instance, a new "School Quality Snapshot" was developed under mayor Bill de Blasio and schools chancellor Carmen Farina. The snapshot provides scores for seven categories: rigorous instruction, collaborative teachers, supportive environment, effective school leadership, strong family-community ties, trust, and student achievement. These categories include measures from surveys of school community members, a review of the school by an educator, and a variety of other data.

It is a good scorecard. Even so, schools are not being held accountable for what is on the scorecard. Instead, they are held accountable for Annual Measurable Objectives (AMOs), which have replaced the Adequate Yearly Progress scores mandated by NCLB. Although AMOs now take into account "acceptable growth towards proficiency" and not merely raw test scores, calculations remain largely based on standardized testing. In short, the strengths of New York City's school scorecard are not integrated into the state's accountability mechanism.

One group did depart from the standard approach to the NCLB waiver process—a consortium of districts organized as the California Office to Reform Education (CORE). As a state, California did not receive a waiver from the Department of Education under NCLB. But this did not prevent the consortium from seeking one, despite the tenuous legal status of a bargain between the federal government and a series of localities. Articulating a desire to go beyond standardized test scores in measuring school quality, the CORE districts began to create a system of accountability "grounded in transparency and capacity-building versus external sticks and carrots."[3]

CORE's School Quality Improvement Index is built around a 100-point scale—60 points allotted for the academic domain and 40 for social-emotional and school culture factors. Within the academic domain, two-thirds of points are determined by test scores, with raw scores and growth scores counting equally. The remaining third of the academic domain is determined by graduation rates.

CORE's real departure from the herd, however, is in the 40 points allotted for social-emotional and school culture factors. In these areas, they rely on a broader range of measures, including how many students are missing significant amounts of school, how many are suspended or expelled, and how many English language learners have become fluent. Once the schools have collected two years of data, they will incorporate climate surveys given to students, parents, and teachers. Finally, CORE's approach differs once more in the design of accountability after the points are tallied up. In the CORE districts, low-performing schools, which are identified as "priority" schools—signaling a concern with capacity building rather than with punishment—are paired with higher-scoring peers, with the goal being to create a "community of practice."

These are promising innovations that challenge the way policy leaders have traditionally thought about school accountability. As

California Board of Education president Mike Kirst commented: "In some ways, these indicators are apples, bananas and oranges. You throw them into a blender and you get a smoothie—I don't see how you get one number."[4] But there are signs of broader uptake. In September 2016, the California Board of Education voted unanimously to include factors such as graduation rates, college preparedness, and attendance in school evaluations. Rather than receiving a single overall rating, schools will receive results for each of several categories, presented in the form of shaded Harvey Balls of the sort used by *Consumer Reports*. As Kirst concluded, "There are many functions of accountability, not just finding schools and districts that are not meeting performance standards."[5]

Still, test scores largely remain the coin of the realm, both in policy and in practice. In the fall of 2016, my daughter's school was downgraded from a "Level 1" school to a "Level 2" school because the test scores of students with disabilities failed to increase at the rate determined by the state. Never mind the fact that suspensions declined to one-fifth of the previous figure, thanks in part to a restorative justice program and an emphasis on positive school culture. Never mind the school's mindfulness program, its use of hands-on science and technology programs, its drama club, or any of the other factors that make it a successful place for young people to learn and grow.

The Value-Added Wars

In addition to being used as measures of school quality, test scores have also been put to use in recent years as measures of teacher quality. Backed by deep-pocketed donors as well as by the U.S. Department of Education, which required states to use standardized test score data in teacher evaluations in order to qualify for NCLB waivers, this shift has transformed conversations about how to measure teaching.[6]

There has long been a desire to evaluate teachers more objectively and more efficiently than through observations by principals. Principals are extremely constrained in terms of their ability to spend time in classrooms. Given that a typical class period is roughly an hour long, and that the average school has roughly forty teachers in it, a principal would need to spend an incredible amount of time watching teachers in order to get a real sense of their abilities. Most principals, however, don't have that luxury. As research indicates, principals have multiple responsibilities, and spend roughly half the day on administrative tasks alone.[7]

There are other reasons to be concerned about principals evaluating teachers. Principals often lack the training to conduct effective evaluations. Evaluation tools have been criticized as subjective, heavily dependent on a principal's particular assumptions and beliefs. And principal-led evaluation has largely failed to create meaningful distinctions among different teachers.[8]

Not surprisingly, most teachers receive positive evaluations from their principals. A recent study of Chicago's schools, for instance, found that 93 percent of teachers were identified as "superior" or "excellent"—a rate that raises questions among skeptics of teacher quality. Only 0.3 percent were identified as "unsatisfactory."[9]

One way of explaining this phenomenon is that the vast majority of teachers are good at what they do. That is quite possible. Another potential explanation, however, is that if principals lack the time and training to do teacher evaluation properly, they would rather err on the side of caution. Dispiriting a good teacher because of a single observation would be counterproductive, not just for that teacher, but for a school's entire staff. It is better to give positive evaluations, even to some ineffective teachers, than to risk giving negative evaluations to good teachers.

Clearly, there are ineffective teachers out there. Teachers themselves do not dispute this. In fact, most teachers will agree that their work is made harder by ineffective colleagues.

Thus, however much confidence one might have in teacher quality writ large, all parties have a stake in identifying ineffective teachers. Many, however, have serious doubts about the use of test scores in tackling this challenge.

Value-added measures of teacher effectiveness, often referred to as VAMs, are created by taking a student's actual test score and comparing it with a predicted test score. The predicted test score is generated by a regression—a formula used by social scientists to determine the influence of different factors in a process. Common inclusions are the student's native language, disability status, poverty level, attendance, and prior-year test scores—factors that are strongly correlated with student achievement. For example, in calculating a student's predicted test score, we could just take the average for all students in that grade. Or we could do that *and* look at an individual student's scores from previous years. Alternatively, we could look at the average for all students at that grade level from a particular economic background, and then adjust that score based on the individual student's previous test scores. It is an imperfect science, certainly, but it is possible to predict student test scores with a surprising degree of accuracy.[10]

The trouble, however, comes when we try to give particular teachers credit, or assign them blame, for student test scores. Students can be nonrandomly assigned to classes, resulting in students of higher or lower ability being clumped together. Learning gains due to one teacher's efforts might not register that year, taking some time to bear fruit. Teacher influence can spill over across classrooms—with history teachers helping students grow as writers and readers, for instance, or science teachers helping students master mathematical concepts. Tests can be ineffectively scaled, making it hard to register the gains of students who are far above or far below grade level. And different choices about which variables to control for will lead to different ratings of teachers.[11]

There are also many problems with VAMs that are due to standardized tests. Since a test can't ask about everything that was taught in a particular year, for instance, there is the chance that some of what students learned won't be on the test, and that some of what they *didn't* learn *will* be on the test. These kinds of errors even out over large distributions of students. However, if test scores are being used to evaluate individual teachers, the sample size of students can often be small enough that measurement error is a real problem.

Perhaps the biggest problem with VAMs as a measure of teacher effectiveness is that we want our teachers to do more than raise student test scores. We want teachers to be role models and counselors. We want them to inspire students and to instill in them a love of learning, as well as to develop strong relationships with students and to look out for their best interests. We want teachers to treat each student as an individual and nurture individual passions and abilities. Test scores will never tell us much about those other aims.

Parents and policymakers intuitively know this, even if they are desperate for easy-to-digest information about teachers. In one survey our research team conducted in Somerville, we asked 400 parents how they believe teachers should be evaluated. Specifically, we asked them to respond yes or no to the desirability of five different methods: student test scores, observation by principals, student feedback, observations by district representatives, and parent feedback.

In general, our survey revealed that parents appreciated the value of several different tools in the teacher evaluation process. Yet, while test scores garnered the support of roughly half of respondents to the survey, the other four tools earned much higher levels of support—from over 75 percent of respondents. One possible explanation is that test scores simply can't capture a great deal of what successful teachers actually do. Consequently, they can't answer the questions parents have about teachers and teaching quality.

It should come as no surprise that moves to implement VAMs have sparked firestorms. By design, far more teachers will be given low ratings under these models than under previous ones. Furthermore, as an unintended consequence resulting from flaws in the methodology, many teachers will be misidentified as ineffective—a phenomenon that has already begun to play out. In one highly publicized case, for instance, a teacher in New York sued the state after her rating flipped from "effective" to "ineffective" in a single year. Highly regarded by her peers, her principal, her superintendent, and her former students, she was outraged that any system would lump her with the lowest performers.[12] In other cases, however, more than pride is at stake. Though not yet the primary factor in any teacher evaluation system, it is already true that value-added scores can play a decisive factor in determining teacher pay, as well as whether teachers keep their jobs.[13]

Some have suggested that the solution is to use VAMs only at the school level, for programmatic improvement. Others have suggested that VAMs might serve as a trigger for a more thorough investigation. But it is important to recognize that however VAMs are used, they will, at best, tell us very little about anything other than the acquisition of academic content knowledge.[14]

Black Holes and Scorecards

Districts and states are now collecting more data than ever before, including measures that go beyond student standardized test scores. Yet they often don't know what to do with the new information—an instance of what David Shenk calls "data smog."[15] Consequently, though it is ostensibly public, much of this information tends to reside in dark corners of school, district, or state web pages.

Even if the data can be located, the numbers can remain impenetrable to laypeople. As the authors of a 2014 review for the Education

Commission of the States put it, information about school performance can be "difficult to communicate clearly to the public."[16] Massachusetts, for instance, uses a value-added metric—the Student Growth Percentile (SGP)—to calculate student achievement. Nevertheless, while SGP is theoretically more useful than raw test scores, its presentation can be confusing to users. An SGP score above 50 is "above average." But many users interpret SGP scores as *percentages* rather than *percentiles*: they mistakenly read an SGP score of 50 as indicating 50 *percent*—a failing grade!—rather than as an indicator that the school is exactly halfway between the highest and lowest performers. To combat this problem, the state has crafted a graphic representation—a dot placed along a set of X- and Y-axes, with one representing raw test scores and the other representing growth on those tests. Needless to say, it does not speak for itself. Additionally, because SGP is expressed as a percentile, all schools are pitted against each other in competition. However successful or unsuccessful they all are, someone will come in first, and someone will come in last.

Knowing the weaknesses of district and state data systems, many of which are simply the product of bad design, third parties have leapt into the fray. Working mostly with publicly available data, web and print media providers have filled a gap in the market—offering simpler and clearer pictures of school quality explicitly designed for public consumption. The problem, of course, is that these providers often lack the capacity to provide rich and complete portraits of school quality. Additionally, their for-profit status often incentivizes them to be both unduly certain and unnecessarily provocative in their assessments, even if it misleads users.

One of the most prominent of the publications ranking schools is *U.S. News and World Report.* Long the leader in ranking colleges and universities, *U.S. News* began rating high schools as a part of its overall shift away from traditional journalism and toward consumer-oriented ratings.[17] But rating high schools is an even more complex task than rating colleges and universities. Whereas there are roughly 2,000 four-year schools in higher education, for instance, there are roughly 25,000 public secondary schools, to say nothing of the 65,000 K–8 schools. And while colleges and universities have an incentive to share data with *U.S. News*—after all, they are competing for clients—public K–12 schools have little reason to cooperate with such ranking efforts.

What does *U.S. News* include in its calculations for rating high schools? It begins with raw standardized test scores, comparing schools against each other to produce a relative ranking. Bonus points are then awarded to schools with the highest test scores among low-income and minority students. Then, schools are judged by "college readiness," which is measured by Advanced Placement (AP) and International Baccalaureate (IB) participation rates and test scores. *U.S. News* also includes student-teacher ratios in its reporting.

This means that the schools ranking near the top of the *U.S. News* list may not actually be the best schools. They may just be schools with high percentages of affluent and middle-class students, schools that have self-selected populations, or schools that weed out low performers. In Massachusetts, the top-ranked schools for 2015 included a charter school that mandates the IB curriculum for all students, thereby ensuring a higher "college readiness" score; Boston Latin School, which uses an entrance exam to select its student body, thereby skewing its schoolwide scores; and affluent Lexington High School, located in a town with a median family income of $165,000 and a median home value of $750,000—an economic variable that predicts higher student test scores regardless of school quality. In short, *U.S. News*'s methodology may tell us very little about the value added by schools. It may even guide parents to schools that employ troubling pedagogies—teaching methods that emphasize test preparation, exam performance, and competition.[18]

U.S. News, of course, is not alone. *Newsweek,* for instance, produces a rival list of best high schools, which each year claims the cover of the magazine. Previously, *Newsweek* had relied on Jay Mathews's Challenge Index, originally developed for the *Washington Post.* The Challenge Index simply counts the number of AP and IB tests given, and then divides that by the number of seniors who graduated. The updated *Newsweek* methodology now measures AP / IB scores instead of participation—a measure that rewards performance but that skews results against populations that tend to score lower on standardized tests. It also uses raw standardized test scores, which have obvious weaknesses in terms of their ability to reveal something about school quality, and SAT / ACT scores, which correlate very highly with family income. It includes graduation rates and a school's counselor-to-student ratio—variables that are interesting but that still tell us very little about what life inside a school is like. And schools earn a "gold star" if their low-income and minority students outperformed the state average on standardized tests. Like *U.S. News's* list, *Newsweek's* is easy to consume, and often comforting to more-affluent parents, whose local schools usually come out on top; but it is also highly flawed.

Other groups have used the Internet to tap into the desire among parents and the public for more information about schools. Perhaps the most prominent of these is GreatSchools.org, whose scores show up on searches through the online realty company Zillow. As Zillow puts it, "GreatSchools is the leading national source of school performance information, reaching 44 million unique users per year."[19] As they calculate it, that amounts to 50 percent of American families with children.[20]

GreatSchools.org rates schools on a 1 to 10 scale. Ratings are based on raw test scores and test score growth, which are weighted equally. For high schools, GreatSchools.org adds in a "college readiness factor," which is measured by SAT scores and graduation rates. The site also includes user reviews—an interesting twist in the age of Yelp, yet one that nevertheless raises questions. Who is posting reviews? Upon what are their reviews based? How representative are they?

Another popular online school rating site is SchoolDigger.com. Unlike GreatSchools.org, SchoolDigger.com relies exclusively on raw standardized test scores, ranking schools by city and state. The site also includes a "Worst 10 Schools" tab designed, it seems, to draw eyeballs, but which also stigmatizes schools in the process. Stigmatizing any school is problematic, making it harder for the organization to improve. But it is particularly troubling to imagine a perfectly good school being stigmatized as a consequence of entrepreneurial mismeasurement.

A more recent entrant into the online school ratings business is Niche.com. Niche allots 25 percent of its weight to test scores—specifically, to the percentage of students at or above proficiency levels on state assessments. It also allots 10 percent for each of the following categories: graduation rates, SAT / ACT scores, the percentage of students enrolled in at least one AP class, and the percentage of students scoring 3 and above on AP tests.

In a departure from its competitors, Niche.com ties 15 percent of a school's rating to the "average score of colleges that students are most interested in or go on to attend." The effort to move beyond test scores is laudable, but the methodological flaws here reveal why so few rating systems include more than low-hanging fruit. First, the method presumes that college rankings matter—something that research has failed to bear out, at least beyond the impact of attending an elite school.[21] Second, it presumes that being interested in a college reveals as much as actually attending it. Third, it presumes that any of this reflects something about a high school rather than about family background. Roughly 40 percent of low-income, first-generation college-going students enroll in college immediately after high school. For students from middle-income families where at least one parent has some postsecondary education, the percentage is nearly double.[22]

Like GreatSchools.org, Niche.com takes advantage of the Internet to include user ratings. Unlike GreatSchools.org, however, Niche.com actually includes such ratings as 10 percent of a school's score. In theory, this is not a bad move. Again, however, their methodology reveals the challenge of allowing a third party to cobble together this kind of data. The minimum number of respondents that Niche.com requires in order to include a user rating score is nine. Imagine a school with 1,000 students, and then imagine that it received only nine user ratings to generate its ranking. Are the reviewers actually students there, and if so, do we want reviews from only a few of them? Are they parents, and if so, do we want them weighing in on issues about which they may only have secondhand information? And what about the other 991 students who may be content enough to not bother writing a review, or, conversely, too despondent to muster the energy?

There is a clear desire among the public for information about school quality. But for-profit third parties have met demand in a manner that often borders on the irresponsible. Their methodologies can be misleading. They can exacerbate stereotypes. And their presentation of results unwaveringly pits schools against each other—as if there are only a handful of decent schools out there, and as if there is a one-size-fits-all school for all young people and all values.

Consequently, even parents who know better can end up relying on problematic data. As one parent in Los Angeles admitted, "I certainly know that the GreatSchools ratings aren't the end-all be-all determiner of school quality; but it is very difficult to avoid putting stock in the ratings." Major decisions, then, can be shaped by information that isn't particularly informative. An alderman in Somerville echoed this, saying: "I can't tell you how many parents of young children I talk to who have concluded—without any serious research or inquiry—that the [Somerville Public Schools] suck. When I ask them how they know, they almost always cite test scores or various rankings, which . . . are based on MCAS scores."

For district leaders like former Somerville superintendent Tony Pierantozzi, the battle between perception and reality was deeply frustrating. "The talk shared by people who do an hour's research on the Internet fits the category of a little information being a dangerous thing," he observed. "Talk to a student or a family that has navigated the system and ask if their kids thrived or if we held them back. That's a conversation that I think would be valuable." Somerville High School principal John Oteri expressed a similar opinion. "People don't know how to interpret the data," Oteri observed. "They get blinded . . . by a raw number that doesn't have any context." When asked for an alternative, Oteri offered advice similar to Pierantozzi's: "If you want to know how good a school is, go through it. Walk through the school. See what the kids are like."

Yet not all stakeholders have the time or the know-how to conduct a detailed walk-through of a school. For their part, policymakers want figures that are more objective, easier to collect, and more portable than firsthand observations. The challenge is to collect that kind of information, to make it standard across schools, and to transform it so that users can engage with easily and quickly.

What We Talk about When We Talk about School Quality

Many members of the public never consult test score data. They don't access state web portals, read magazine rankings, or consult online rating tools. Instead, they talk to neighbors, make best guesses, and judge by readily observable criteria such as the physical condition of the building or, more troublingly, racial demography.[23]

In fact, perhaps the chief factor that parents weigh when they choose a school for their children is convenience.[24] Particularly for parents with limited access to transportation, and who themselves need to get to work—often via public transportation—driving a child to school is simply not an option. For these parents, location trumps all else in choosing a school. That isn't to say that better information about school quality is useless. Such parents could still benefit from knowing more about the schools their children attend—in order to advocate for their kids, support the school, or demand resources from district and state leaders. Nevertheless, it is important to recognize that convenience matters.

The next most influential factor shaping how parents choose a school, as well as how they perceive its inner workings, is probably word of mouth.[25] This makes sense. When I'm choosing a restaurant, I often ask friends about their experiences. When I'm considering a particular car, I'll talk to those who have owned a similar model. Why would it differ with schools? Word of mouth is also much easier to come by than many other forms of knowledge about a school.

Word of mouth can be a very powerful tool for gaining information about a school. After all, even the best data system can only imperfectly anticipate the questions users will have. Face-to-face conversations, on the other hand, can be tailored to the exact needs and concerns of those involved, and there is far more potential for depth and explanation in a conversation. The problem, however, is that for word of mouth to be an effective tool, those sharing information need to be well informed, and that isn't always the case. People share their views about schools whether or not they know much about them, often asserting that a school is good or bad without having ever set foot inside the door. If such misinformation were easily identified, it would be of little consequence. Yet information networks, as scholars like Mark Schneider have shown, are of highly varying quality. Thus, as former secretary of education Arne Duncan put it, parents often end up accepting "legend, intuition and chance" as sources of information.[26]

Even among those with firsthand experience, however, word of mouth can be complicated. After all, parents don't spend the day inside the building—their children do. Thus, when parents share their views about a school, they are likely to know less than they might assume. In Somerville, for instance—as in many places—a handful of teachers have outsized reputations among parents and are highly requested at the beginning of each school year. But are they better teachers? In one case, two elementary school teachers engaged in almost identical teaching practices. One, however, engaged in more parent-oriented activity—e-mailing with parents, roaming the playground in the morning to talk with them, and maintaining a class blog. These are all positive behaviors, but they may not make this teacher more effective in the classroom, as many parents presumed.

Word of mouth can also be complicated because it is always grounded in a series of unspoken assumptions and based on an incredibly small sample size—a parent's own child. Parents don't say things like "This school worked well for my child in a few ways, which have a great deal to do with who she is, and it didn't work for her in other ways, which also had to do with who she is." Nor do they articulate their own, often unique, priorities and values. Instead, they tend to bury their assumptions about what makes a good school, and they tend to discuss the school in general terms without particular reference to their own children's strengths and weaknesses. This isn't to say that a parent is wrong when he or she says that a school is good or bad. But we do need to remember that a school is rarely good or bad in *all* ways or for *all* kids.

A third complication worth discussing is that related to our propensity to fixate on negative information, even when it is outweighed by positive information. Recently in Somerville, a would-be public school parent wrote an e-mail to an education-oriented listserv, asking for advice. "I was recently talking to some friends," she wrote, "and I realized that my knowledge of the Somerville school district is mostly based on rumors." She then asked a series of thoughtful questions. One parent responded that her girls received a good education in the district and found themselves well prepared for college, adding that "the girls had the most diverse group of friends one could imagine." As she concluded, "suburban and private schools" are simply "much better at public relations" than urban districts like Somerville. Several others chimed in with their own anecdotes—most were positive, though by no means were they unrealistic in their assessment of the district. One user, however, commented, "If I were you, I would invest by having your children go to private schools."

The experiences people shared via e-mail were quite powerful. They indicated a strong knowledge of what actually goes on inside the schools, and they were clear about their own values and assumptions. Still, that negative comment seemed to carry more weight than all of the positive ones. Why? As it turns out, we tend to focus on extremes, particularly negative ones. In the psychological literature, this phenomenon is often called "negativity bias." The brain, as scholars like John Cacioppo and Daniel Kahneman have shown, reacts more strongly to negative stimuli, influencing our attitudes more strongly.[27]

So which schools are most likely to be mentioned in a negative light? Weak schools, certainly—schools where students do not feel safe, cared for, or academically challenged, and where teachers are not supported by administrators and colleagues. However, given the mixed quality of word of mouth—often shared by those without a real sense of what is going on inside a school—and given stereotypes about urban schools, we might also expect some unfair things to be said about otherwise good schools with diverse student bodies, particularly in cities. Conversely, we might expect to hear some uninformed positive characterizations of schools with wealthier or less diverse populations, particularly those in leafy suburbs.

Finally, we should remember that none of these conversations—in person or on the web—take place independently of test scores, which people frequently use to support their beliefs about school quality, or which they have to fight against. Nor are perceptions of school quality independent from policy rhetoric, which political leaders employ for many reasons—most frequently, to position themselves as leaders, or to generate political will—but which is often disconnected from reality on the ground. And all of these ideas are bound up in issues of race and class.

How Race and Class Shape Our Perceptions of School Quality

At the most basic level, our demographic characteristics—such as race and class—shape our experiences. And our experiences, insofar as they shape who we are, influence our perceptions of school quality.

But characteristics such as race and class also exert a more direct influence on how we view schools. Consider, for instance, how demography shapes our social networks. Rather than being demographically representative, social networks tend to be characterized by homophily—association among individuals who share similar characteristics. Not surprisingly, race and ethnicity tend to produce the biggest differences in American social networks. According to one estimate, only 8 percent of American adults have someone of a different race in their social network with whom they "discuss important matters." Class also has a powerful impact on social networks, particularly when it includes not just income, but also variables like educational attainment and occupational status.[28]

Given these trends, when parents turn to their social networks for information about schools, they are drawing on a particular set of assumptions, experiences, and values. The result is that individuals tap into separate pools of knowledge about school quality—pools that may not provide new or high-quality information. Additionally, people end up being drawn to schools attended by the children of their friends. Thus, without any real intent, they reinforce the demographic character of schools, creating a kind of feedback loop.[29]

Race and class also shape the degree to which parents engage with test score data. White, higher-income families, for instance, tend to belong to social networks that traffic in educational data more comfortably than do families of color and lower-income families. And they tend to be drawn to schools with higher test scores, even if there are no substantial differences in school quality. To be clear: this does not mean that white, middle- and upper-class families have a better sense of which schools are of high quality; rather, it means that race and class influence which kinds of information people use to make decisions. Their social networks provide limited, and different, windows to the world. As a result, they tend to share beliefs about which schools are good and which are not.[30]

Of course, the influence of race and class is not always so subtle. Research, for example, indicates that parents will often consciously consider the racial demography of a school. To a certain degree, this is quite rational. Very few parents want their children to be minorities in a school—out of concerns about racial isolation, as well as about home / school "fit."[31]

But parents also engage in a much more problematic practice—relying on race as a proxy for school quality. Insofar as that is the case, they often seek out schools with lower minority populations. In the words of scholar Amanda Bancroft, "good" schools are usually those with "a majority of white, affluent students."[32]

This is not necessarily a reflection of bigotry. Survey work has shown that most parents aren't particularly interested in racial homogeneity for its own sake.[33] Instead, preference for predominantly white schools is often the product of people engaging in amateur acts of social science; unfortunately, they tend to commit errors in the process. Many, it seems, begin with an observation: schools serving students of color have historically been underresourced. This observed pattern is reinforced when they see students of color streaming in and out of a dilapidated school, ignoring the fact that many students of color do not attend dilapidated schools, and ignoring the fact that many white students attend such schools. They then create a rule of thumb: that when students of color are present, quality is lower. And, finally, they create a working theory—that school quality can be gauged by the racial makeup of the student body. This isn't always a completely conscious process, but the impact on perception is likely not much different whether or not it is.[34]

That said, it is also important to note that societal views toward young people of color are highly fraught. Young people of color, and particularly African American males, are far more likely to be perceived as threatening than their white counterparts. Such attitudes can exist consciously or unconsciously, and are in both cases deeply consequential. They lead to segregation, unequal opportunity, and stigma.[35]

Parents also use social class as a proxy for school quality. Again, this likely starts with more general, and often unconscious, observations. It is hard not to notice, for instance, that the quality of so many consumable goods in the United States is tied to price. And it is reinforced through observed correlations, such as the fact that schools in higher-income areas tend to score higher on tests than schools in lower-income areas, or that students at expensive private high schools often attend high-status colleges. A general rule then emerges: that the higher the income of the families in a school, the stronger the school. No wonder that segregation by income is greater among families with children than among other households.[36]

It is certainly true that money matters in education, but it is quite possible that a school may have adequate funding while also serving a high percentage of low-income students. It is also possible that a school with relatively modest resources can produce powerful learning outcomes. It is even possible that a school with tremendous resources can fail to hire strong teachers, promote a positive school culture, or nurture a full range of characteristics in students. Additionally, the assumption that school quality might be improved by the mere presence of high-income students, or harmed by the presence of low-income students, is a false one. Having some wealthy students in a class does not help others in the class learn; having poor students in a class does not keep learning from happening. Similarly, white students do not score higher when they are around more white students.[37]

Powerful as these latent and often unconscious theories about school quality can be, they do not stand alone in the minds of parents. Instead, they are linked with a constellation of other ideas and beliefs. Some of this comes through political rhetoric about the presumed failures of American schools—rhetoric that often focuses particularly on urban schools. However, some of these ideas and beliefs come from the world of fiction and can be quite powerful in their influence on the way people view schools. Movies like *Stand and Deliver, Lean on Me, Dangerous Minds, Freedom Writers,* and *Coach Carter* appear every five to ten years, sending a message that urban schools are frightening places where learning is a rarity. This, of course, has more to do with the nature of screenwriting than with the reality of schools—to create dramatic story lines, screenwriters invent heroic teachers and drop them into dire situations. Fictional though they may be (even those ostensibly based on true stories), these images affect people, particularly if they have never been in an urban school. After all, most of us have gone to only a few schools in our lifetimes and have little sense of what most other schools are like.[38]

None of this is to say that there is no connection between demography and school quality. Generations of racial discrimination and economic inequality have ensured that there is a clear link between the two.[39] But schools can certainly have substantial populations of color, or of low-income students, and still be outstanding places to get an education. They just can't be overwhelmingly segregated; that's when real problems set in. Students at such schools often recognize that those with the resources to leave have chosen to do so—a powerful realization that can severely undermine motivation.[40] Teachers and administrators at such schools become unable to give higher-need students extra attention, because so many of their students have additional needs. And it is harder for highly segregated schools to tap into pools of political, social, and economic capital.

Unfortunately, believing that they are acting in the best interests of their children, many white and high-income parents actively avoid demographically diverse schools. And by chasing after test scores or one of several other highly problematic proxies for school quality, they enact a self-fulfilling prophecy. Though it is certainly not their intention, they play a role in stigmatizing and segregating schools.

Good School Realty

Buying a home means buying a school. That's because, in the vast majority of districts, student assignment at a particular school is determined by one factor: a family's address. The fact that home buyers are selecting a school when shopping for a home, then—when combined with the absence of good information—exacerbates stereotypes and assumptions about school quality. It is an extremely high-stakes decision that people do not want to get wrong, that they are often unprepared to think through, and that they frequently don't have a great deal of time to answer.

Realtors have long known that schools are central in many people's decisions about home buying. Just a few miles from my house, in fact, are the offices of the somewhat preposterously named Good School Realty. Yet realtors have no inside line on good information. Instead, they often select easy-to-access information about schools and present it as if it were insightful. A friend looking at an open house in a nearby suburb, for instance, shared that the realtor had left out a school fact sheet for prospective buyers—listing the school's standardized test scores and, to my friend's astonishment, its racial demographics. This may qualify as information; but it certainly doesn't inform, at least with respect to school quality.

Increasingly, many people are doing their own calculations—using the Internet to investigate the quality of the schools that particular real estate listings are zoned for. As the online real estate company Zillow put it in an announcement about its partnership with the school rating tool GreatSchools.org, "At Zillow, we know how well school and real estate information go together."[41] The general practice of pairing schools with real estate is certainly not new, but the availability of searchable school data has already begun to change the way that particular groups seek housing. With the ability to toggle a "Great School Rating" bar, for instance—setting it to reveal only high-ranking schools—a prospective buyer can eliminate whole neighborhoods from consideration without ever setting foot inside a school. Recognizing this, investors have begun to use those data systems to guide their real estate acquisitions. The Blackstone Group, for instance, recently spent $10 billion to spruce up foreclosed homes in fourteen metropolitan areas, "using data to choose properties in desirable school districts."[42]

Of course, not all parents are locked into a school once they settle into a home. In Somerville, for instance, parents have the benefit of intradistrict school choice. What that means is that any child can attend any school in the city.[43] Most districts, however, do not have this option. Charter schools have changed this picture a bit, as a child can attend any charter school in the state within which he or she resides. Yet, unlike a school district, which must serve everyone, charter schools usually have limits on their enrollment. Consequently, parents cannot necessarily count on their children being admitted to the charter school of their preference. Nor can they necessarily count on charter schools being any better than traditional public schools, despite the outsized reputation of charters. Additionally, research has found that white, advantaged parents are more likely to navigate school choice systems in a way that exacerbates stratification and separation of students.[44]

Parents can also elect to send their children to private school. Though accounting for only a fraction of enrollments—roughly 10 percent from year to year, primarily within Catholic schools— private schools represent a free market for those who can afford the cost of tuition. Like charters, however, private schools have limits on enrollment, and can also select their student bodies; thus, there is no guarantee of admission. Additionally, there is the issue of cost—from under five figures at many Catholic schools, to upwards of $50,000 annually at schools like Andover and Choate—which can be a deal breaker for many families. Finally, and again mirroring the charter sector, private schools are often no better than their public school counterparts, despite the hype.[45]

Thus, while there are exceptions, the connection between home-ownership and school quality is a powerful one. Ask a subset of middle- or upper-income earners how they chose their homes and most will likely say something about the schools.[46] But it is a high-stakes decision that many parents have to make without great information, and they often make it before they really know who their children are as students. Consequently, they end up seeking some abstract, universal "good" school rather than a school that fits their children's needs and interests. Not surprisingly, many end up overwhelmed. In a recent poll of Florida residents, for instance, half of respondents said that they considered test scores and school-level report cards to be the most important factors when deciding on a school. Yet the majority said they didn't know very much about interpreting either set of data.[47]

Of course, it is important to note here that not all parents have this luxury. Many do not engage in the search for a "good" school because they are tied to a particular community because of their jobs or their need to care for their families. They live where they live. Their children will attend school wherever they have been assigned. They are, however, no less concerned about their children, and no less invested in their futures.

Generally speaking, though, helping people think more deeply about school quality when they are seeking homes is a matter of critical importance. Almost as an afterthought, parents can rule out areas with perfectly good schools. And once the decision is made, it is rarely unmade.

A Little More on Private and Charter Schools

Most people imagine themselves to be making informed decisions about their children's futures, at least among those with the privilege to decide. Yet they often end up making decisions that reflect the limited nature of their information.[48] Why is that? To get a better handle on the issue, it is useful to look at the examples of charter and private schools.

According to a 2012 Gallup poll, 78 percent of Americans believe that private schools provide a good or excellent education, and 60 percent believe the same about charter schools. Traditional public schools, by contrast, elicit that response from only 37 percent of the populace.[49]

How accurate is the picture Americans have of private and charter schools? It's a hard question to answer, not only because running a true experiment—taking a large number of children and randomly assigning them to different kinds of schools—is impossible, but also because school quality is such a multifaceted concept. Many scholars have tried to work around this problem, using pseudo-experiments and statistical techniques to measure traditional public schools against their counterparts in the private and charter sectors. But findings are anything but consistent, and it cannot be universally claimed that one kind of school is superior to the others. Just about the only conclusion we can safely draw is that some schools in each sector—whether private, charter, or traditional public—will be of high quality; others will not.

How can that be? Private schools send almost all of their students on to college—a substantially higher percentage than traditional public schools. Just ask their college guidance counselors; or simpler yet, look at their websites. Groton, for instance, has a web page listing colleges where five or more of its students have matriculated over the past five years.[50] On that list are schools such as Harvard, Yale, Dartmouth, Princeton, Columbia, Brown, and Penn. Fact sheets like this can be quite persuasive, as can the advertisements known as "look books" sent to prospective families. At one New England private school, the 2016–17 look book—a seventy-five-page glossy magazine, which cost the school six dollars just to mail—closed with a list of colleges attended by graduates, as well as the colleges attended by faculty.

Yet it is quite possible that the admissions edge private school students seem to have is not due to schooling. Roughly 80 percent of students from high-income families, regardless of the kind of school they attend, immediately enroll in college after high school; that is true for only about half of students from low-income families. Among households with incomes under $50,000, only 6 percent attend private schools. By contrast, 26 percent of households with annual incomes of $200,000 or more send their children to private schools.[51] Thus, we might reason that when we look at private schools, we are really just seeing the effects of concentrated privilege.[52]

This is not to say that there are no differences between private schools and public schools, especially when the private schools in question are elite institutions with massive endowments. But many of the differences between private schools and public schools are magnified out of proportion. Parents often believe, for example, that private schools offer much safer environments for their children, or that class sizes in private schools are significantly smaller. According to the National Center for Education Statistics, however, crime rates and incidents of bullying are roughly the same across all kinds of schools, and average class sizes are nearly indistinguishable at both the elementary (20.3 public, 18.1 private) and high school (18.6 public, 18.4 private) levels.[53]

Charter schools, too, maintain solid reputations among the American public. As with private schools, though, this may not be due to any real difference in quality. Like their private counterparts, charters have self-selecting populations. This can be due to pull factors, such as well-crafted messages sent to would-be parents, or to push factors, such as strict rules and high academic expectations. In either case, however, it complicates what we can say about the value added by a charter school. And though thoughtful researchers have tried to account for this by using a variety of methodological approaches and statistical techniques, it can be very hard to pinpoint which results are due to the student's school and which to the student's family. Thus, the only generalizable thing we can say about charters is that quality varies from state to state and from school to school. Some cities have stronger charter sectors than others, and some charter firms have more coherent practices than others.[54]

Unlike private schools, which are not required to give standardized achievement tests, charters are public schools that must adhere to state guidelines. Consequently, we have some data about performance. But here, too, we are limited in what we can determine about charter school quality. Even if we control for differences in population, there is tremendous variance across schools, networks, and states. As one team of scholars concluded, the only thing we can conclude across traditional public schools and charters is that "students perform similarly across the two settings in most locations."[55] Yet even if that weren't the case, and charter schools did uniformly produce higher test scores, we would be left asking, At what cost? How are those scores being achieved? And what else is going on inside the school?

Without particularly clear or useful data about schools—whether public or private—we end up leaning heavily on anecdotes, observed correlations, and assumptions. Often, we simply fall back on general brand attributes that may have nothing to do with actual effectiveness.

Private and charter schools, always vying for clients, are well aware of this. Not surprisingly, they work to bolster their brands by investing in technology, creating impressive faculty biographies on their websites, posting high-touch photos, and even launching advertising campaigns. For their part, traditional public schools tend not to engage in such practices. Why would they? Most have never had a shortage of clients.

The impact of exclusivity is also worth considering. Research from consumer psychology indicates that people disproportionately value products that are perceived to be scarce.[56] If that is the case, private schools and charters are at an inherent advantage over their traditional public school counterparts. Private schools are generally small in size and carefully cultivate the image that they are selective in their admissions. Many, of course, are genuinely difficult to get into. Others, however, ask students to complete a lengthy application process even if they are virtually guaranteed entrance; even if it's a sham, the process creates a sense of accomplishment for the families that are accepted.

Charters play this game, too. As public schools, they are prohibited from employing selective admissions procedures, but they can recruit more applicants than they have spaces for, thereby forcing a lottery for available seats and triggering a sense of scarcity. In Ohio, for instance, state audits suggest that some schools spend more than $400 per student to attract them away from public schools, employing sophisticated marketing schemes. And in New York, the Charter School Center supports multimedia campaigns in support of charter schools. The results have been powerful—over one million names on waiting lists.[57]

A final factor worth discussing with regard to opinions about charter and private schools is the impact of choice. As a wealth of psychological research indicates, people prefer making their own choices.[58] And, more importantly, people tend to be happier with outcomes if they have had a hand in shaping them. To be clear: this does not mean that people are happier because they made *good* choices. Rather, these studies have found that simply having been allowed to choose creates happier customers. Thus, even if they don't produce markedly better results, private and charter schools hold a powerful advantage in generating positive perceptions.

None of this is intended as a takedown of private and charter schools. Many do good work, and they should be valued for their contributions. Rather, the point is that public schools do not have the same advantages with regard to perceptions of their quality. And the result, for many public schools, is that people believe them to be worse than they actually are. Some of these factors cannot easily be changed. We cannot wave a magic wand and install a more privileged clientele in every school, for instance. Nevertheless, there is much that we can do to measure school quality more fairly and more accurately.

Questions Worth Asking

One day a local resident of Somerville asked me if his child would be well served by his neighborhood school. His suspicion, he told me, was no.

As he explained it, student growth scores at the school were high, but overall scores were middling. He reasoned that this was bad for kids like his—high achievers with lots of at-home support. The school, he noted, had a large population of students from low-income families, who tend to enter school with lower test scores than their more affluent peers. He presumed that a school with more low-income students would be an easier place to produce test score growth, so the growth scores could be dismissed. And the lower-than-average *overall* test scores, he concluded, were evidence that students from traditionally higher-scoring backgrounds were underachieving.

He clearly had done far more homework on this issue than most parents. But his interpretation wasn't necessarily right.

The state of Massachusetts SGP score, which measures test score growth, attempts to create an apples-to-apples comparison by measuring students against similar peers, not against everyone. Consequently, students with low prior-year test scores are compared against *other* students with low prior-year test scores. And students with high prior-year scores are compared against peers with similar testing histories. At least theoretically, then, all schools should be equally able to promote test score growth, regardless of population.[59]

Additionally, the middling overall test score average did not indicate low performance among traditionally high-achieving students. Instead, it could be seen as a product of the school's very high level of diversity. Only roughly one-third of students at the school were from middle- or upper-income families—students who, statistically speaking, tend to score higher. Thus, although they constituted a sizable minority, there were not so many of these students that the average test score for the entire school would equal that of schools with *uniformly* middle-class or affluent student bodies. We looked at the scores, broken down by demographic subgroup, and non-low-income students at the school in question were scoring as highly as students in nearby suburban schools.

The test scores, in other words, looked good.

Even so, there were other questions to consider. I asked him if he knew anything about the school other than the test scores. What about the arts, or school culture, or how students fared once they moved on to high school?

He smiled. "Yes, I want to know about that stuff, too." I knew that students received instruction in each subject once per week. Such is the case in the vast majority of elementary schools. Only 10 percent of elementary schools offer music three or four days per week, and a lower percentage of schools offer art that frequently. Music and art instruction take place every day at only 5 percent and 2 percent of schools, respectively—often at specialty schools with particular missions.[60] "Does the school offer electives?" I asked. "Are there after-school clubs?" We both jotted down reminders to look into the matter.

"How about the teachers? How do I find out if they're good?" he asked. I glibly suggested that he sit through their classes for a while until he figured it out. Then we brainstormed some other ways to try to get at the question. He could talk to other parents, though I cautioned him not to listen to parents about teachers their children *hadn't* had, and urged him to try to find multiple sources for each teacher. He could try talking to some teachers, which I assured him wouldn't be a weird thing to do. He could ask the principal what the teacher turnover rate was like; and while he was at it, he could get a feel for her leadership style—something that might tell him a great deal about the school.

I asked if he had been inside the building. "Just outside," he said. "Looks fine. But some of the paint is peeling off." Sometimes the exterior conditions of a school can be an important indicator. Does the school look like students respect it? That's probably a pretty powerful thing to take note of. But the paint, in a harsh climate like New England's? Maybe not.

"OK," he said. "Imagine I get inside the building. What then?" He made it sound like a spy film, perhaps not knowing that schools arrange tours for prospective parents all the time. Again, we brainstormed together. He could look at student work posted on the walls to get a sense of what children were doing inside the classroom, as well as to get a sense of the range of abilities at each grade level. He could peek inside classrooms to see how students engaged with each other and with teachers. He could watch students as they passed through the halls, getting a snapshot of their moods, as well as of the kinds of rules enforced by the school. He could look in the teachers' lounge to see how adults in the building interacted with each other.

I suggested he walk by the school at recess, too, as it might give him a sense of the culture of the place—who the kids were and how they acted. As I said this, he pulled up a school lunch menu on his phone.

He had begun a deep dive into figuring out what the school was all about.

Around the same time, a friend in Los Angeles asked about a high school that her oldest child might attend. The L.A. public schools offer a graphically rich report card for every school, and the report card for her prospective school, which she e-mailed to me, included data more important to her than standardized test scores. Only 38 percent of students, we learned, earned a C or better in the core courses required for admission to the University of California system. Students were achieving "below predicted growth" according to the district's AGT (Academic Growth over Time) value-added calculation, and 60 percent of students—the district average—had attendance rates of 96 percent or better.

These data seem pretty clear, but the numbers also have to be interpreted for the particular type of student planning to go there. Sixty percent of students at that school were attending more or less every day. As I told her, I would worry about sending my child there if he or she *wasn't* surrounded by positive messages about the importance of school—messages that come from family, community, and culture. Clearly the school wasn't succeeding in interrupting predispositions like that. If my child were likely to cut school, I'd worry about a school where she'd find a substantial peer group of like-minded students to fall in with—students not that into school. That said, the school was serving a population in which 74 percent of students were classified as "economically disadvantaged"—so clearly it wasn't *totally* failing to motivate kids to show up, since students from such backgrounds are far more likely to miss school on a regular basis.[61]

Among the 60 percent of students at school almost every day, then, roughly two-thirds were on track to be eligible for admission to the University of California system—the top-tier public system in California. These figures weren't particularly impressive, but a balanced assessment, it seemed, would be that the school was probably not to blame for many of its shortcomings. At the same time, we might fairly say that the school didn't seem to be changing the course some kids were headed on. I reasoned, perhaps unhelpfully, that for a child already inclined to take school seriously—as was the case with her child—this particular school might be perfectly fine.

Now, it is worth briefly discussing the importance of peer groups. Peers matter, and they can have an effect on a student's experience in school. Friendships, particularly, are important—for reinforcing particular values, modeling new ones, and exerting social influence. Friends can exert a prosocial or antisocial influence on each other, can set standards for academic engagement, and can help determine the degree to which young people engage in high-risk activities.[62] It is important, consequently, for parents to help their children choose good friends, whatever kind of school they attend.

What about the composition of a school? Do schoolmates matter as much as friends do? After all, students teach one another, influence classroom standards, and take up varying amounts of teacher attention. But research indicates that schoolwide effects are less significant than classroom effects. And the primary influence appears to be generated not by the race, ethnicity, income, or parental education of one's classmates, but rather by their levels of academic achievement. What this means is that a school needs to be diverse enough that there is a critical mass of engaged, high-achieving students in each class, though it does *not* indicate that students benefit from homogenous classrooms. Although research tells us that a critical mass of disruptive students is problematic, it also reveals that racial diversity can have a positive influence on all students.[63]

When applied to our discussion of this L.A. high school, the research on peer groups offered three relevant lessons. First, overall school demographics and achievement levels were probably not that important as long as the school was relatively diverse, which it appeared to be. Second, it struck me as unlikely that a child with a parent so deeply engaged would end up falling in with the wrong friends.[64] And third, it seemed like a good idea to ask about how classes were constituted—What kind of class would a relatively focused and high-achieving student be placed in?

The L.A. report cards offer more information, too, so we continued to dig deeper. Some 90 percent of the staff said they felt proud of their school. Ninety-five percent of students said they felt safe on school grounds. Eighty-five percent said that the material in class required "a lot of thinking." Obviously those results seemed good.

So I told her that, depending on the child, I wouldn't rule out the possibility that the school was just fine. But she wanted to know so much more, and she didn't have much time to conduct her own research. She didn't have the bandwidth to e-mail teachers, grab students on their way home from school, or walk the school grounds during the day. She still felt that she needed to know more. Some of her questions couldn't be answered without sending her child there. Would her child be comfortable? Would she make friends? Would she discover her passions? No school data system in the world will tell you that. Other questions, however—Would the classes be challenging? Would there be access to technology? Would adults function as role models?—should have been easier to answer.

The Kids Who Will (and Won't) Be Fine Anywhere

The two parents referenced above were from middle-class families with a strong orientation toward education, and they were asking lots of good questions about school quality. That said, the overwhelming likelihood—as evidenced by their concern with education—was that their children would be academically fine almost anywhere.

As researchers have continued to emphasize, out-of-school factors account for a significantly greater share of a student's academic achievement and attainment than do in-school factors. Relative to family background characteristics, for instance, school factors pale in comparison, explaining only about 20 percent of achievement.[65]

Parents are the driving force in a child's academic orientation and self-concept; as a result, young people with parents who care about education will, themselves, care about education. This happens because children absorb their parents' values, but it also happens because children are strongly influenced by community expectations. In short, if young people are surrounded by people who expect them to succeed in school, they'll work hard to meet that expectation.[66]

Additionally, children with active and education-conscious parents come to school ready to learn—entering kindergarten with pre-reading skills, huge capacities for language, and early mathematical reasoning abilities. Whatever the particular nature of the learning environment, such students are well prepared to soak up new knowledge.[67]

Still, many white, middle-class parents opt out of particular schools, believing that their children would be poorly served there. In some cases, as in areas of intense segregation, they are right—not because of any innate factor related to race or class, but because of the impact that segregation can have on schools and children. In many other cases, however, they are merely making assumptions.

For low-income families and families of color, this kind of segregation poses a far more serious problem. Often lacking the resources to send their children elsewhere, these families are dependent on schools that bear outward signs of abandonment. Students at such schools are well aware of the fact that the privileged are educating their children elsewhere. They feel all too acutely the stings of segregation and resource scarcity.

Limited data that disproportionately denigrate the quality of schools with large populations of low-income and minority students exacerbate this problem by further scaring away well-resourced and quality-conscious parents. Already inclined to doubt the quality of schools with large populations of less-advantaged students, such parents—unwilling to take a risk on the education of their own children—err on the side of what they believe to be caution. In seeking out people like themselves, they often inadvertently foster higher levels of school segregation.[68]

Thus, even if schools with high percentages of low-income and minority students do not face formal sanctions—as they no longer will under the Every Student Succeeds Act in the way they did under NCLB—they remain far less likely to attract parents positioned to advocate for stronger schools and who themselves constitute an important subgroup in any diverse school.[69]

This is not to say that schools need white students, or middle- and upper-income students, to be successful. Rather, the point is that schools with high concentrations of less-advantaged students are more likely to be sites of low social, political, and economic capital; they are more likely to have more high-needs students than they have the capacity to serve; and they are more likely to be populated by students who look around and see that those with the power to leave have already left.

The limited nature of most educational data also directly affects lower-income parents. Though they may not be as trained as their higher-income counterparts in the interpretation of data, such parents nevertheless care equally about the education of their children. After all, though income is strongly correlated with school preparedness, there is no correlation between income and parental love. However, love is not enough to help many parents engage in a powerful and direct way with schools. Without an ability to engage with the state's school information system, such parents are at a disadvantage when trying to advocate for their children or for their children's schools—a fact that should keep designers of educational data systems awake at night.

What Would Better Data Do?

Better data, and better presentation *of* that data, might help parents make well-informed decisions about where to send their kids to school. In many cases, this would bring about no change at all—people would continue to send their children to the schools they already attend. In other cases, however, better educational information systems would lead parents to think twice before jumping to conclusions— good or bad—about schools.

More robust and more carefully designed information systems might also help parents and members of the public engage more fully as key stakeholders in the schools. Parents, for instance, often know about the experiences of their own children in school; but they rarely know how those experiences relate to those of others. This is fundamentally disempowering because it means that any advocacy tends to be viewed as personal in nature rather than as a campaign on behalf of the whole community. Personal advocacy, of course, is fine; but it does little to create systemic change. Community members, for their part, often operate with far less information. Many, at least in the abstract, would like to support the schools, but aren't sure how.

Just as importantly, better information about school quality would have a significant impact on our schools. Our schools would be better off if we measured all of the things we care about and not just the things that are convenient. Our schools would be better off if state-determined measures did not unfairly denigrate schools with high percentages of students from low-income and minority families. Our schools would be better off if those measures did not pit schools against each other, as if only a handful can be truly "good." And our schools would be better off if educators did not operate in fear that matters beyond their control will lead to their firing or to sanctions for their schools.

3

What Really Matters: A New Framework for School Quality

WHAT DOES a good school do?

If you could know anything about your child's school, or the schools in your community, what information would you wish for?

On the back of a napkin, could you write down four things? Eight? A dozen?

The answer is probably yes. Each of us might use different terminology, and we might place greater emphasis on some factors than others. Generally speaking, though, almost everyone—parents, policymakers, educators, and the public—can name a wide range of inputs and outcomes that characterize good schools.

Unfortunately, that information is mostly unavailable, which has had a host of troubling consequences for our schools.

While the high stakes introduced by No Child Left Behind exacerbated the consequences of limited data, the underlying problem of insufficient information is hardly a new one. For two generations, we have talked about school quality as if it were a unitary concept. And in casting our judgments, we have relied heavily on a narrow range of evidence that often tells us very little about what is happening inside a school.

Perhaps it is time to take a shot at this problem, not by pecking at the margins but by addressing it head-on—by proposing a new framework for measuring school quality.

The challenge, of course, is that any school quality framework will be imperfect. The task is a large one. Our tools are still limited. Not every value will be shared by all members of the public. And the work is inherently subjective.

Despite this, there is also much that we can agree about. Nearly a quarter-century ago, Philip Jackson, Robert Boostrom, and David Hanson wrote a book called *The Moral Life of Schools.* In it they made the following observation:

> To anyone who takes a close look at what goes on in classrooms it becomes quickly evident that our schools do much more than pass along requisite knowledge to the students attending them (or fail to do so, as the case may be). They also influence the way those students look upon themselves and others. They affect the way learning is valued and sought after and lay the foundations of lifelong habits of thought and action. They shape opinion and develop taste, helping to form liking and aversions. They contribute to the growth of character and, in some instances, they may even be a factor in its corruption.[1]

A generation later this is still true.

Not everything can be measured, of course, and many of us have become rightly skeptical of efforts to measure schools. As one online commenter observed: "I think we are too overloaded with data as it is. How about we go back to how we taught 30+ years ago."[2]

Still, there remains significant demand—among parents, policy-makers, and the public—for information about how schools are doing. As Somerville superintendent Mary Skipper put it, "Our students deserve a broad portfolio of measurements." The reality is that most criticism has been leveled not at the collection of data per se but at the collection of incomplete or misrepresentative data.

Even educators, who have generally resisted quantification, have not been entirely opposed to measurement and accountability. As one Somerville teacher observed: "I'm not opposed to data. I'd just like that data to actually reflect what's going on in my classroom." And as a Somerville principal put it, "If I could show that the teaching environment was weak—that I didn't have the time to be an instructional leader . . . I could make a case for resources; for resources that would fix those weaknesses."

The task, then, is to determine what a more complete and balanced way of measuring school quality might be. If not test scores—or, at the very least, if not test scores *alone*—then what?

The Somerville School Quality Framework

In the summer of 2014, our team began to build a new framework for assessing school quality.

The easiest option was to look at the data available and then, working with those pieces, to assemble as coherent a picture as possible. However, we had tried that approach with the *Boston Globe* Dreamschool Finder project and had been dissatisfied with the results. So were many others. As one parent wrote in an e-mail to a Somerville listserv: "I think your goal is good. You just need to find more data which represent the things that parents and students actually do dream of, and I *do* object to selling it as a 'dreamschool finder' when you haven't done that."

Instead of working with available data, then, we decided to begin with a simple question: What do stakeholders—teachers, parents, policymakers, and the public—care about?

We began by looking at polling data. Organizations such as Gallup, Pew Research, the Associated Press, and Editorial Projects in Education have done extensive polling on attitudes and values—providing indicators of what key stakeholder groups feel is important in public education. We were also able to lean heavily on our colleague Rebecca Jacobsen, who, along with Richard Rothstein and Tamara Wilder, wrote *Grading Education: Getting Accountability Right.*[3] In their project, they polled a large and representative sample of Americans, seeking to identify what people care about most in education.

We also recognized that we needed to dig deeper than national polls. So, with a general sense of what Americans value in education, we began interviewing and surveying Somerville residents. In one early survey form, we asked just one question: What are the five things that you think make a good school? Our goal was to see how well the factors identified in our examination of national polls held up in a community like Somerville.

Given how closely Somerville's demography matches that of the nation, we felt confident that our emerging framework—if it could build on academic research *and* generally reflect the city's values—would serve as a starting point for similar efforts elsewhere.

That said, it is worth noting that Somerville is a small city, with a population of roughly 80,000 people. That size makes face-to-face relationships practical in a way they simply can't be in a larger city. The city also has had incredibly stable leadership. Before stepping down, outgoing superintendent Tony Pierantozzi served ten years in the position, and in 2016 Joe Curtatone began his seventh term as mayor, with what one school committee member called "the full-throated support of a very engaged community." Perhaps most importantly, civic and education leaders in the city have a sense of shared purpose that another school committee member called "stunning." Although our later efforts to adapt the framework in other Massachusetts cities and towns were relatively straightforward, it should not be assumed that just because something works in Somerville it will work everywhere.[4]

Eventually, we compiled a long inventory of essential factors distilled from polling, research, and conversations with Somerville community members. The result was a hodgepodge in desperate need of organization. Some of the factors seemed to repeat each other, differing primarily in language. In those cases, we simply selected the factor with the clearest wording. Another problem was that many of the factors on our list seemed to be of different grain size—if some were factors, then others were umbrella concepts for multiple factors. In those cases, we retained the smaller, specific items and set aside the umbrella terminology for later in the process.

Soon we had distilled three dozen separate factors, which, if they were to function appropriately, needed to be organized into a hierarchical taxonomy. Consequently, we began to pair similar measures, such as "student sense of belonging" and "student-teacher relationships," into subcategories—in this case, "Relationships." Next, we nested our sixteen subcategories under five major categories. The "Relationships" subcategory, together with the "Safety" and "Academic Orientation" subcategories, formed a major category: "School Culture." This approach allowed us to preserve a high level of complexity while also respecting the limits of working memory.[5]

Throughout this process, we conducted focus groups with students and teachers, with all of the district's principals and key administrators, with community members, and with the district's community liaisons—a group tasked with reaching out to families from traditionally underrepresented cultural backgrounds, with one liaison assigned to each of the city's schools. Ultimately, we ran fourteen focus groups—one with students, four with teachers, three with principals and administrators, and six with parents and community members.[6] Ultimately, though professionals and laypeople may have different priorities and concerns, it continued to surprise us how much they tended to agree about things. As one of our research assistants concluded after analyzing results from focus groups with principals and community members, "There was virtually no disagreement between the two groups."[7] We found similarly strong overlap with results from our other focus groups.

Once we had incorporated all of the suggestions from our stakeholders and had determined that there were no significant disagreements among them, we sent a copy of the framework, reproduced in Figure 3.1, to the district for its approval.

The five major categories of this framework, we believed, represented a coherent model of a good school, balancing inputs and outcomes.

The first three categories, broadly construed, are inputs. A school with a strong teaching environment, healthy school culture, and sufficient resources is quite likely to produce positive outcomes. A school lacking those elements will likely struggle.

As Figure 3.2 illustrates, these categories are not entirely independent of each other. Insofar as schools are ecosystems, each component affects the whole—something we found empirical evidence of when analyzing correlations between categories.[8] Yet the constructs are also independent enough from each other to merit separate categories. For example, even schools with problematic cultures and inadequate resources often employ great individual teachers. By the same token, a school may have a strong culture even if some of its teachers are weak and its resources limited.

ESSENTIAL INPUTS

1. Teachers and the Teaching Environment

   1A. Knowledge and Skills of Teachers
      1A-i: Professional qualifications
      1A-ii: Effective practices
      1A-iii: Professional disposition

   1B. Teaching Environment
      1B-i: Professional community
      1B-ii: Support for teaching development and growth
      1B-iii: Effective leadership

2. School Culture

   2A. Safety
      2A-i: Student physical safety
      2A-ii: Student emotional safety

   2B. Relationships
      2B-i: Sense of belonging
      2B-ii: Student-teacher relationships

   2C. Academic Orientation
      2C-i: Valuing of learning
      2C-ii: Academic challenge

3. Resources

   3A. Facilities and Personnel
      3A-i: Physical spaces and materials
      3A-ii: Content specialists and support staff

   3B. Learning Resources
      3B-i: Curricular strength and variety
      3B-ii: Cultural responsiveness
      3B-iii: Extracurricular activities

   3C. Community Support
      3C-i: Family-school relationships
      3C-ii: Community involvement & External partnerships

KEY OUTCOMES

4. Academic Learning

   4A. Academic Performance
      4A-i: Test score growth
      4A-ii: Performance assessment

   4B. Student Commitment to Learning
      4B-i: Engagement in school
      4B-ii: Graduation rate

   4C. Critical Thinking
      4C-i: Problem solving emphasis
      4C-ii: Problem solving skills

   4D. College and Career Readiness
      4D-i: College-going and persistence
      4D-ii: Career preparation and placement

5. Character and Well-Being

   5A. Civic Engagement
      5A-i: Civic mindset
      5A-ii: Appreciation for diversity

   5B. Work Ethic
      5B-i: Perseverance and determination
      5B-ii: Growth mindset

   5C. Artistic and Creative Traits
      5C-i: Participation in arts and literature
      5C-ii: Valuing creative and performing arts

   5D. Health
      5D-i: Social and emotional health
      5D-ii: Physical health

Figure 3.1. Somerville school quality framework

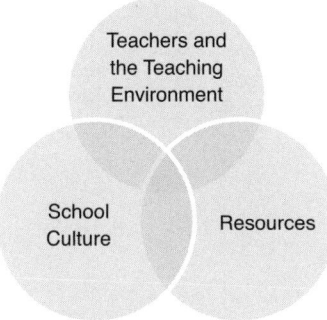

Figure 3.2. Essential inputs

Still, the overlap among these categories is worth noting because a good school must pay attention to all three. In other words, it is impossible to achieve ambitious goals in one category without targeting deficiencies in the others.

The fourth and fifth categories in our framework—Academic Learning and Character and Well-Being—represent outcomes, as shown in Figure 3.3.

As mentioned earlier, a school with strong inputs is quite likely to produce positive outcomes. Teachers employing effective practices, for instance, or a school culture that promotes a sense of belonging, or a strong and varied curriculum—all inputs—will have a positive effect on outcomes such as student engagement or social and emotional health.

All components, in other words, work together. After all, no element on its own, whether an input or an outcome, can singularly define a good school.

Yet it is important to actually measure those outcomes: first, because it is conceivable, if improbable, that a school might earn high ratings for inputs but not outcomes; and second, because a school may be succeeding more in one direction than another. A school may have

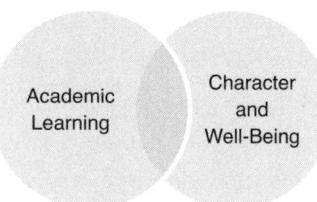

Figure 3.3. Key outcomes

great teachers, a positive culture, and adequate resources, for instance, and it may be channeling those strengths into academic learning alone, neglecting the character and well-being outcomes valued by parents, educators, and the public. As we found in Somerville, the correlation between these two categories, at each school, tended to be quite small, indicating a clear need to measure both. Other researchers, similarly, have found that different kinds of outcomes can be surprisingly independent of each other, even within individual classrooms.[9]

The categories in our framework are also balanced with regard to the exogenous (*external* to the school) and endogenous (*internal* to the school) nature of their influence. Good schools benefit from much that is outside of their control—financial support from the state, for instance, or high levels of parental engagement.[10] That should be recognized in any representation of school quality. Too much reliance on exogenous factors, however, can send misleading messages about the work being done inside a school. Consequently, some balance is necessary to ensure that, in discussions about school improvement, stakeholders articulate well-rounded solutions that do not simply dump undue responsibility at the school's doorstep.

Of course, something as complex as education can never be perfectly measured, no matter how detailed the framework. Schools are highly complicated systems with thousands of components. And a measure that captures *everything,* despite its accuracy, would cease to be useful as a tool, because it would perfectly replicate reality in all of its messiness. It calls to mind the Jorge Luis Borges story "On Exactitude in Science," in which the pursuit of cartographic precision drives the creation of a 1:1 scale map—a map as large as the empire itself. If it is going to be useful, a map can't capture everything; but it should capture the things most valued by its users.

Whatever its shortcomings, this framework offers a clear and comprehensive model for thinking about the quality of a school. Though it can be used to guide formal school- , district- , and state-level assessment, it is equally useful for parents and community members who wish to have a better understanding of other schools. These are the things that matter—the things that every one of us should be seeking to promote in our schools.

Hopefully, anyone looking at this framework will see its various categories and subcategories as both important and relatively comprehensive. But this framework should not be viewed as if it were carved in stone. Instead, it should be understood as a living document that can, and probably should, be updated and amended to match the values and concerns of different communities and the new challenges that await us in the future.

One way that it can be tailored is across *space.* This framework was designed for a diverse and relatively representative community; but it is certainly possible that a community could interpret particular components of this framework as inappropriate, or that they might identify something missing from it. Inasmuch as that is the case, potential users should ask the same questions we asked in Somerville—about what is missing, confusing, overemphasized, or errantly included. We don't imagine much will change; but, of course, that's exactly why it is important to ask.

The other way that this framework can be tailored is across *time*— as values shift over the years, and as our knowledge base expands.

Though this framework reflects what we know about school quality and public values today, that will certainly change in the years to come. Some measures, for instance, will reveal themselves to align too closely with race, ethnicity, and social class.[11] Others will become outdated as new techniques and technologies allow for more precise and accurate assessment.

It is also worth noting that we have not placed weights on any of the framework's categories or subcategories. That is not because each component is equally valuable. Rather, it is because the way a community values particular components may differ from place to place. Should more emphasis be placed on Academic Learning than on Character and Well-Being? In some places, yes; in other places, no. It depends on the values of stakeholders.

Finally, it is important to note here that many people may use different terminology to describe similar concepts. In such cases, differences in language might be mistaken for differences in values. Thus, while it is our hope that the meaning of each category and subcategory of this framework is relatively self-evident, it is worth taking the time to clearly define each of these constructs and describe their individual importance. The sections that follow, then—organized by the framework's five major categories—are designed to answer any lingering questions, and may even reveal something new about what matters in measuring school quality.

Teachers and the Teaching Environment

The quality of teachers and the teaching environment is a seemingly obvious factor in the success of a school—one commonly recognized by Americans as essential. In a 2013 poll, for instance, 96 percent of parents cited teacher quality as "extremely" or "very" important to them.[12] We heard this repeatedly from stakeholders in Somerville, perhaps most clearly from teachers. As one teacher put it, "I need other teachers, and my principal, to do their jobs so I can do my job." Not surprisingly, teachers and the teaching environment are also commonly recognized by scholars as an essential input for any successful school. As one commonly cited research study put it, "No other measured aspect of schools is nearly as important in determining student achievement."[13]

Teachers and the teaching environment clearly matter. But what, specifically, should we be looking for? As one group of scholars asked, "Most parents want good teachers, but what indicators reflect the actual quality of the teaching staff—seniority? advanced credentials? salary?"[14]

One seemingly easy measure would be the percentage of teachers who are "highly qualified" according to the definition established by No Child Left Behind—a figure that is already collected in every state. One problem with this approach, however, is that the vast majority of teachers possess the credentials—a bachelor's degree, a state-issued license to teach, and demonstrated subject matter competence— required to earn "highly qualified" status. The larger problem, however, is that although research raises questions about the effectiveness of teachers who *lack* these qualifications, it does not indicate that teachers who possess them are, in reality, effective teachers. We should not be comforted, in short, merely by the fact that all of the teachers in a school are licensed.[15]

Many people also look at teachers' academic credentials—the prestige of their alma maters and the number of degrees they possess. On the face of it, such factors seem like good proxies for teacher quality. Knowing this, private schools almost always include faculty bios on their web pages, hoping that the advanced degrees possessed by teachers will entice parents into paying tuition. Yet although these would be relatively easy variables to measure, they don't tell us a great deal about teacher quality. Graduates of higher-prestige colleges do not appear to be more effective in the classroom than other college grads; and those with graduate degrees do not appear to be more effective than those without. If we think about it, this makes some intuitive sense. The factors that help someone gain admission to an elite college do not closely align with the factors that lead to success in teaching elementary or secondary school students. Furthermore, graduate programs are highly variable in their relevance to classroom instruction. Additionally, because roughly half of teachers possess graduate degrees—in part because some states require a master's degree for a full teaching license—such measures make for a weak sorting mechanism when it comes to quality.[16]

Training does matter. Scholars have found that possession of degrees in relevant content areas can have a significant effect on student achievement. Content coursework in math and science, specifically, appear to improve a teacher's performance, particularly at the high school level. Relatedly, research has shown that teachers who know how students learn and who know how to facilitate learning are significantly more effective in the classroom. It seems to make sense, then, to gather information about these factors through queries of the district, as well as through survey questions addressed to teachers themselves.[17]

What many would like to know most, though, is whether or not teachers engage in effective practices in the classroom. After all, relevant content knowledge and knowledge of pedagogy are valuable because they predict classroom effectiveness among teachers. So what about measuring effectiveness directly?

That turns out to be quite challenging. The best way would be to have a team of highly trained professionals engage in multiple observations of the teachers within a school. That, however, can prove infeasible given limits on school funding, as well as the sheer scale of the enterprise—we have over three million teachers in American public schools. It is also complicated by the fact that effective teaching can take many different forms. That said, there are promising models from other countries worth considering. New Zealand, for instance, has developed a teacher observation system built around key practices that help students learn. Britain has developed a much-lauded school inspection system that has been replicated on a smaller scale in places like Charlotte, North Carolina. Additionally, advances in technology—primarily video—may make it easier to observe teachers directly. Thus, despite the challenge, researchers and educators will no doubt continue working on such models across the next decade.[18]

Survey questions of students can also begin to unpack, at least in some general fashion, whether a teacher engages in practices that are associated with student learning and positive classroom environments. Of course, the questions need to be specific enough that they produce answers about actual teaching *practice* rather than the popularity of the teacher. A well-designed survey scale goes through substantial testing in order to determine how highly it correlates with the things we think it should align with. Thus, rather than merely guessing, we can actually determine through empirical evidence whether or not survey questions work.[19]

In addition to teacher pedagogical practice, our focus groups convinced us that we needed to include teachers' professional dispositions as a subcategory. Principals and teachers told us that educators should possess the ability to work with students who have a wide range of needs, be sensitive to student cultural background traits, and have positive attitudes in the workplace. In short, they were identifying a professional disposition as an instrumental good—valuable because it improves classroom instruction and strengthens the teaching environment. Not surprisingly, research substantiates this thinking.[20]

In focus groups with parents and community members, however, teacher disposition was often described as something valuable in its own right. They expressed strong preference for teachers with character traits such as patience and compassion, not because such traits would lead to better academic performance among students, but because they would be good for young people. Briefly put, they wanted their children to be taught by role models who would treat students with appropriate care and respect.

Of course, teachers do not work in a vacuum. While much of teacher success can be attributed to individuals, much is also due to a school environment that is supportive of educator growth and development. In other words, however good teachers are, they need support to maximize their potential. As research indicates, teachers can grow a great deal across the full arc of their careers, and their professional environments can exert a powerful influence on growth. According to one study, teachers working in schools with high professional environment ratings improved student math achievement nearly 40 percent more than those working in schools with lower ratings. Additionally, research has shown that supportive environments can promote teacher development, enhance collaboration, and reduce burnout. Consequently, striving to create schools that structure this kind of professional learning environment should be a top priority.[21]

How would one go about evaluating the quality of the teaching environment? By using surveys, it is possible to ask teachers directly. What is the quality of the school's professional community? Is it collegial and collaborative? Do teachers get along with and help each other? Such questions can be paired with other measures, such as the rate of teacher turnover not due to retirements, to piece together a fairly robust picture of the professional community.[22]

If teachers are to reach their full potential, they need more than just a strong community of fellow educators—they need targeted and effective professional development (PD). The research on PD is not always uniformly positive, because PD programs are often implemented ineffectively. Still, research does indicate that PD can be a powerful lever for helping teachers develop their skills and stay engaged in the process of their own growth. And when a PD program is implemented in a way that stays true to the program's core, PD is associated with higher-quality lesson plans and higher student achievement; it is also relatively cost-effective. Determining a district's commitment to PD, then—and particularly by asking teachers about the quality of their PD experiences—is an important aspect of determining a school's teaching environment.[23]

In addition to support for development, teachers also depend on effective school leadership in order to do their jobs well. As one teacher put it in a focus group, "Teachers also need support, not just students." Research substantiates this insight, indicating that school administrators play a significant role in creating a strong teaching environment, perhaps chiefly by establishing a positive and focused instructional climate. Successful administrators support both novice and experienced teachers in their work, foster collaboration and trust, raise teacher effort, enable teachers to collaborate and learn from each other, and increase willingness to engage in reform efforts. Administrative support is also strongly correlated with factors like student achievement, school safety, school climate, and teacher satisfaction. Again, by asking teachers direct questions about these issues, it is possible to begin to gauge the degree to which a school's leaders are creating a strong environment for teaching.[24]

To review, Figure 3.4 shows the full framework for Teachers and the Teaching Environment.

Not every school will be equally strong in these areas. Still, it is important to note that factors in this category are not dependent on student demography the way that test scores tend to be. Consequently,

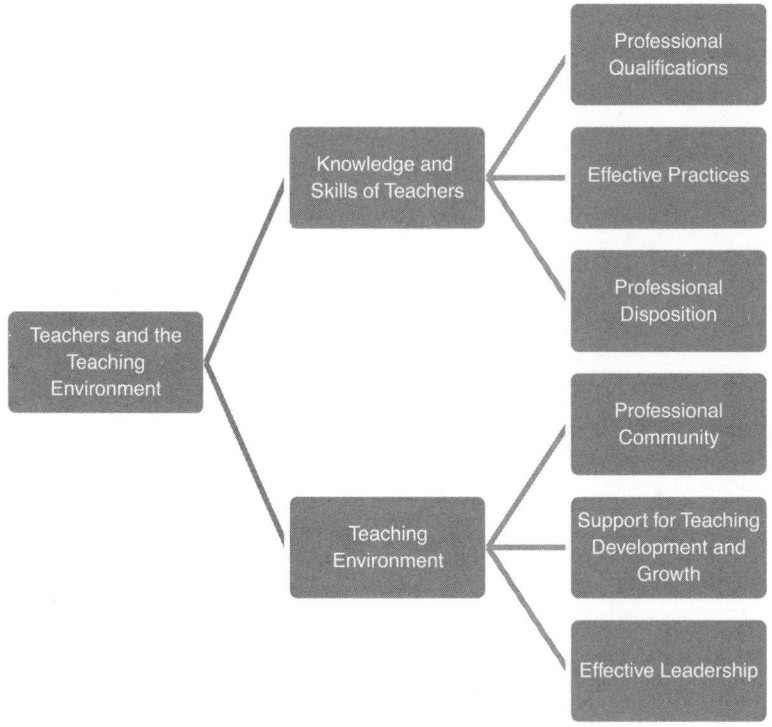

Figure 3.4. Teachers and the teaching environment

it is perfectly reasonable to establish the expectation of relative parity with regard to these variables and to demand an account for inequities. Thus, while state officials and district administrators might use data about teachers and the teaching environment to guide policy and practice, parents and educators might use them to advocate for their schools.[25]

In the absence of such data, however, it is still possible to piece together more useful information about teachers and the teaching environment—whether individuals are just learning about a school or seeking to be better and more informed advocates. Here, then, are a series of questions one might ask, organized by the category of person best qualified to answer them. Though they will not produce "data" per se, they may lead to better kinds of conversations about school quality.

Teachers and teaching environment questions to ask a school's principal:

What grade levels and subject areas have you had to hire for in the past two years?

What does it typically look like here when teachers try to engage students?

What stories can you tell me about how invested teachers are here? How does the school promote that kind of investment?

How much turnover has there been in the teaching staff over the past two years? What explains it?

What is your top priority as the person responsible for helping teachers grow?

Teachers and teaching environment questions to ask teachers:

How many of your colleagues are teaching the children and the subjects that they're best qualified to teach?

How much are teachers encouraged to use different kinds of teaching strategies to engage students in class?

To what extent are your colleagues personally interested in the students and invested in their futures?

How much do your colleagues trust the principal here?

How much has your principal helped teachers improve? What kinds of things has s / he done?

Teachers and teaching environment questions to ask parents at the school:

What does your child say about his or her teachers?

Do you get the sense that teachers use different kinds of teaching techniques here?

Is it your impression that teachers at this school are invested in
the kids?

How much turnover is there in the teaching staff from year to
year?

Do you get the sense that teachers here enjoy working with each
other? What does that look like?

School Culture

Another key element of school quality to monitor, and the second
major category in our framework, is school culture. What are the
norms of a school? How does it feel? What is the nature of relationships between community members? Those are critical aspects of
school quality, and standardized test scores tell us very little about
them.

At first blush, "school culture" can seem a vague, catchall category.
Relative to a seemingly more nuts-and-bolts input like teacher quality,
it may even seem like a frill. Who needs school culture when you've
got great teachers?

Yet, as scholars have shown, school culture is an essential aspect of
school quality. It shapes the experience students have in a school, influences their effort, and strengthens their commitment to the process
of learning. And in doing so, a positive school culture can begin to
even out some of the out-of-school influences that lead to disparate
levels of achievement. Additionally, schools with strong cultures are
also more attractive workplaces for teachers and easier organizations
for administrators to manage.[26] As one principal told us, "That's my
main goal right now—creating a building-wide culture where everyone
is on the same page and excited to be here."

Parents and community members also tend to identify school culture as an important input in schools. They use different words and

phrases, certainly, but very few engaged members of a school community disagree with the fact that the character of a school and the relationships forged within its walls are of great consequence. They know intuitively that the feel of a school can attract or repel teachers, inspire or suppress student effort, and promote or inhibit teamwork. They know that the way students interact with each other matters, as does the way students interact with teachers, and that both kinds of relationships influence every aspect of life inside a school, learning included. And they sense that students will realize their full potential only if they attend a school imbued with hope, trust, and a sense of shared purpose. Not surprisingly, researchers have found that school culture is generally linked to a number of important outcomes, such as higher levels of academic achievement and school-level improvement efforts.[27]

How would you track a concept as nebulous as school culture? You know it when you step inside a school. As one Somerville parent put it, "You can just tell, by the sound ... people in the hallway ... if they're happy to be there, if they like each other, if the teachers are talking to kids; that's a good school." But how could that possibly be included in a systematic measure of quality?

Scholars have identified several key elements of school culture— including student sense of belonging, discipline, liking of school, peer relations, and teacher support—that can be more clearly delineated and measured. And though it is true that some schools will have an easier time than others in promoting particular aspects of school culture, it is nevertheless possible for all schools to create environments conducive to learning. Insofar as that is the case, school culture data may tell us more than test scores do about how a student will fare there, as well as about whether intervention and support are required.[28]

Perhaps the most fundamental aspect of school culture is student physical safety. This is a basic concern, particularly for parents. As one

Somerville mother put it, "That's my absolute number one priority, all the time." But physical safety also matters because of what it is associated with in schools. Student perceptions of victimization, for instance, are predictive of lower levels of engagement and achievement. Feelings of safety, by contrast, are associated with a range of positive outcomes. In short: if students aren't safe, they aren't relaxed and focused. Schools struggling to ensure this basic prerequisite for learning are probably not paying sufficient attention to other components of school quality.[29]

Because it seems so straightforward, people often seek to measure safety informally. They might elicit anecdotal evidence, for instance, or look at a school's exterior conditions. Yet anecdotal evidence is likely to center around high-profile incidents, which may not indicate a tremendous amount about the general safety of a school. And building conditions, though they can affect student learning, do not appear to have a direct impact on safety. Most troublingly, those seeking to informally gauge a school's quality may use racial demography as a proxy for school quality in general, and for safety in particular. As research has demonstrated, however, the presence of students of color does not make a school feel less safe. In fact, research has found that the schools most successful at making their students feel safe may be those with high levels of diversity.[30]

As it turns out, school safety can be measured in relatively straightforward fashion. By combining student and teacher survey responses with data from the district about reported incidents, it is possible to assemble a much clearer picture of how physically safe students are at a school.

Of course, safety is much more than freedom from physical violence. In fact, some of the worst forms of bullying involve no physical threats at all—creating a feeling of dread among students that can lead to distraction and even serious depression. Bullying, for example, can keep students out of school, with as many as 160,000 American students a year staying home on any given day because they are afraid of being tormented. And a recent study of more than 2,000 students found that those who witnessed bullying reported more feelings of depression, anxiety, hostility, and inferiority than either the bullies or the victims themselves.[31] Asking students and teachers about this is critical, because it can happen at all kinds of schools.

Accurately gauging student emotional safety requires more than just tracking bullying. After all, we don't merely want schools to be characterized by an absence of a negative factor; we want them to be characterized by the presence of a positive factor. Good schools, when we close our eyes and imagine them, are places where students and teachers share a collective sense of responsibility for each other and, in turn, allow themselves to depend on others in the community. Academic research bears this out, finding that high levels of trust in school are associated with a range of positive outcomes for both teachers and students.[32] Like bullying, relational trust can be measured through teacher and student perception surveys. Together, such figures can give us a relatively clear sense of how emotionally safe a school is—a critical element of a positive culture.

Because we cannot understand school culture without understanding the bonds that exist among students, teachers, and administrators, relationships became our second major subcategory, and we decided to measure it in two ways. The first is a student's sense of belonging. Connectedness to school and feelings of belonging are what many of us remember about our own schooling experiences when we reflect back on them—often far more clearly than we remember the degree to which we were challenged academically, though obviously that matters as well. We remember whether or not we were cared for by our peers and our teachers. We remember whether or not a school felt like home.

Not surprisingly, research has found that student sense of belonging in a school is generally associated with positive outcomes. Individual students' perceptions of belonging, for instance, are predictive of academic performance, emotional well-being, mental health, social confidence, and behavior control. Decreased school connectedness, accordingly, is associated with lower levels of learning and involvement, as well as declining health status.[33]

Do you know "belonging" when you see it? Probably—but, again, it is easy to jump to conclusions with regard to the kinds of schools that foster belonging. Certain populations, people may assume, are inherently disconnected from school. Yet, as research has found, *any* school—not just affluent schools with abundant resources—can promote a strong sense of belonging among students.[34] While that doesn't mean that all schools are actually succeeding in this dimension, it does mean that we should collect the evidence before reaching conclusions.

The second half of the "relationships" subcategory is student-teacher relationships, which shape the experiences of students and teachers alike, leading to higher rates of effort and retention for both groups. Not surprisingly, these relationships are also significantly related to academic engagement and performance. Students reporting strong relationships inside schools, for example, tend to report higher levels of motivation and confidence in completing their work.[35]

Of course, it is worth noting that although strong student-teacher relationships are predictive of student achievement, they are equally important for promoting the development of happy, healthy young people. Teachers serve as friends, mentors, and role models for students. As research indicates, strong relationships with teachers are linked to lower rates of alcohol and tobacco use as well as to lower levels of depression and violence, even when students do not feel a general sense of belonging in school. Perhaps not surprisingly, these relationships appear to be particularly important for students from traditionally underserved backgrounds—students who lack the social and institutional supports common among their more privileged peers.[36]

A school that has high levels of perceived physical and emotional safety and that fosters strong relationships between young people and adults will have a positive culture. Yet there is a difference between a positive culture, in general, and a positive *school* culture. After all, a day camp can be a safe and caring place where people have strong relationships. The difference between a day camp and a school, though, is that a school is explicitly oriented toward helping students expand their academic knowledge and skills—it helps them discover their intellectual passions, strengths, and interests. Consequently, our third subcategory in the school culture cluster is academic orientation—the degree to which students see school as a place of learning and are invested in the learning process.

One way to measure academic orientation is by tracking regular attendance. Regular attendance, of course, is an outcome, but it is also a precondition for learning, as students frequently absent from school are unlikely to be committed to building their skills. Attendance is also a proxy for the degree to which students value learning. As 98 percent of American teachers and administrators agree, good attendance is a characteristic of highly engaged and motivated students. And as one Somerville teacher put it: "Are you showing up every day? Then I know I've got a shot at teaching you something." Now, it is true that students from some demographic backgrounds are more inclined than others to attend school regularly. Those with college-educated parents, for instance, or from higher-income households, are more likely to be in regular attendance through graduation. Nevertheless, schools with positive atmospheres and effective practices encourage students to attend, whatever the nature of a student's family background.[37]

Of course, students may regularly attend school for a variety of reasons. Consequently, if we are using attendance figures as a proxy for the degree to which students value learning, we should pair them with a more direct measure of that construct. Again, a well-designed survey scale seems an appropriate tool. How intrinsically motivated are students? To what degree do they identify as learners? How much does school matter to them? Such questions can tell us a great deal, particularly when paired with an objective measure of whether or not students are showing up every day.

The other half of the academic orientation equation is the degree to which a school and its teachers challenge students academically. Academic challenge, as researchers tend to define it, is the degree to which educators push students to learn and grow, though not beyond what is reasonable. In schools with strong levels of academic challenge, teachers set high but achievable goals, they believe in the ability of students to succeed, the school environment is orderly and serious, and all stakeholders respect hard work and accomplishment. When academic challenge is coupled with other measures—such as consistent attendance—it has also been linked to higher levels of academic achievement.[38]

To review, Figure 3.5 shows the full framework for school culture.

These are important pieces of school quality that all stakeholders should be invested in. And though such a framework may lend itself naturally to a formal data system—inside a district, say, or at the state level—it is also of use to anyone interested in broadening their conversations about school quality. Parents searching for schools or looking to become better advocates, educators seeking to improve their schools, or community members wanting to get involved all stand to benefit from a more detailed and more clearly defined map of what constitutes a "good" school. What follows, then, is a series of questions that anyone might ask, regardless of position or expertise.

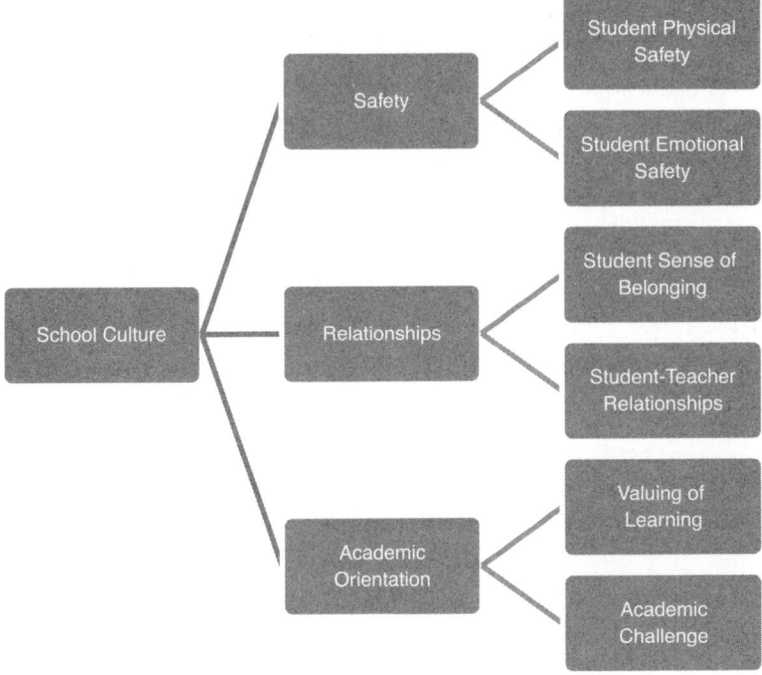

Figure 3.5. School culture

Once again, they have been organized by the category of person best qualified to answer them.

School culture questions to ask a school's principal:

Can you describe a safety challenge here and how the school responds to it?

What does the school do to build trust among community members? Can you provide specific examples?

How does the school help students feel at home here?

How much effort does it take to get students focused on learning here? What kinds of schoolwide efforts are in place?

How does the school encourage students to meet high expectations? Who sets those expectations?

School culture questions to ask teachers:

How safe are students in the hallways, bathrooms, and playgrounds here?

How much bullying do you think goes on here? What accounts for it?

How connected are students to this school? Can you tell me any stories?

How strong are relationships between teachers and students here? Why are things that way?

How much do your colleagues focus on challenging students? Can you describe a particular example?

School culture questions to ask parents at a school:

How safe does your child feel at school?

Has your child ever talked about being bullied or about observing students being unkind to each other at school?

How close are your child's relationships with adults at school? What is his / her closest adult relationship there?

What is your child's attitude toward school? What do you think accounts for it?

How challenged does your child feel at school? Can you tell me any stories?

Resources

The next major factor in our framework, and the last of our three essential inputs, is resources.

For many people, the word "resources" means one thing: money. After all, money is essential in securing many of the resources essential for educating students. Even great teachers working in a school with a positive culture need access to working facilities, support staff they can count on, solid curricular materials, small enough classes to develop relationships with their students, and support from community members. And though not all schools currently have access to equitable resources, it is quite possible to foster conditions in which they do. Tracking these data might help us not only to recognize well-supported schools but also to identify gaps that can be filled.[39]

That said, the impact of school funding is not always proportional. We cannot say, for instance, that a school with annual per-pupil expenditures of $10,000 is bad merely because that figure falls below the national average. Nor can we say that a school with per-pupil expenditures of $20,000 is twice as good as one with per-pupil expenditures of $10,000.[40] Additionally, many important school resources, such as parental involvement, have no price tag associated with them. Relatedly, many school expenditures have only indirect effects on student learning. A roughly $1 billion outlay for iPads in Los Angeles, for instance, appears to have done little more than provide students with easier access to games and social media. Finally, different schools may have different needs. A school with a large Special Education population, for instance, will require substantially more funding to meet the needs of its student body than a corresponding school with very few Special Education students.[41]

How, then, to measure resources? Again, money is perhaps the easiest metric to go after, and there is a substantial body of scholarship indicating that money is important. A major review of the literature by scholar Bruce Baker, for instance, found that per-pupil spending is positively associated with higher student outcomes. Another study, by Rob Greenwald, Larry Hedges, and Richard Laine, concluded that a broad range of resources were positively related to student outcomes, including academic achievement. And as C. Kirabo Jackson, Rucker

Johnson, and Claudia Persico found, a 10 percent increase in per-pupil spending across a student's K–12 experience leads to 7.25 percent higher wages.[42]

In short, money matters, yet it fails to tell a clear story. Consequently, measuring a school's access to resources may make more sense than tracking expenditures. But which particular resources matter?

Ask a teacher and you're likely to hear something about physical spaces and materials. Academic research supports this position, indicating that in schools with inadequate spaces and materials, the focus on academics tends to be less clear, the learning environment is less likely to be seen as orderly and serious, and there tends to be less community support for teaching and learning. In other words, if the physical spaces and materials at a school are inadequate, it can be hard to convince teachers and students that they are actually engaged in a process that matters. Additionally, research has shown that facility quality is an important predictor of teachers' decisions to switch schools, even after controlling for other contributing factors.[43]

Class size also matters. Now, some will suggest that the research on class size is mixed, and in a certain sense that is true. Reducing class size across the board often doesn't accomplish much, at least as measured by test scores. First, this is because reducing class size often means hiring new teachers—many of whom had not previously secured teaching jobs because they lacked skills or qualifications. Second, smaller class sizes can fail to make a difference if teachers are not trained to capitalize on them. Yet, research does suggest that smaller class sizes support more individual teacher-student interactions and higher levels of student engagement, particularly for lower-achieving students. As one study recently concluded, "Research supports the common-sense notion that children learn more and teachers are more effective in smaller classes." There are, of course, diminishing returns to consider. If a teacher cannot keep track of more than twenty-five students in a room at once, a reduction from thirty to twenty is perhaps more critical than one from twenty to ten. It may also be that there is such a thing as classes that are too small. Nevertheless, class size is a "physical space" issue worth measuring and continuing to conduct research on.[44]

Teachers also talked to us a great deal in focus groups about the importance of high-functioning content specialists and support staff. That came as no surprise. Good schools must account for the varying needs of students, meeting those needs with appropriate support that often goes beyond what teachers can provide. Parents understand this as well. According to an Associated Press–NORC poll, 82 percent of parents see the availability of support resources such as counselors as extremely or very important. College counselors play a vital role in helping students craft their postsecondary plans, and ensuring that counselors have adequate time to advise students on course taking can improve postsecondary success. School-based mental health counselors have been linked in research to lower rates of student course failure, absence, and disciplinary referral, as well as to higher grade point averages. And for young people who require Special Education services, support personnel can make or break their school experiences. It is important, then, both to track the number of specialists and counselors at a school and to ask teachers if their students have adequate access to trained and knowledgeable support personnel.[45]

Learning resources—those directly related to the curriculum—are also critical to school success. One key question to ask concerns curricular variety and strength. In short, is the curriculum rich, diverse, and challenging for all students? All students, regardless of background, benefit from a diverse curriculum, and students are less likely to be bored and disengaged when the curriculum is challenging. Yet test scores tell us nothing at all about the extent to which the curriculum is varied and strong. It is quite possible, for instance, that a school might produce high scores by narrowing the curriculum and by orienting classroom instruction toward state-mandated exams. Consequently, it is important to measure curricular diversity, and one simple way to do this is by counting the number of instructional hours in each subject per student, to ensure that a sufficient range of courses is being taught. Curricular rigor, though somewhat more difficult to operationalize, can be tracked by measuring advanced coursework offered through programs like Advanced Placement or International Baccalaureate, at least at the high school level. Both concepts—curricular diversity and rigor—can also be measured by surveying teachers and students.[46]

Another key question to ask about the curriculum concerns the degree to which it is culturally responsive. There may be, as some scholars have argued, a core of knowledge that all students should be exposed to. But it also appears that historically marginalized students are engaged and empowered by a curriculum that explicitly values their cultural backgrounds. Some critics have dismissed the concern with cultural responsiveness as being bound up with self-esteem rather than with curricular rigor; others have cautioned that too much emphasis on cultural particularity can be divisive. Advocates of culturally responsive curricula, however, have made a compelling case that the traditional school curriculum is not neutral, and that an orientation toward the dominant culture has had a detrimental effect on the most vulnerable. Only by accounting for that, they argue, can the curriculum be made equitable—an observation we heard from our focus group participants in Somerville.[47] Thus, it seems appropriate to consider not only the rigor of the school curriculum but also the degree to which it engages and empowers all learners.[48]

Our third "resources" subcategory is community support. All of our focus group participants seemed to embrace the idea that good schools are fully integrated within the larger community, concurring that good schools are not just supported *by* parents, but also frequently reach out *to* parents. There was also widespread agreement that good schools maintain ties with neighborhood residents and businesses. In other words, participants in our focus groups agreed that good schools support the community and vice versa. Such support can be an animating spirit in a school, even if it lacks physical resources; and schools that are rich in other kinds of resources can often fail to realize their full potential if they lack support from families and the community.

Family involvement is perhaps the most obvious form of community support and can manifest in a variety of ways—from parents volunteering at the school, to communicating with a child's teacher, to supporting a child's learning at home. All of those forms of involvement, research indicates, matter to a school's success. That is because children with involved parents get the support, guidance, and encouragement they need to succeed in school. But it is also because when parents and school staff work with each other, they can collaborate to share information, coordinate expectations, and align support for students, thereby more effectively managing behavior and enabling academic success.[49]

Many parents know this intuitively. "Schools can't do it without families," one Somerville parent acknowledged. According to an Associated Press–NORC poll, 96 percent of parents see the amount of parental involvement in a child's education as "extremely" or "very" important. Teachers know this, too. When surveyed by the Education Week Research Center, teachers rated "parental support and engagement" 4.5 on a 5-point scale. Not all schools, of course, will have equal success in engaging parents; some communities—specifically those with more affluent, college-educated, English-speaking parents—are simply more likely to get involved than others, because they have the privilege to do so. But schools can do a great deal to foster engagement through communication and outreach. Knowing this, we should not only expect schools to engage families; we should also track family involvement as a resource—enabling schools with low ratings in this category to demonstrate their need for assistance.[50]

Broader community involvement is also a critical resource for schools. At first blush, this may not seem as inherently important as parental involvement. What impact does a local business owner, for instance, have on the quality of a school? Yet the stability of a community and a school's connections with community leaders can play a key role in cultivating an environment of trust—trust among educators that the school will get what it needs to support the children enrolled there, and trust among community members that the school has the best interests of its children in mind. Ultimately, the responsibility for children's educational development is a collaborative enterprise among parents, school staff, and community members.[51]

More concretely, community members can volunteer in the school, support it financially, and foster school spirit. Anyone who has sat through a sold-out theater production, squeezed into an overflowing athletic event, or inched through a lively science fair knows the power that community support can have. Community members can also help foster social capital among students—expanding who they know, what they have access to, and how they envision their futures. Finally, connecting with the community can make school more relevant for students. School and community partnerships, for instance, foster community-based learning that provides young people with real-world experience, and that can help school feel more important in their lives. So why not ask teachers about the degree to which they feel supported by parents and community members? Though such support is not under the complete control of a school—and therefore should not be a part of any accountability calculation—it is an important resource that should be tracked, because it might lead to smarter activism and intervention.[52]

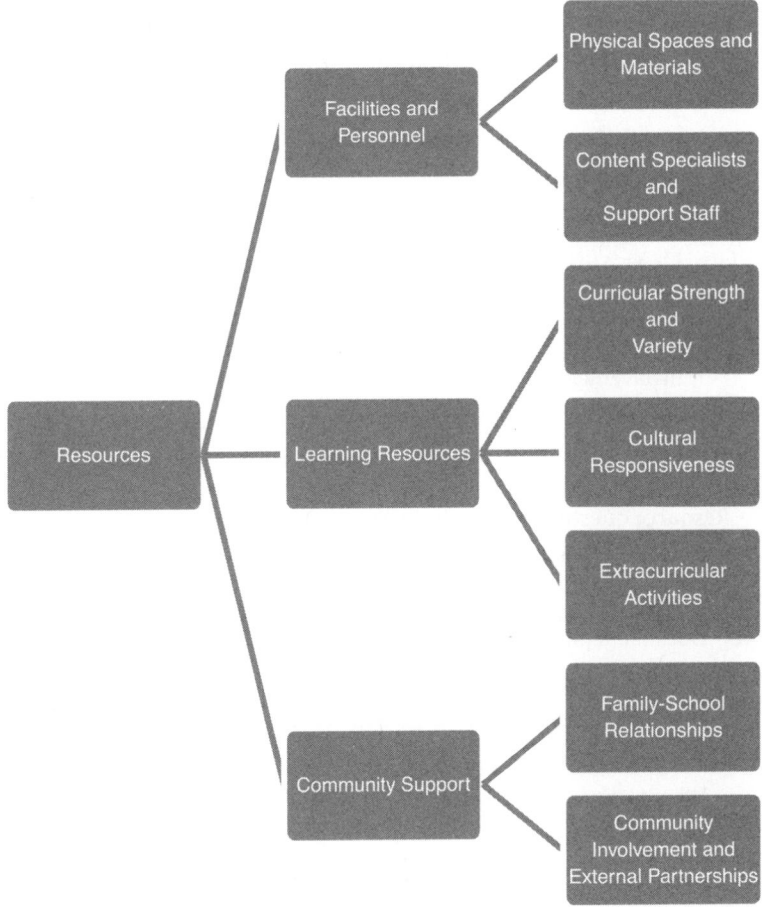

Figure 3.6. Resources

To review, Figure 3.6 shows the full framework for school resources. Another series of questions follows, designed for those seeking to expand their conversations about school quality. Once more, questions are organized by the category of person best qualified to answer them.

Resource questions to ask a school's principal:

What are the biggest resource challenges the school faces? What are your strategies for dealing with those?

What kinds of support do students typically receive from nonteaching staff, such as counselors?

How much curricular diversity is there here? What's your dream for the curriculum? Where would you like to see it five years from now?

How involved are parents at this school? What forms does their involvement take?

How involved is the community? What is the impact of that involvement on students?

Resource questions to ask teachers:

To what extent do you have access to the resources you need to be successful?

Does the school have enough specialists and support staff? How do they support you?

How well-rounded is the curriculum that you and your colleagues teach? What makes it the way it is?

What is the average class size here? How does that shape your teaching?

How much do parents support your work as a teacher? What does their support look like?

Resource questions to ask parents at a school:

Are the school's facilities adequate? Has there ever been an obvious issue that parents were concerned about?

Does your child have an art teacher, a music teacher, and a physical education teacher? What can you tell me about them?

How much time is spent on test prep? How much does your child talk about testing?

How involved are parents in supporting the school? How does that support affect student experiences?

How often does your child have an opportunity to engage with the community outside of school? Is that important at all?

Academic Learning

Listening to policymakers, one might get the sense that academic learning, as measured by test scores, is the only thing that matters in education. That isn't true. And it is even less the case when we include the modifying phrase "as measured by test scores." Yet, across multiple polls, Americans have ranked academic learning as either the first or second most important outcome of schooling, meaning that it must be included in any measurement framework.[53]

So what indicators of academic learning do we have?

As it turns out, not many, which is why standardized test scores may be somewhat useful indicators. Of course, raw test scores remain highly problematic as measures of what a school adds to a student's ability. As former Somerville superintendent Tony Pierantozzi put it: "What do their high scores tell us? That you didn't screw their path up. But they were on that path already." The reverse is true of schools with large populations of low-income students—schools that may have low raw standardized test scores but that may nevertheless be perfectly good.

This is what makes measuring outcomes, such as student learning, more challenging than measuring inputs. Inputs, of course, present their own difficulty, in that they do not tell us about actual results. But inputs are also less tied to a student's home life than outcomes are. If the full range of inputs—across Teachers and the Teaching Environment, School Culture, and Resources—is roughly equal at two different schools, we can be fairly confident that a student would have a relatively similar experience at each. A student's academic achievement level, by contrast, may not tell us a tremendous amount about the educational experience.

Even so, it is important to collect data on student outcomes, even if they are strongly influenced by background variables such as race and family income. One way of approaching this problem is to look for measures that can be applied evenly across different populations. Looking at college enrollment rates, for instance, is not a fair way of comparing high schools, which may have less influence on students than do out-of-school factors. Looking at persistence rates of college-bound students, on the other hand—rates indicating how adequately prepared students were for college-level work—might create more of an apples-to-apples comparison. Particularly if efforts were made to control for family background, as well as for the type of college attended—two-year schools having much higher attrition rates—we might learn a great deal about college preparation.[54]

Another way to approach the problem is to track growth. Where do students start, and where do they end up? Looking at both of these data points, rather than exclusively at the latter, might allow us to gauge, however roughly, the influence of school.[55] In the case of standardized test scores, this is both particularly important and surprisingly easy. Of course, as discussed in Chapter 2, value-added scores are highly questionable measures of teacher competence. A body of scholarship does, however, support the use of value-added scores when the school, rather than the teacher, is the unit of analysis.[56] By looking at how student scores change from year to year, we can learn a great deal more than if we look only at final scores.

So growth scores are better than raw scores. But a standardized test is still a standardized test, no matter how you slice it.

In light of this, it is worth experimenting with performance assessments—examples of student work that reflect a fuller range of what students know and are able to do. Can students write a compelling essay or a poem? Can they paint or play an instrument? Can they produce a lab report? These are the kinds of questions that might be targeted through performance assessment and gathered in a student portfolio in order to track growth from year to year.

Such an approach also has other upsides. One immediate advantage over state-run standardized testing is that students can actually learn from the process. When sitting for tests—a process that lasts twenty to twenty-five hours per year, according to one estimate—students are effectively learning nothing. But when working on a research project, or a science lab, they are actively building their skills.[57]

Another advantage is the amount of information such assessments provide. Standardized testing, often conducted at the beginning and end of the year, and reported in a pair of scores—one for English and one for math—offers very little usable information to parents and educators. Performance assessments gathered together in a portfolio, by contrast, provide more evenly collected snapshots of a student's ability. Additionally, by looking at work samples, educators and parents can more clearly identify concrete areas of student strength and weakness. Such snapshots can also be empowering to students—showing them clear evidence of their growth.[58]

Now, actually *pursuing* portfolio assessment requires significant investment of time and energy—establishing rubrics for performance tasks, training raters to evaluate them, finding the funds to pay those evaluators, and building that entire process into the school year. It can also be draining work for teachers to motivate students to fully invest in the process. Nevertheless, performance assessment is possible. New York's Performance Standards Consortium, which came together in the 1990s, has been successfully using alternative assessments in place of standardized tests for two decades. And in New Hampshire, a consortium of districts is currently working with classroom teachers to design common tasks and use common benchmarks to determine student competency. Even a stripped-down version of one of these models, in which a cross-section of student portfolios at each school was assessed by a team of trained raters, might do a great deal to enrich data systems with a clearer picture of student work at a school.

Our second subcategory for indicators of academic learning is student commitment to learning—a factor linked to a range of positive outcomes. One way to measure such commitment is by tracking student engagement. Engagement, after all, is a visible sign of one's commitment to learning, and it is also closely tied to the larger aim of academic achievement. Elementary students with high levels of self-reported engagement, according to one study, were 44 percent more likely to achieve high levels of academic performance and commitment than average students; at the middle school level, the increase was 75 percent. It is also possible to engage students of different backgrounds, as long as we are careful to avoid overgeneralizing about what "engagement" looks like.[59]

Like other elements in this framework, student engagement is also important in its own right. Certainly it appears that engaged students will learn more. But it also stands to reason that engaged students will enjoy their days more. Given the fact that young people spend roughly 12,000 hours in school before high school graduation, this seems a matter of self-evident importance. As one Somerville parent said, "I want my kid to get up in the morning excited to go to school." Insofar as it is hard to imagine a parent who feels otherwise, it is important to ask students and teachers questions about classroom engagement, as well as to begin conducting observations and developing other measures.

Another way of gauging commitment to learning is by looking at graduation rates. This, of course, tells us much more about high schools than about elementary or middle schools, but it also tells us something of great importance: about whether students were committed enough to complete their journeys through the K–12 system. Like several other measures in this framework, a school's graduation rate will inevitably reflect conditions beyond the school. As research indicates, living in poverty can have an impact on a child's likelihood of high school graduation, as can parental attitudes and behaviors. Nevertheless, research indicates that educational attainment is not solely a product of family background. Although schools cannot control family structures and living conditions, they can do a great deal to promote completion by setting high expectations, facilitating academic success, and keeping students interested in school. These kinds of "protective factors," as scholars refer to them, cannot mitigate all of the detrimental effects of poverty, yet it does appear to be the case that they can quite effectively keep students in school through graduation. Particularly if it were to account for student inputs, then, it seems that a school's graduation rate is a fair and appropriate measure of performance in general, as well as of student commitment to learning in particular.[60]

When asked about the educational outcomes they value, Americans consistently rank basic skills in core subjects—the kinds of things often measured by standardized tests—at the top of their lists. Not far behind, however, is "critical thinking." Certainly the phrase is challenging to define; people often use it without a particularly crisp meaning in mind. Many of the parents in our focus groups, for instance, would voice support for critical thinking and, when asked to define it, engage in the verbal equivalent of a shoulder shrug. When asked follow-up questions, though, they generally agreed on a few things. They agreed that it isn't enough for students to excel at reading, writing, and mathematics. And they articulated a vision that aligns with research on critical thinking—a vision of young people learning to analyze and interpret information, and applying their knowledge to new situations.[61]

Given these feelings, critical thinking seems important to measure. But there is also another reason to include critical thinking in a school quality framework: as a way of affirming its importance. This is true for all of our categories and subcategories—if they are measured they will be less likely to fall out of the spotlight. Critical thinking is an exemplary case in this regard because it is so abstract. After all, the more abstract an aim is, the less likely it will be to drive specific action. Rather than leading to concrete shifts in behavior, an abstract aim is most likely to affect how people *talk*.[62] This, consequently, helps explain why, even though school officials and the public talk a great deal about critical thinking, most students historically have not scored well on tests that measure their ability to recognize assumptions, evaluate arguments, and appraise inferences.[63]

That said, we can define critical thinking, and we can also begin to track the degree to which schools are helping students develop the skills associated with it. In our framework, we operationalized critical thinking by including measures of a school's emphasis on problem solving, as well as a measure of the problem-solving skills that students possess. Research indicates that a problem-solving emphasis in the curriculum is aligned with many of the other factors in our framework—leading to gains in content knowledge, student engagement, and student valuing of learning. Research additionally indicates that problem-solving *skills* are related to improved study habits, general academic performance, and higher levels of achievement at the college level.[64] Thus, even if we operationalized critical thinking in a particular way, it at least appears that this definition squares with other aims and values in the framework.

The final subcategory we included in the domain of academic learning relates to the long-term outcomes of college and career readiness. Again we have to begin with the caveat that college enrollment figures may indicate more about student background than about elementary and high schools. Most private colleges and universities are not need-blind, giving an advantage to higher-income students. Most favor "legacy" candidates in the admissions process, giving the children and siblings of alumni an advantage, and thereby disadvantaging low-income families less likely to have college graduates in them. Higher-income families have the resources to help college applicants pad their resumés, perfect their SAT or ACT scores, and secure private tutoring. And, of course, higher-income families headed by college graduates are more likely to set a tone, from the time a child first starts school, emphasizing the importance of school success and college attendance. College acceptances, then, may tell us more about student family backgrounds than they do about K–12 schools.

By and large, however, schools and districts stand to benefit a great deal from tracking students into college. District leaders might learn, for instance, that their students are generally unprepared, or that they tend to fail in particular subject areas. Furthermore, though it might never yield a completely fair apples-to-apples comparison, this kind of information can certainly be interpreted within the context of a particular community. Data on college enrollment and persistence can be adjusted for student background variables, with particular attention to factors such as family income and parental educational attainment.

A final way of measuring fairly across schools would be to look at career readiness alongside college readiness. Tracking placement into jobs aligned with high school Career and Technical Education programs—and not merely into low-wage, low-skill jobs—is one way to do this. One can also imagine a series of performance tasks that might begin to capture career readiness as well.[65]

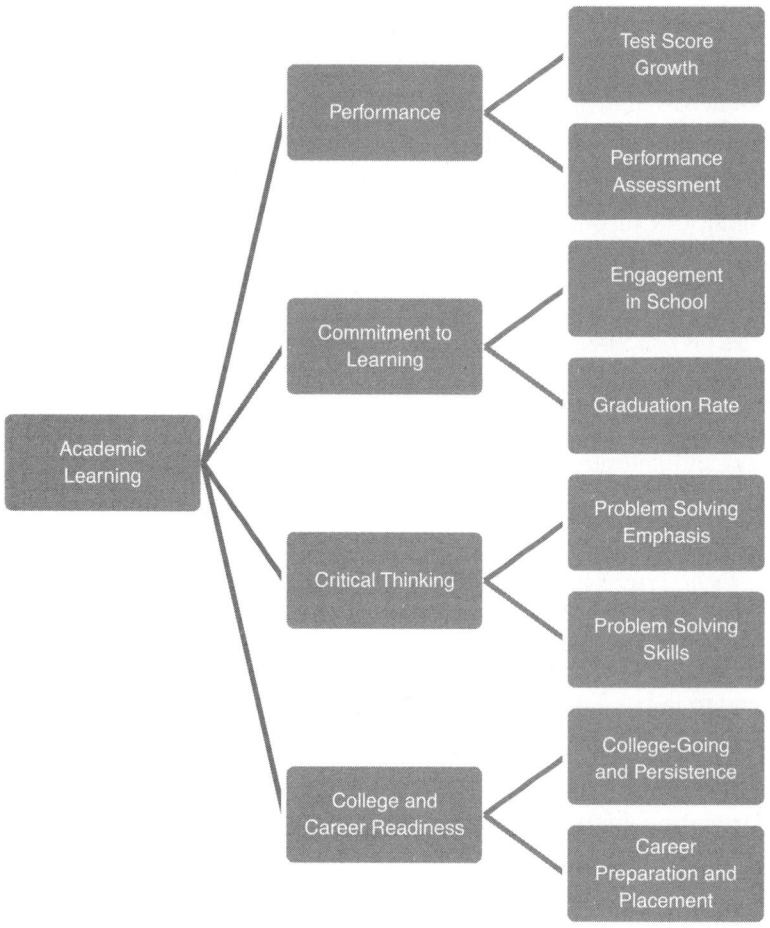

Figure 3.7. Indicators of academic learning

To recap, Figure 3.7 shows the full framework for Academic Learning.

Once more, here are some questions that parents, educators, and community members might ask, organized by the category of person best qualified to answer them.

Academic learning questions to ask a school's principal:

How do you know students are learning here? What are your sources of evidence?

How should I interpret this school's test scores? What are they telling me? What are they *not* telling me?

What does student engagement here look like? How will I recognize it if I take a tour?

How often are students at this school able to solve problems and apply their knowledge?

How much do you know about how students fare when they leave this school? How does that shape your goals for the school?

Academic learning questions to ask teachers:

How should I interpret this school's test scores? What are they telling me and not telling me?

How engaged are students in a typical class? What does that engagement look like?

How much freedom do teachers have to engage students in authentic problem-solving tasks? Can you give me an example of one?

How much emphasis do your colleagues place on critical thinking? What kinds of things do they do to promote it?

What are teachers preparing students for, in terms of the future?

Academic learning questions to ask parents at a school:

What kinds of projects and assignments do you remember your child completing? What was your impression of them? What was your child's impression?

How excited is your child about what he or she learns each day in school? Can you remember a time when he or she told you about what happened in class?

How important is school to families here? Why do you think that is?

> How much of your child's learning involves memorizing, and how much involves other kinds of brainpower?
> How confident are you that your child is growing academically? Why is that?

Character and Well-Being

For the past several decades, character and well-being outcomes have received short shrift in policy discussions. Yet they remain as fundamental today as they did when the American school system was founded nearly two centuries ago. Central to the foundational vision of public education, as Horace Mann argued in 1848, was the idea that schools would protect society against "intemperance, avarice, war, slavery, bigotry, the woes of want and the wickedness of waste," while also cultivating "the sufficiency, comfort, competence, of every individual."[66] Briefly put, Mann's idea—one that won support for public education in the young republic—was that good schools would develop good people. That still rings true today.

Whatever the narrow focus of policy elites in the past few decades, the American public has continued to see schools as places for fashioning engaged and active citizens who are prepared to thoughtfully participate in their communities. When we send our children off to school, many of us hope that the process, at the very least, supports the general work being done at home—nurturing both virtue and happiness among young people. Most of us want our children to come home and describe their days to us, and we long to hear not just stories of academic triumph but also of kindness, integrity, diligence, and responsibility. Somewhat more ambitiously, many of us hope that our children are developing competencies that we as parents may not be able to support—becoming better than us.

Polling indicates widespread support for this general aim among parents and nonparents. In a 2016 Phi Delta Kappa poll, for instance, 26 percent of Americans identified "prepar[ing] students to be good citizens" as the primary goal of public education—a figure surpassed only by those who cast their votes for "prepar[ing] students academically." In an earlier poll, conducted by NPR and the Kaiser Family Foundation, 34 percent of respondents indicated that developing character in the schools was even *more* important than developing academic skills and knowledge.[67] We heard more or less the same endorsement from educators and community members in Somerville. As one teacher put it: "Parents still expect us to help their kids grow up. Not just ace [the state standardized test]. But grow up."

Developing character and well-being outcomes is an aim important in its own right. Yet it is also true that, as with the other factors in our framework, pursuit of this aim does not conflict with the aim of promoting academic achievement. In fact, as research indicates, enhancing social, moral, civic, and emotional behaviors can have a strong impact on success in school.[68] It only stands to reason, then, that schools should make this a priority.

Although Americans generally support a core set of character and well-being outcomes, variability is bound to exist. After all, there is no such thing as the "right" set of qualities. Additionally, any set of measures will reflect the culture and worldview of the people selecting them. Consequently, it is important that stakeholders have a say in the identification of character and well-being outcomes. This might be done at the district level, through a consortium of districts, or possibly at the state level. Insofar as it is possible to identify general outcomes that most stakeholders will agree upon, such work might even be done at a larger scale. Only research and engagement of the public will fully clarify this.

That said, many character and well-being outcomes are public goods—designed not just to empower individuals but also to benefit society as a whole. One example of this is the cultivation of a civic mind-set among students—an outcome of schooling highly prized by the public.[69] In light of this, it is important to gauge the degree to which students will acquire essential citizenship skills, which our research team defined not as mere knowledge of the law, but rather as the ability to understand and work with others. Good citizens, after all, don't merely know their rights. They also organize members of their community, make persuasive civic arguments, contribute when they can, and display strong commitment to their fellow citizens.[70] Participants in our focus groups endorsed a highly active vision of citizens—one that includes such things as community service, volunteer work, engagement in public affairs, and a respect for the public good.

While schools cannot be held entirely responsible for the civic attitudes and dispositions of their students, they are the institutions most directly responsible for imparting citizenship norms. Given that charge, it is worth considering what, exactly, is possible. Schools may not be able to do everything with regard to developing citizens, but they can cultivate particular kinds of relevant attitudes and behaviors.[71] Specifically, a good school might use the curriculum, school rules, and school culture to help students better understand others, their actions, and their worldviews.[72]

Now, teaching young people to accept and understand difference may sound to some like inculcating a personal value—one that, like religious affiliation, should not be taught in school. But whereas young people are free to make their own choices about how they worship, it is difficult to imagine them navigating social and economic life in the United States without an ability to engage with those from different racial, ethnic, and class backgrounds. This was true in the first years of the republic. George Washington, for instance, believed that schooling would encourage tolerance and appreciation for diversity in the newly created United States by helping young people understand that there is no basis for their "jealousies and prejudices."[73] And it remains true today, with polls revealing strong support for the aim of teaching students "to work with people from diverse backgrounds and cultures"— not only because such skills are important in our society, but also because they are instrumental for gainful employment.[74]

Another character and well-being outcome highly valued by the public is work ethic. In a survey by the Roper Center for Public Opinion Research, 92 percent of respondents indicated that a good work ethic is a very important trait for schools to cultivate. And according to a study by Richard Rothstein and Rebecca Jacobsen, work ethic placed third among all possible school outcomes when ranked by parents and the public. Only basic academic competencies and critical thinking skills ranked higher.[75]

For our purposes, we divided work ethic into two categories. The first of those is long-term academic perseverance, which research indicates to be a predictor of school success. As measured by "grit," for instance—the most popular operationalization of the concept— perseverance is even more predictive of high achievement than intelligence and ability. And it appears to be the case that perseverance can be supported by schools through training in positive mind-sets and learning strategies. Still, it may be that schools cannot foster this characteristic, and given that possibility, experiments in measurement must be carefully tracked and consistently adjusted.[76]

Our other work ethic construct addresses a student's belief that he or she can achieve things through effort. Students with what is often called a "growth mind-set" believe they can develop their intelligence over time. Insofar as such an attitude is a precondition for work on challenging intellectual problems, a growth mind-set is an important outcome of schooling. Additionally, students with a growth mind-set are more likely to respond to obstacles by remaining involved and trying new strategies. When students are encouraged to see their intelligence as malleable rather than fixed, they maintain psychological engagement with academics, and their grades improve; they also report greater enjoyment of schooling. Students with a growth mind-set also seek out learning opportunities, develop deeper learning strategies, and strive to identify areas for self-improvement. Encouragingly, this appears to be true across all demographic characteristics. That said, mind-set data, like other survey measures, might become subject to gaming in a high-stakes accountability system.[77]

Our third subcategory for character and well-being outcomes is the cultivation of artistic and creative traits. Appreciation for the arts is one of the top eight aims that parents and the public want schools to produce.[78] Though policy structures do not reflect this, such support should not be surprising. After all, although it is true that students will grow up to become citizens and employees, it is equally true that they will have to build fulfilling lives for themselves. Insofar as schools are charged with preparing young people for their lives, part of their task is to cultivate creative and artistic ways of seeing and interacting with the world.

One way to measure the cultivation of artistic and creative traits is to track exposure to the arts—something that districts can easily do. Such transparency might do a great deal, in fact, to empower stakeholders who place high value on the arts.

But what about outcomes? Can something like creativity be measured? And is it a fair metric to include, when students bring widely differing levels of interest and talent? Genius, of course, cannot be taught, and not every student will become a Picasso. Creativity, however, when defined as a habit of mind rather than as a gift, appears to be a teachable trait as well as an outcome complementary to the other constructs in our framework. Additionally, efforts to measure creativity are rapidly evolving. That said, until there is more scientific consensus around how to measure creativity, it may be prudent to measure the degree to which students *value* visual art, music, dance, drama, and other modes of artistic expression. Setting aside the question of talent and ability, we can ask students about the degree to which they see the arts as a part of their lives, as well as about their collective sense of self-efficacy in pursuing their artistic interests. Once more, a well-designed survey scale is an appropriate tool.[79]

The final subcategory under character and well-being outcomes is health—social and emotional as well as physical—which research into public attitudes has shown to be highly valued by the public. Though schools alone are not in control of these outcomes, they can do a great deal to help young people develop into healthy, self-reliant adults, empowered to make good choices.[80]

The first aspect of health in our framework is social and emotional— a measure of the degree to which young people are happy, energetic, and optimistic. Again, schools cannot be held entirely responsible for developing well-adjusted young people. Still, they clearly have a role to play. And teachers, who might be most likely to resist this notion, given that they are already tasked with so many responsibilities, actually appear to embrace it enthusiastically. According to a 2013 survey, for instance, 95 percent of teachers agreed that social and emotional skills are teachable. The public, too, has rated student psychological health highly, and research indicates its importance in school success and life outcomes. In our work in Somerville, we included survey measures developed by the National Institutes of Health; but there are also other ways of collecting information about social and emotional well-being, whether based on student self-reports, teacher observations, or the surveying of parents.[81]

Schools can also do a great deal to promote physical health among students, and can do so without disrupting other efforts. In fact, research has shown that physical activity in general has a positive effect on academic achievement and that exercise can improve executive functions.[82] It also has obvious effects that extend beyond the school walls—potentially addressing obesity, substance abuse, and other risk-associated activities. Data for physical health, in many districts, are collected through the Youth Risk Behavior survey, which we drew upon for our work. Additionally, as with emotional outcomes, rigorously developed survey scales from the National Institutes of Health can help gauge student health by asking students direct questions about how they feel and what their days are like.

To reiterate: schools alone are not responsible for these outcomes, and schools must draw the line somewhere with regard to the scope of their missions. Yet educators are *already* addressing student social, emotional, and physical health, and many are experiencing great success that extends across domains. Thus, rather than distracting from other core functions, the pursuit of aims such as social, emotional, and physical health can be viewed as a way of strengthening other aims, such as academic learning. Additionally, though it would be misguided to expect equal outcomes across vastly different cultural and economic settings, it is not unreasonable to expect equal levels of school support for student health, and perhaps equal levels of student growth. Developing a set of measures that works will take time, and no measure will ever be perfect; but there is enough evidence to indicate that we can begin this work now and continue to refine our efforts through trial and error as well as through carefully orchestrated research.

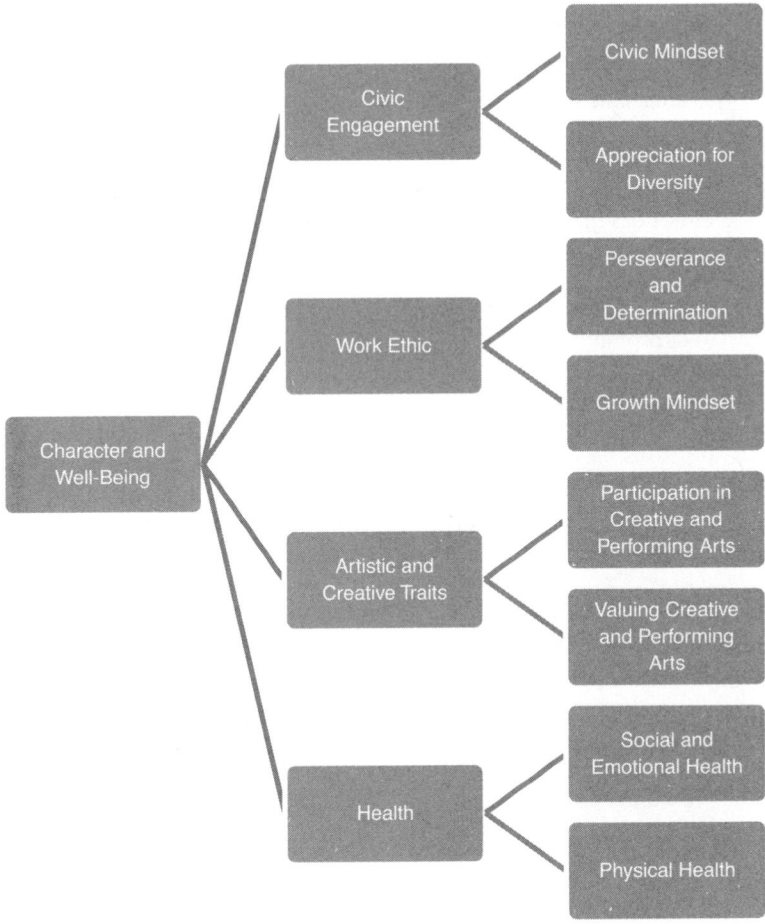

Figure 3.8. Character and well-being outcomes

To review, Figure 3.8 shows the full framework for Character and Well-Being.

Here is a final series of questions that stakeholders might ask, organized by the category of person best qualified to answer them.

Character and well-being questions to ask a school's principal:

What does the school do to help students understand people who aren't like them? What kinds of consistent and ongoing efforts does the school make?

How is diversity a strength of this school? How is it not?

How does the school get students to work hard? What does hard work look like?

How much of a priority are the arts here? What does the school do to promote them?

What does the school do to promote emotional health? How do you know if what you're doing is working?

Character and well-being questions to ask teachers:

How does the school's diversity play out in the classroom?

How much do teachers here help students focus on growing as learners? What else do they focus on?

How much do students at this school get to work on artistic or creative pursuits?

How well does the school foster emotional health for its students? What makes you say that?

How often do students engage in physical activity here? Is that enough?

Character and well-being questions to ask parents at a school:

How diverse is the school, and how does that play out for students?

How much do you think your child's work ethic has been fostered by the school?

How often does your child get to work on artistic or creative projects?

How happy is your child? How has the school played a role in that?

How much does your child get to move around at school? How much does he or she *need* to move around?

A Coherent Model for a "Good" School

Our framework represents the values expressed by Americans through polling data, as well as through extensive work with various stakeholders in a highly diverse community. Additionally, the framework is supported by scholarly research demonstrating the degree to which included factors promote or correspond with valued outcomes. It captures the full range of what good schools do, without placing undue burden on what schools alone can accomplish; and it includes both essential inputs and key outcomes.

Still, this is not a perfect and universal framework for understanding school quality. Some people may place more emphasis on particular categories, value factors not in the framework, or disagree with what has been included. And whatever our efforts to account for broader socioeconomic inequities, it is impossible to keep them from spilling over into any measure of school quality. This is particularly true of outcomes; but is true for inputs as well.

That said, many of the factors in this framework can be addressed through local, state, and federal support, meaning that even if there are current inequities, transparent data might help marshal political will. And many other factors, though perhaps harder to achieve parity in, are at least not chiefly predicted by student background characteristics, particularly when growth is the target of analysis. It is also important to note that, given its breadth and the specificity of its measures, this framework is more likely than lists of standardized test scores to spur change in our schools. Once we have identified shortcomings, even if they are not under the complete control of the school, we have a much stronger understanding of the scope of the problem and a better sense of how to address it. Ultimately, however, it bears repeating that this framework is a starting point that will need to be refined over time as our knowledge about educational ecosystems continues to expand.

While our framework might quite reasonably be tinkered with or adjusted, though, it is not a menu of à la carte items, and users should resist the temptation to winnow it down. It would be quite easy to look only at information that is readily available, or to focus only on a few concrete aspects of school quality. Yet we must remember that the availability of educational data, at least at present, is not an indication of their relative importance. We might also recall that placing too much emphasis on any individual variable will distort our understanding of school quality, which is inherently multifaceted.

Users of this framework should also take care not to view the factors included in it merely as instrumental goods designed to raise achievement scores. Certainly it is true that a variable such as teacher professional community is connected with student learning. Yet, like most other factors in the framework, a positive professional community is also valuable in its own right. Teachers should enjoy coming to work and feel a sense of collegiality in the workplace, for a number of reasons, but not least because we value them. Similarly, students should be happy not just because it will lead to them working harder and presumably learning more, but also because they deserve to be happy. Some things are valuable, in other words, simply because they are good.

Finally, we must remember that no school will be perfect, even in a single category. Ultimately, education is a system in which each constituent part affects the others—less like a vast machine than like a rain forest. Insofar as that is the case, we need to look across a wide range of measures, and not just at test scores. By doing so, we can produce a more accurate picture of our schools. But perhaps more importantly, such work might improve our discussions about schools—expanding our understandings of what is possible, challenging problematic assumptions, and empowering stakeholders. Whatever the inherent challenges, the work is worth the effort.

4

But How Do We *Get* That Kind of Information? Making Use of New Tools

IT'S ONE THING to generate a framework for measuring school quality. It's another thing altogether to fill in that framework.

After all, most of the information we wish we had about schools is not simply sitting around, waiting to be integrated into a data system. Instead, it must be collected. Thus, our new framework presented a twofold challenge. First, we needed to identify measures that aligned with our new organizational scheme. Second, we needed to go out and collect new data.

As it turns out, some information *is* actually sitting around waiting to be used. Massachusetts is hardly alone, for instance, in making public the average class size in each district. Many states have data for chronic absences—students who miss 10 percent or more of school days—and for on-time graduation. Many also track the number of teachers who are teaching in their area of licensure.

Massachusetts also produces a number of useful measures not found in every state. Wading through the state website, one can find the percentage of students in each district who complete the core college-preparatory curriculum, the percentage of graduates who require college remediation, and the percentage of graduates who persist beyond their first year in college. All of these are helpful indicators of school quality.

Though not always compiled at the state level, a great deal of information is also collected by districts, though much of it is not available to the public. Any well-organized district, for instance, knows its rate of teacher turnover as well as the number of teacher departures not due to retirements. Districts generally know how much they spend on professional development, how many specialists and support staff they have per student, and the number of students they suspend each year. They also know the number of hours students receive instruction in art, music, and physical education each week.

Some useful information is collected by organizations other than the district. The Youth Risk Behavior Surveillance System (YRBSS), organized by the Centers for Disease Control and Prevention, is an example of a survey that produces lots of rich data, and the Somerville schools conduct it every other year. The YRBSS can tell us the percentage of students who were bullied at school, who skipped school because they felt unsafe, who were threatened or injured with a weapon at school, or who were in a physical fight at school in the past year.

The YRBSS also tells us about a number of important student health outcomes. It compiles the percentage of students who are overweight or obese, the percentage of students who are physically active sixty minutes a day for at least five days per week, and the number of days students have access to physical education each week. It also provides a window into how many students eat breakfast before school, how much television they watch, and how many of them use alcohol and tobacco.

Theoretically, then, a motivated individual might cobble all of this information together to produce a clearer picture of schools than might be gained through test scores alone.

Doing so, however, requires tremendous effort. It entails knowing what is available—through the state education web portal, the school district, and other government agencies—and then collecting the relevant information, often through formal data requests. Even then, the limits of what is available will emerge quite quickly. The data are incomplete, providing insight into some aspects of a school but not others. They are poorly organized. And the numbers are not always easy to interpret, leaving nonexperts wondering what constitutes good or bad performance.

With regard to our framework for school quality, it was clear that although we would not be starting from scratch, we would have to begin collecting a great deal of new data. That would mean counting things that the district doesn't traditionally count—the number of art classes per student per week, for instance. It also, as we soon realized, would require tapping students and teachers for their perspectives. Who, after all, knows a school better than the people who spend their days in the building 180 days a year?

If You Want to Know, Just Ask—Surveys as Measurement Tools

Our team was hardly the first to realize that commonly available data offer only a limited picture of school quality. In fact, many large school districts produce annual school-level report cards that include a great deal of useful information about schools, much of it drawn from a relatively simple source: students and teachers.

That seemed promising. After all, if we could fill gaps in our framework simply by talking to students and teachers, it would make data collection relatively simple. How safe do students feel? How strong are student-teacher relationships? How adequate are the school's resources? Those inside a school generally have the answers to these questions, so why not ask them?

The most common tool for such work is the survey, which is relatively easy to administer. Now, it is true that interviews and focus groups can provide deeper and richer information than surveys, and they can allow participants the opportunity to share their views in a relatively unscripted way. But interviews and focus groups are extremely time-intensive.[1] Imagine spending an hour with each student and teacher in an average school. It would take a research team months just to collect the data. Then they would face a second challenge—trying to assemble all of those different opinions in a coherent way. In light of all this, it should come as no surprise that surveys are often the default tool for large-scale questioning.

Surveys have other advantages as well. They are inexpensive, particularly when administered electronically. They are exactly the same from person to person, making for uniform measurement. Perhaps most advantageously of all, surveys are generally easy to compile—using computer software, a data analyst can see aggregate results immediately. Imagine, by contrast, trying to compile the results of several hundred focus groups in a clear and consistent way.

Still, much can go wrong with a survey.

Consider, for instance, what researchers call "construct validity"—a measure of how accurately a survey question measures the thing it is supposed to measure. A question that asks students how much they like a teacher, for instance, might seem like a good one. We all want students to like their teachers. But what if a student likes a teacher as a person but not as an educator? What if a student dislikes a teacher personally but has learned a great deal in that teacher's classroom?

What if a student has recently been given a bad grade and is temporarily upset with that teacher? What if a teacher is well liked because he or she never assigns challenging work? In short, the way a question is asked will have a potent effect on the response it produces. And it is quite possible for a poorly framed question to elicit information about the wrong construct.

Another way a survey question can go wrong is by being too general. All of the students in a school, for instance, might agree that their teachers are "excellent." But what makes an excellent teacher? Are the students saying it because they like their teachers? Are they saying it because their teachers push them to work hard? Are they saying it because they're actually learning something in their classes? Certainly it would be welcome news to know that so many students appreciate their teachers, but what else, beyond this general sentiment, would we actually know?

Similarly, survey questions can go wrong if they are too open to interpretation or depend too much on an individual's frame of reference. If we are interested in the adequacy of school facilities, for instance, we can ask students and teachers, and we can expect that they will honestly share their perceptions. But we also need to recognize that different people—within a school, or perhaps more likely, *between* schools—may have different expectations that will invariably shape their responses. Those who have gone their entire careers without functional electronic technology, for instance, may be thrilled to have access to a single working computer. Those who are used to up-to-date machines, by contrast, may have very different expectations.[2]

Conversely, a survey question can be too specific, forcing respondents to make hard choices between what they think is being asked and what a question actually says. In seeking to determine the adequacy of the school facility, a survey designer might include a question about working heating and cooling systems. A school in San Diego, however, where the average temperatures in December and June are practically indistinguishable, may not have either a heating or a cooling system. In such a case, a respondent might reasonably answer either yes or no to the question and still be telling the truth.[3]

Survey questions can also lead to this kind of dilemma if they are double- or triple-barreled—packing multiple questions into one. A question about a teacher who is "kind and generous," for instance, overlooks the possibility that a teacher may be kind but not generous, or generous but not kind. A question about whether professional development opportunities for teachers are relevant and consistent, similarly, assumes that those two factors will always go together. And when they do not coincide, a survey respondent cannot answer the question honestly.

Survey questions can be too vague or confusingly worded. Questions can be too long or have too many components. They can also be biased—suggesting to respondents that there is a right answer and inadvertently nudging them in a particular direction.

In short, there's a lot to watch out for.

And even in a best-case scenario, there is always the fact that surveys rely on the reports of fallible human beings. We forget. We protect our reputations. We can be vengeful. We sometimes lie.

Knowing all this, survey designers have developed a range of techniques for mitigating threats to survey validity and reliability. Perhaps chief among them is the survey scale, which functions as a kind of safety net. By asking several relatively similar questions—all designed to target the same construct—survey designers can ensure that responses aren't skewed by a single bad question.

The obvious downside to asking questions in the form of scales is that it makes surveys substantially longer. Rather than asking a single question about student engagement, for instance, we included eight different takes on the theme:

How closely do you listen to what is said in class?

In this class, how much do you participate?

How often do you come to class ready to learn?

When you are not in class, how often do you talk about ideas from class?

How often do you get so focused on class activities that you lose track of time?

How excited are you about going to this class?

Overall, how interested are you in this class?

How often do you take time outside of class to learn more about what you are studying in class?

A scale of this length provides quite a safety net. Just as importantly, it serves as a research tool for improving the survey. After all, however well conceived a survey initially is, careful development always requires revision. A scale allows survey designers to see how well particular questions cohere, and can be measured by looking at the degree to which responses to scale items are correlated with each other. If they tend to capture about 70 percent of the same signal—allowing room for 30 percent "noise"—the likelihood is good that you are measuring the same core construct. If a question fails to correlate with the other items on the scale, though, it is likely not measuring the same thing. In such a case, the question should usually be dropped or revised.

Other kinds of analysis can also improve the effectiveness of a survey. For instance, we examined how much student and teacher responses varied within each school and how much those responses varied *between* schools. Constructs such as teacher quality are likely to vary more within schools than between them, at least in a small district like Somerville. But other factors, such as the adequacy of the school facility, or the school's culture, should produce relatively consistent answers from students and teachers at the same school— answers that are likely to differ somewhat from those in other schools.

Other kinds of analyses can be conducted after initial results are in. Our team, for instance, examined results across demographic factors including race, gender, and age. We explored ways to cut down on survey scales and substituted new questions for those that didn't appear to be working. We also introduced a series of A / B tests, to see if one scale might work better than another. Overall, however, the guiding principle was relatively simple: keep tinkering.

Won't People Lie?

Many readers may have their doubts about asking K–12 students— young people ages five to eighteen—to weigh in on their teachers and their schools. Certainly they spend hundreds of hours with their teachers and thousands of hours in their schools. But the degree to which students can provide fair and reliable feedback is far from obvious.

Like all measurements, questionnaires are imperfect. Even when surveys are anonymous, respondents can offer misleading responses. This is particularly true with highly personal and potentially threatening questions about criminal or taboo behavior that can induce cognitive dissonance in people—heavy drinkers who do not view themselves as alcoholics, for instance, may underestimate the number of drinks they consume in a week.

Similarly, people vary in their introspective abilities. Thus, when answering questions about deeply held assumptions and beliefs, some people are more likely than others to select a response that does not reflect reality.

Still, scholarship in social and cognitive psychology has shown that people generally communicate their true opinions if they have been asked reasonable questions. In most cases, people have no reason to lie; so they don't. Additionally, well-constructed surveys are remarkably predictive of objectively measured outcomes. Briefly stated, when some aspect of reality can be measured by researchers, and then compared with the reality presented by survey respondents, the two tend to align.[4]

This applies to young people as well. Recent research has revealed that, in keeping with this more general finding, student perception surveys produce reliable data.[5] Ratings of teachers, for instance, tend to be consistent within the class but different across classrooms. That means that not all teachers are simply getting the same rating, and that students tend to be in agreement about whatever they are saying. Additionally, student ratings of their schools tend to be consistent across grade levels, racial / ethnic groups, and gender, indicating that if students are lying about their teachers or their schools, they are all managing to tell the same lie.[6]

Roughly two dozen states now encourage the use of perception surveys to assess K–12 teachers, and as time goes on, more will use these surveys to supplement test scores for the purpose of measuring school quality. This, consequently, has begun to raise questions about gaming. Will principals pressure teachers to issue high ratings of their leadership? Will teachers pressure students to issue high marks for classroom instruction?

Anonymity is a strong check on potential gaming efforts by teachers and administrators. However, in the context of a hypothetical accountability structure, it would also be prudent for states to oversee the administration of surveys, as well as to conduct checks through on-site visits—visits that might include focus groups with students and teachers.

Additionally, it would be important to assemble a range of measures—some of which do not rely on self-reports—for the purpose of corroborating evidence. Teacher responses to questions about a school's principal, for instance, could be analyzed alongside the teacher turnover rate. If teachers were being bullied by their principal into falsely reporting positive perceptions of his or her leadership, a higher turnover rate—a likely possibility in such a hostile work environment—would serve as a kind of red flag. Or with regard to student character and well-being outcomes, brief, age-specific performance tasks might be deployed to produce a picture of what students can *do*—a picture that could then be compared against what students *say*. Such a multimethod approach to measurement can, as research has demonstrated, dramatically increase the reliability and validity of data.[7]

Finally, states would want to structure accountability systems such that no student or teacher felt pressure to give falsely positive responses. Stigmatizing labels, restriction of funding, and school closures, if connected to survey results, will undoubtedly have an effect on the kinds of responses given at schools in danger of being sanctioned. Thus, it may be the case that data systems are most powerful when they have only low stakes, or no stakes at all, attached to them. The power of information, we might recall, is rooted in its accuracy. And though we can imagine data influencing schools without the use of carrots and sticks, it is hard to picture an accountability system having a positive impact if the data underlying it are inaccurate.

A final concern worth addressing with regard to the truth basis of perception surveys is the ability of younger students to complete them. Can a five-year-old complete a seventy-item online survey? No. Yet researchers like Harvard University's Ron Ferguson have been adapting survey instruments for fairly young students and doing so with success. Questions for young students would need to be pared down to a small handful—perhaps five to ten—and administered by a trained adult who was not that child's teacher. Though this process is obviously more time-intensive than asking students to complete an online survey, it does not present an insurmountable challenge.[8]

Would younger students only weigh in on five to ten questions? Yes and no. In an average-size school, survey administrators could conceivably ask each student to answer only about half of all questions. By randomly selecting a batch of, say, ten questions to ask each student, administrators could compile answers to a set of perhaps twenty questions. If those twenty were carefully chosen as the most representative questions from a series of survey scales—having been adapted into language that younger students could understand, of course—the survey might satisfactorily distill the longer version administered to older students.

As is probably clear, this is not an exact science. Nor is it easy work. But there is reason to believe that perception surveys can produce reliable information about schools, particularly if they are conducted in conjunction with other measures and with a commitment to constant improvement.

What Should We Ask?

Given how labor-intensive survey creation can be, the best strategy can often be to adopt a set of scales that have been thoughtfully designed and tested over a number of years.

In education, the most well-established source of perception surveys may be the University of Chicago Consortium on School Research—a partnership between the University of Chicago and the Chicago Public Schools. For two decades, their research on the "five essentials," stemming from work by Tony Bryk and his colleagues, has been consistently improved and refined. The consortium makes its survey questions available for no cost, asking only that their work be credited.[9]

There are other good surveys out there, too. Although we considered picking and choosing from multiple providers, we decided that consistency was also important. So when using borrowed instruments, we worked as much as possible with the Chicago scales, adapting them as necessary to better match our categories and subcategories.

Most of our survey scales, however, came from a member of our team—Hunter Gehlbach, an expert on survey design who, at the time, worked just a stone's throw away from Somerville, at Harvard University. Many of the survey scales that Hunter and his team had developed worked perfectly with our framework. In the cases where they didn't, we simply adapted them.

Hunter's survey scales weren't just useful because they addressed the right constructs. After all, I could sit down at my computer and generate several dozen relevant questions. They were also useful because they were well designed, through a painstaking process that will likely become standard practice in education.[10]

Hunter's first step is to conduct a review of the scholarly literature. The primary reason for doing this is to more clearly define the construct. By looking at how others have conceptualized a construct such as "student-teacher relationships," we can establish clear boundaries for talking about it. This is particularly important because it helps ensure that we don't accidentally target *other* concepts. Hunter likes to sketch Venn diagrams showing overlap with other related but distinct constructs. He also likes to focus on "grain size"—the level of abstraction at which to measure the concept.

After the literature review, the next step—and a bit of an unusual one in survey development—is to look at the population of interest. How do *they* think about the concept? This was particularly important to us because we wanted to create measures that all stakeholders would view as valid. We had spent a great deal of time conducting interviews and focus groups to build a framework that everyone in the community would buy into; so it was particularly important that the data feeding into our framework had the community's endorsement. During this step, Hunter considers the vocabulary stakeholders use, the way they define terms, and the way they understand key concepts. Interviews and focus groups can help ensure that questions are being asked the right way and that nothing extraneous has made its way into the scale.

The third step in the survey development process is to begin reconciling differences between the scholarly literature and the input from stakeholders. The goal here is to develop a concept and related survey questions that both sets of people will agree on. The first move is to merge the two lists—using the vocabulary of stakeholders, rather than scholars, whenever possible. The next move is to take a close look at the items that cropped up only among one group. Did stakeholders miss something important that scholars had pointed out? Had scholars totally overlooked something critical to stakeholders?

The fourth step is to begin writing particular survey questions, trying to capture the fullness of a construct in a handful of questions. The task here isn't to ask absolutely *everything* about a concept. Instead, the task is to get the right sample of questions that are *representative* of it. This, of course, involves professional judgment, but it is always possible to begin fairly conservatively, with more items, and then to cut down on the number of questions after testing them out.

With draft survey items in hand, the next step is to spend some time with experts and scholars. Does the scale have construct validity? In other words, do the questions seem to align with the concept being measured? Are there any obvious omissions? Is any of the language obtuse or misleading? It might even be a good idea to have scholars complete a survey *about* the survey items, rating each one for its quality.

By this point, a decent-looking survey scale should have emerged, making it possible to do some "cognitive pretesting" or "cognitive interviewing" with a focus group.[11] By having participants talk through the items, it is possible to get a sense of how respondents will approach the survey when they sit down to do it. This kind of process allows you to "see" people thinking as they go through the survey. That can help reveal that something has been asked too vaguely, that the particularities of a subgroup—Special Education students, for instance, or kindergarten teachers—have been overlooked, or that key instructions have been omitted. This process can at times feel strange for respondents. Additionally, having them spend too much time talking about an item can lead to red herrings. Overall, however, it generally leads to better questions that people are better able to process when taking a survey.

Finally, it is important to spend some time constructing clear and logical answer banks for questions. For example, when asking students a question such as "How curious are you to learn more about things you talked about in school?" it would be simple enough to attach a 1–5 scale and a note that higher numbers align with higher ratings. A better approach, however, might look like this:

How curious are you to learn more about things you talked about in school?

Not at all curious
Slightly curious
Somewhat curious
Quite curious
Extremely curious

Including something from the question in the answer sharpens respondents' focus—they get a clear reminder about what the core of the question is about, and they don't have to try to remember what the 1–5 scale means. Constructing the answer bank to echo the question also gives respondents one more opportunity to reflect on the question. Am I quite curious to learn more about the things we talk about in school, or am I *extremely* curious?

After all this, it is time for a pilot test run. Administering the survey to a target population, it is possible to see how each question functions within the scale of similar questions, as well as to see how the scales function relative to each other. With results in hand from this test run, it is then possible to refine the survey for a wider audience.

Of course, the process of refining should never stop. We found out after our first year that the survey was too long. Most perception surveys take less than thirty minutes to complete, but ours was taking significantly longer, so we made a plan to analyze survey results and determine which questions aligned best with averages for the whole scale. We also realized that we should create an error rating for each student's survey responses, since not all students had completed the entire survey with the same level of focus and attention. Other issues continued to come to our attention, and each time we simply added another line to our to-do list.

Example Survey Scales

What do these scales of survey questions come out looking like? Perhaps a few examples, for those interested in diving deeper, will help clarify our general approach to surveying. Those less interested, of course, can skip ahead. Insofar as an overview of this process may help all parties think in more complex and nuanced ways about school quality, however, it may be useful even to those who never plan on administering a survey.

Let's start by looking at our efforts to measure teacher qualifications and abilities. Current data systems, of course, offer several measures of teacher qualifications. In the wake of No Child Left Behind, for instance, all states began reporting on the number of teachers who possess a bachelor's degree and a state-issued license to teach. Yet, as discussed in Chapter 3, almost all teachers possess these qualifications, and research doesn't make a strong case for relying heavily on these factors as indicators of teacher preparedness. Additionally, though rigorous observations by trained professionals would tell us a great deal about teacher quality, there is great variance in the capacity of states and districts to conduct these.

To dig deeper into this issue, we developed a scale designed to measure what we called "professional preparation." It consisted of three short questions:

Given your preparation for teaching, how comfortable are you
   teaching at the grade level you have been assigned?
How prepared are you for teaching the topics that you are expected
   to teach in your assignment?
How confident are you in working with the student body at your
   school?

Certainly it is true that teachers could lie in their responses. But provided that their responses are anonymous and low stakes, why would they? Our questions don't ask them how well they teach or how effective they are in the classroom. No teacher would want to report anything negative about questions like that. But if the issue in question is one of *fit* rather than ability, it might be possible to elicit honest and accurate responses. We included them, deciding it was worth an experiment.[12]

We also asked students about their teachers. One of the scales from Hunter's research group—about "pedagogical effectiveness"—is designed to piece together a picture of teaching technique by asking students about their experiences in the classroom.[13] Given the scale's alignment with our framework, and given how sensible the questions seemed—both to us and, critically, to teachers from our focus groups—we decided to include it. The scale's nine questions asked:

> Overall, how much have you learned from this teacher?
>
> For this class, how clearly does this teacher present the information that you need to learn?
>
> When you need extra help, how good is this teacher at giving you that help?
>
> How well has this teacher taught you about the topics of his or her class?
>
> How good is this teacher at teaching in the way you personally learn best?
>
> How well can this teacher tell whether or not you understand a topic?
>
> How comfortable are you asking this teacher questions about what you are learning in his or her class?
>
> How interesting does your teacher make the things you are learning in class?
>
> How good is your teacher at helping you learn?

To fully round out our picture of teacher effectiveness, we also included questions about the degree to which students feel known and cared about by their teachers. The scale's six questions asked:

> When your teacher asks how you are doing, how often do you feel that he / she is really interested in your answer?
>
> How interested is this teacher in what you do outside of class?
>
> How interested is your teacher in your career after you finish school?
>
> If you walked into class upset, how concerned would your teacher be?

If you came back to visit class three years from now, how excited
would your teacher be to see you?

If you had something on your mind, how carefully would this
teacher listen to you?

These kinds of questions, when coupled with other data—the percentage of teachers working outside their areas of licensure, for instance, or the rating of a trained evaluator—can reveal a great deal about a school's teaching staff. And though each measure on its own is imperfect, the full range of measures collectively present a relatively clear and stable picture of what is going on inside a school.

Let's consider another example: school culture.

Measuring a concept such as school culture is somewhat different than measuring teaching quality. Whereas teachers and students may feel some discomfort responding to questions about teaching effectiveness, questions about the whole school carry much less baggage. Finding the right questions to ask, however, can be quite challenging.

The Youth Risk Behavior survey offers a glimpse into school culture through questions about bullying, violence, and substance abuse. Additionally, the state collects data on school attendance, suspensions, violent incidents, and the like. But we wanted to know more.

To assemble a fuller picture of school culture, we began by adapting the Chicago Consortium scales about two of its subconcepts: peer victimization and its opposite—peer support. Consequently, we included questions for teachers like the following:

How often are students bullied at school?

How much do students at this school care about each other?

How well do students at this school get along with each other?

How often do students at this school decide on their own to help
each other?

We also wanted to ask students for their perspectives, so we adapted the Chicago "safety scale" to ask questions like these:

> Are you worried that you will be the victim of violence in school?
> How physically safe are you outside of the classroom in this school?

Such questions gave us a sense of bullying, safety, and trust in a school. But that didn't give us a full picture of school culture. In a school with positive culture, students and teachers feel a sense of attachment to and comfort in the place, and they develop strong personal relationships. Seeking this kind of information, we added questions like these:

> Overall, how much do you feel like you belong at your school?
> How connected do you feel to the adults at your school?
> How close are your relationships with others at this school?
> How caring are your teachers towards you?

Finally, because school culture should be oriented toward learning, and not just safety and happiness, we wanted to know if students were being challenged academically. Consequently, we asked students to think about a particular teacher, and then to respond to questions like these:

> When you feel like giving up on a difficult task, how likely is it that
>   this teacher will help you keep trying?
> Overall, how high are this teacher's expectations of you?
> In this class, how hard does this teacher make you think?
> How often does this teacher take time to make sure you understand
>   the material?

The point here is not to run through all of the survey questions we used in our work but rather to illustrate our general approach so that interested parties—even parents, though perhaps through less formal means—can replicate this kind of research.

Given that aim, it is worth revisiting a few basic rules of thumb:

1. Question wording matters. How a question is asked matters tremendously. This is true not only for researchers constructing perception surveys, but also—as the next section will discuss in greater detail—for parents and community members seeking to learn more about their schools.

Asking a good question is not always easy. I have seen formal school surveys, for instance, that asked students to respond "yes," "no," or "sometimes" to the statement "My teacher is a good teacher." What is a "good teacher"? How many different constructs are packed into that statement? A student might respond "yes" without reflecting on whether he or she has learned anything from that teacher, thinking merely about how much fun class is. Or a student might say "sometimes" because he or she occasionally gets into trouble. The question is simply too general and open-ended to be of much use.

In our work, we worded our questions very intentionally—choosing words and phrases that would be clear and that would evoke a very particular idea among survey respondents. Consider the following two questions:

How much do students at this school care about each other?
How well do students at this school get along with each other?

On the surface, the questions may seem identical, yet they aren't. It is quite possible, for instance, to "get along" with people without caring about them. And, as many of us have experienced at family holidays, it is also possible to care about people without managing to get along with them. Consequently, it seems that both questions are important. We want all students to get along with each other at school, and we also want them to feel invested in each other. In sum: anyone concerned with gaining insight into a school can learn a great deal simply by asking questions; but they have to be both clear and specific.

2. Scales are better than single questions. A scale of survey questions is generally a safer bet than a single question. This is true for a number of reasons: first, because a single question about a concept would have to be so general as to be highly problematic, and second, because a single question might be interpreted differently by different people.

There are other reasons to ask questions in the form of scales. Most concepts of interest in education, for instance, are fairly complex. If we are interested in school culture, we will want to know about students' sense of safety and belonging, community-wide trust, the academic orientation of the school, and the degree to which students have positive relationships with teachers and peers. Briefly stated, to get a full picture of school culture, we need to ask questions about its constituent parts.

Finally, asking questions in the form of a scale will increase the accuracy of the information elicited. If someone answers a single question thoughtlessly, that answer will be smoothed out by the answers to other questions in the scale. The average for the scale, in other words, will be more reliable than the answer for any particular question on its own.

3. Ask multiple sources. Even if we are primarily concerned with the student experience, it still pays to ask others for their insights. Teachers, for instance, work with 20 to150 students a day and are often aware of general phenomena that students don't see from their perspectives. Parents, too, can offer a useful perspective on what is happening in a school. Certainly it is important not to ask people questions they might have only secondhand evidence about; parents, for instance, are probably not the best source for information about a teacher's pedagogical style. But looking at an issue from different vantage points can help assemble a more well-rounded picture.

In our work, we tried to provide students and teachers with the opportunity to weigh in on each concept. Though each party will often see things the same way, there will also be times when they do not. Insofar as that is case, it is essential to get both sets of perspectives. Additionally, while survey designers can use common sense to determine which group—students or educators—should answer a particular question, it isn't always obvious. Asking both groups allows you to cover your bases.

4. Corroborate the evidence. Surveying the members of a school community for their perceptions can provide a much clearer picture of schools than test scores can. But it is also important to remember that surveys alone are not enough. Particularly if you are gathering responses in a less than systematic way—as a parent, say, seeking to learn more about a school—relying exclusively on self-reports increases the chances of getting things wrong. The trick is to blend survey responses with other kinds of information—adding them together, and checking them against each other.

It is worth noting here that the checks run both ways. Although it may not be entirely obvious, the ostensibly "objective" data provided by a district or the state may actually misrepresent reality. In such cases, survey responses can be an important corrective. Take the example of student safety, for instance. Certainly states and districts collect data on student safety, largely organized by the number of "incidents" reported at each school; these measures provide a relatively objective picture of school safety. Yet these measures can be misreported, whether intentionally or unintentionally. Additionally, they provide very limited information, telling you only the number of incidents.

The addition of survey questions helps address both problems. If a school has a low number of reported incidents, but students and teachers each report feeling consistently unsafe, we have reason to dig deeper. Perhaps incidents aren't being adequately reported, or perhaps something else is going on. And if the evidence *does* align, there's still the likely possibility that a single number—in this case violent incidents—is not giving us a picture with the full depth and clarity that we can get by pairing it with student and teacher voices. In short, corroborating evidence is always a good idea, however reliable one particular figure might seem.

Cutting the Cord—The Future of School Surveys

Many parents and community members interested in learning more about how a school is doing will have to rely on their own ingenuity to gather information. Increasingly, however, states and districts are developing the kinds of tools described in this chapter. Still, surveys take time—time that otherwise would have gone toward instruction— and require serious organization. And, traditionally, the expense of surveys has not been trivial, as they require paper, pencils, and often a contract with an outside provider to compile all of the data.

Given these potential drawbacks, we wondered if there might be ways to leverage technology in order to improve upon surveying. What if we asked one question each day instead of fifty to seventy questions in a single sitting? That could be accomplished in seconds, without the need for organizing the entire student body, as well as the faculty, and asking them to spend thirty to forty minutes filling out surveys. But how would we get students and teachers to stop by a sur- veying terminal each day to answer a single question? It was impos- sible to imagine.

If we sent survey questions to students and teachers via text mes- sages, however, they could respond after the school day was over— sometime between 3 p.m. and evening. It wouldn't take any instructional time away, nor would it require organizing members of a school community every day.

Methodologically it made sense, too, at least at first blush. If you ask a student how curious he or she is to learn more about the things that were talked about in school, the answer might differ depending on the day. The answer to many questions, similarly, might differ depending on the time of year that students or teachers have been asked—near the beginning of the year, for instance, or near the end. An answer might also differ depending on where in the survey a question falls. On a long survey, respondents can simply begin selecting random answers just to bring a merciful end to a drawn-out process.

Asking a single question multiple times over the course of the year, then, might provide several advantages. First, it might produce a "truer" answer. In other words, ask me about my school only once, and you may catch me on a bad day, but if you ask me several times, that single "bad day" will be averaged out by the more honest answer. If each respondent was randomly assigned a different question each day, we might get an even more diversified snapshot for each question on the survey.

As an additional benefit, asking a question multiple times might give teachers and administrators a sense of how attitudes change over time—over the course of the year. You could even begin to track growth more carefully on a day-to-day basis. All of this could potentially be done at no cost if someone were to create open source software, and if all students had their own phones.

This more frequent approach to surveying is called Ecological Momentary Assessment (EMA). The technique has shown great promise in recent years in social science research, smoothing the error associated with self-reports and easing the data collection burden.[14] Our short-term vision was to apply EMA to education—sending text messages to students and teachers on each of the 180 school days.

Our first step in this experiment was to convert our survey questions so they could be sent as texts, and one obvious challenge was length. The standard limit for text messages is 140 characters—roughly the length of the previous sentence. That meant we had to figure out a way to text each question, as well as the answer bank for the question, in a way that made sense on a cellphone.

Smartphones don't have this limitation. In fact, questions can be delivered through a custom-built app, thereby avoiding text messaging altogether. One of our partners agreed to put our questions into an app. The problem with this, of course, is that smartphones and their associated data plans cost quite a bit more than basic cellphones. Consequently, the pool of potential participants in a smartphone survey might not accurately reflect the economic diversity of a community. With teachers this is less of a concern. Teachers generally work under a collective bargaining agreement that provides equal pay to those with equal training and experience. Certainly it is true that younger teachers would earn less than more experienced teachers. But younger cellphone users are, on average, more likely to own smartphones—so we figured it was a wash. We used the smartphone application with teachers.

With students, however, we developed a text messaging program called EdContext for use on any cellphone. If students did not have phones already, we purchased low-cost phones with texting plans for them. By doing this, we could assure a relatively representative group of participants.

After thinking through the limits of 140 characters, our next step was to choose which questions we wanted to ask. Our student survey, in its draft form, consisted of nearly one hundred questions, and we could have asked each of those twice over the course of the school year. While that would have solved some of the challenges associated with traditional approaches to survey taking, however, it would fail to capture some of the potential upsides of EMA. We felt we needed to ask each question at least three times.

We narrowed our list by selecting particular scales to include—our highest-priority survey questions. We then chose particular questions, selecting those that had produced average scores roughly equal to their relevant scales. In other words, we chose a few representative questions from each survey scale.

The next step was to change the language of the questions. When converting items to EMA, the procedure is to incorporate a time frame, such as "today," "this week," or "in the past few days." The objective is to take a general item, such as "How often do you stay focused on the same goal for several months at a time?," and revise it so that it focuses on a specific time period. When possible, the question should also reflect behaviors and actions rather than feelings or perceptions. This item, then, becomes "How often did you stay focused on the same goal this month?"

The trick to choosing a time frame is to consider how likely something would be to occur within a given period. For example, on any given day it is unlikely that a student would either succeed or fail to reach an important goal. Thus, when we converted the question "If you fail to reach an important goal, how likely are you to try again?" we revised it as "If you failed to reach an important goal this week, did you try again?"

After developing our questions for texting, the next challenge was to set up a way to actually deliver the questions to students. The system we built made it possible to schedule questions—sending them out on school days only, and at particular hours after school—as well as to randomize the order of the questions being sent. The system was designed to collect all student answers and store them in a secure spreadsheet that could be downloaded at any time to check progress.

Generally speaking, we found that both students and teachers were game for this approach to surveying. The vast majority of participants in our small-scale texting and smartphone experiments responded to a daily question, providing proof of concept that such a model might work if the technologies were all in place. Some even articulated side benefits to the practice—one teacher, for instance, cheerfully observed that she was paying more attention to the things she was being asked about each day.

Conducting surveys in a way that minimizes the drawbacks associated with them might dramatically expand the number of schools and districts doing such work, leading to a future in which student and teacher voices become ordinary components of any school quality assessment system—as common as standardized test scores are today.

We can also imagine even more radical changes if we look even further into the future—changes brought about both by a diffusion of best practices and expected advances in technologies. At the school level alone, it is easy to imagine data being used in ways that are currently unimaginable. Principals, for instance, could log into their computers in the morning to check real-time data on their schools. How is the community feeling? What are perceptions of safety like? How engaged is the student body this week? Having data about such matters might help school leaders more effectively align their priorities with what is happening each day in their schools. Moreover, constantly updating such information would allow school leaders to track progress on goals or examine the impact of particular interventions, leading to more evidence-based decisions.

Of course, such systems could be used for other kinds of communication as well. Teachers, for instance, could ping their students with reminders. Schools could text parents important updates or schedule parent-teacher conferences. Enrolling in school lunch programs or after-school activities could be done with the push of a button. In short, even if costs were to remain high—an unlikely possibility given historical trends—investing in this kind of communication platform might pay dividends in multiple ways.

But What Can You Actually Do? Performance Assessment

Surveys, of course, have their limits. What, for instance, would a survey of student academic performance look like? Multiple-choice questions sent via cellphones? Information about student learning is essential to any educational data system, and neither a standardized test nor a survey scale is sufficient to capture it.

In the past few years, schools and districts have begun to experiment with performance assessment as a measurement tool. Unlike current assessment systems, which begin with multiple choice as a format and then adapt it to the competencies we want to measure, performance assessment begins with the competency to be measured and allows the form of testing to follow. It asks students to perform a task—generating a scientific hypothesis, say, or conversing in a foreign language—rather than to fill in a bubble with a number two pencil.

This is not a new idea. Nearly a quarter-century ago—a decade before the passage of No Child Left Behind—the U.S. Department of Education endorsed performance assessment as a testing methodology. As a 1993 federally funded consumer guide put it:

> Because they require students to actively demonstrate what they know, performance assessments may be a more valid indicator of students' knowledge and abilities. There is a big difference between answering multiple choice questions on how to make an oral presentation and actually making an oral presentation.
>
> More important, performance assessment can provide impetus for improving instruction, and increase students' understanding of what

they need to know and be able to do. In preparing their students to work on a performance task, teachers describe what the task entails and the standards that will be used to evaluate performance. This requires a careful description of the elements of good performance, and allows students to judge their own work as they proceed.[15]

In the early 1990s, a handful of states were active in developing and implementing performance assessment. In Vermont, for instance, fourth- and eighth-grade students were assessed in writing and math through a portfolio, a "best piece" from the portfolio, and a set of performance tasks. As the state's director of planning and policy development put it: "We wanted kids to be engaged in doing interesting work. And we wanted to give teachers a test that was worth teaching to."[16] Leaders in other states, including California and New York, articulated similar concerns.

The greatest progress in developing performance standards was made by a group of twenty-six public schools in New York City. Formed in 1997, the New York Performance Standards Consortium assesses student work through four tasks—an analytic essay, a social studies research paper, a science experiment, and an applied mathematics problem—as well as through supplementary tasks in the arts, foreign languages, or internships. Each task requires that students complete an oral defense, and all tasks and defenses in consortium schools are scored by external evaluators using common scoring guidelines. Samples of student work are independently rescored to evaluate the reliability of evaluations and the challenge level of the assignments.[17]

With this lone exception, however, performance assessment never took hold. Why not? As the U.S. Department of Education noted, authentic assessments "come at a price."[18] Performance assessments are more complex to develop than multiple choice tests, and they present logistical challenges with regard to ensuring that assessments are consistent across schools and fair to all students. They are also time-intensive and complicated to evaluate, requiring vast numbers of trained adults, whereas scoring a multiple-choice test requires only a computer scanner. As a 1992 review of performance assessment noted: "Despite all that has been written and attempted with performance assessment methods to date, there remain two prominent concerns: 1) the *administrative time* to execute the methods, whether one-on-one, in small groups, or station-by-station, is very lengthy compared to alternative methods, and 2) the *costs* associated with development, administration, and scoring are extremely high compared to alternative methods."[19]

Yet there are examples of nations where performance assessment has grown and prospered. In the mid-1970s, for instance, England developed a test that integrated performance tasks—a test that eventually morphed into the General Certificate of Secondary Education. According to a 1992 article, every subject tested "contained some element of performance assessment: investigational work in mathematics, oral work in English and in modern languages, portfolios in English, and projects . . . mostly in the humanities and the social sciences."[20] In Finland, evaluation of elementary and high school students is conducted via school-based performance assessments developed by teachers. And in Singapore and Australia, national evaluation systems include performance-based assessments. In fact, as a 2010 report by the Stanford Center for Opportunity Policy in Education noted, "Assessment systems of most of the highest-achieving nations in the world are a combination of centralized assessments that use mostly open-ended and essay questions and local assessments given by teachers, which are factored into the final examination scores."[21]

Recently, states and districts have begun experimenting again with performance assessment in the United States, in part because there are now so many models of success to draw on, and in part because the wind-down of No Child Left Behind allowed for greater flexibility. When the U.S. Department of Education offered waivers from NCLB, for instance, New Hampshire received one that allowed a group of districts to pilot performance assessment. Participating districts still conducted standardized testing at grades four, eight, and eleven, but at all other grade levels, schools transitioned to teacher-created performance assessments. By training teachers to design, administer, and score standards-based performance tasks—as well as to field-test, score calibrate, and revise them—the New Hampshire collaborative laid the groundwork for a sustainable model.

The feasibility of performance tasks has also improved in recent years. Increasingly, the best tasks cut across domains, yielding scores for different dimensions of performance. By using a single challenge to measure reading and writing competency, for instance, assessment developers can cut down on the overall number of tasks, thereby reducing the amount of time devoted to assessment, as well as the time burden of scoring those assessments. Technology has also created efficiencies that make performance assessment more possible at a large scale. By using computer simulations, developers can ask students to engage in a true performance task while limiting the cost of administration; once uploaded, those tasks can be e-mailed to teachers, who can score them at almost any time.[22]

In the future, we might expect to see more states developing performance assessment systems. The upside, after all, is tremendous, as performance assessments might offer students, families, and educators much greater insight into student learning. There are other advantages, too. If done well, performance assessment can be integrated into what teachers are already doing in their classrooms, eliminating external testing altogether. Thus, we might not only get a clearer view of student learning—with more snapshots over time—but also lose less instructional time to testing.[23]

As time goes on, we might also expect performance assessment to be used for a wider range of purposes. Certainly this means using performance measures to track student competencies beyond core academic content areas. But it also means using performance assessment for purposes such as teacher evaluation. The Stanford Center for Assessment, Learning and Equity, for instance, has created a set of tools for use in licensing teachers and accrediting teacher education programs. Such efforts will no doubt continue to evolve, improve, and expand over time.[24]

There is one more issue worth discussing with regard to performance assessment, and that is cost. Though performance assessments promise to produce information that is both more accurate and more actionable than standardized test scores, they will also come at greater expense, at least initially. Detailing and resolving this financial challenge is beyond the scope of this book. Still, supporters of performance assessment have made some creative suggestions about where to locate funds, and at least one of them is worth mentioning. Currently, school districts spend billions of dollars each year on professional development (PD) for teachers, often producing little in the way of results. Researchers have argued that this is because PD is often divorced from what teachers are teaching, fails to connect teachers with each other, and offers little in the way of ongoing support. With rich and reliable data about how teachers are doing with regard to helping students meet performance standards, however, districts might organize more effective PD experiences—developing a shared conception of high-quality instruction, offering concrete support for specific lessons, and pairing teachers in successful mentoring relationships. Thus, funds for PD might be rationally allocated for the creation and support of performance assessment systems, and would almost certainly cover any increased cost.[25]

The DIY Method—How Parents Can Do School Quality Reconnaissance

What if you are a parent, and you aren't looking to overhaul the entire data collection system in your school or district? Are there any lessons in this chapter worth gleaning? Is there anything you can do yourself?

Setting up a SurveyMonkey account and then e-mailing out a link to the entire school community is probably a bad idea if you're a parent—a good way to ensure that teachers and parents direct your future correspondence to their spam folders. And it is unlikely that teachers or students would be willing to comply with a parent implementing his or her own performance tasks. These are perfectly reasonable activities for a school or district to take on, however, and insofar as that is the case, parents might take the initiative to advocate for new kinds of measurements and ask to be included in any related planning process.

It is also possible to take some of the practices outlined in this chapter and apply them informally—asking better questions and making more careful observations in the quest to understand how a school is doing. The whole process involves quite a bit of work; still, even minimal efforts are likely to bear fruit.

The first step in DIY school quality evaluation is to determine what you value. That might seem obvious, yet it takes a surprising amount of effort to think through questions like who you want your child to be, what his or her strengths and weaknesses are, what kind of community you want to live in, and what you think is possible in 180 seven-hour school days. Certainly there are basic elements that almost everyone can agree on—students should be safe and comfortable, enjoy themselves, and learn something. But what else matters? What is your ideal school culture? How would you like to see teachers and students interacting? What kind of character traits would you like to see being developed? How important is art and music instruction?

Next you'll want to figure out what your data sources are. Who or what will help you assemble a picture? Where should you look? Just by asking this question, you'll go far beyond what most people do. But remember to be skeptical about what is immediately observable. Does the size and sheen of a school's computer lab have anything to do with the school's overall quality? Likely not. Yet that's exactly the sort of thing that many parents unconsciously collect data on as they walk through schools. So it is important to be on guard against unfocused judgment.

Where is the right place to look, and who are the right people to ask or observe? The school is a good place to start, and the people inside the school probably know more about it than anyone else. However, getting information isn't as simple as asking a few students if they like their school. A better approach is to ask them something more specific—a question that targets the issue you're exploring. Do you think your teachers will be excited to see you if you come back after graduation? Do your classmates make it easier or harder to concentrate? Are there classes you wish you could take or wish you didn't have to take?

As you do this, you'll want to remember some of the ways questions can go wrong. A question may be intended to reveal one thing, but may actually reveal another. If we ask students a question like "How long does an average homework assignment take?" we may be uncovering something about the level of challenge. But assignments may be lengthy without being challenging. Just ask any student who has ever been tasked with an hour of busywork. So for each question you come up with, try to think of other, more precise ways to ask it—there's almost always a clearer and more exact way to ask.

In seeking information about schools, you also want to use multiple sources to avoid skewing your results one way or the other. Don't just ask students; ask parents, community members, teachers, and administrators. Talk to teachers at different grade levels and in different subject areas. And when you talk to parents, don't just talk to those who are demographically similar to you. The more voices the better.

Seeking multiple sources also means going beyond conversation. Spend some time on the state data portal. Look at school demography, remembering that more diversity is rarely a bad thing. Look at student achievement scores, but avoid looking merely at the overall average of raw scores for the school. Instead, look at how various student subgroups—organized by race, income, gender, and Special Education status—perform relative to state averages for those groups, focusing particularly on growth. Look at the attendance and graduation rates. Examine teacher turnover.

Most schools will also gladly arrange a tour for parents or prospective parents. Take one, and remember to go in with a specific set of things to look for—performance tasks, of a sort.

Are you interested in academic achievement? Take note of student work posted in the hallways and try to work backward to determine what it says about teaching and learning. Ask to spend some time inside classes at a few different grade levels. While there, take note of classroom norms, of the pacing of instruction, and of how teachers interact with students. Are students of different ability levels being challenged? Are they thinking, and not merely completing seatwork? Does the classroom have a positive, work-oriented energy?

Interested in arts education? Ask to meet an art teacher, to see a studio, or to drop in on a class. Interested in STEM subjects? Head to a science classroom or ask to see the kinds of projects students are completing with technology. Curious about health and nutrition? Visit a recess period, a physical education class, and the cafeteria.

For culture and resource issues, pay attention to hallway interactions between students and teachers, and between students and their peers. Take note of how clean the school is as well as how well cared for it seems—even if it is old, it may be well loved. Take note of how large the classes are, remembering that smaller is not always better, but observing whether every student has a desk and sufficient opportunity to participate. Ask to see a typical daily schedule, a schedule for that week, and a list of afterschool activities.

These kinds of observations are best done with a checklist or a set of notes about what to look for. After all, there are thousands of things to observe inside a school. Begin by sketching out what matters to you, and then try to imagine what a school might look like if it were doing those things well or poorly. What would you see? What would you hear?

Constant Communication

The kinds of tools described in this chapter offer school and district leaders a chance to incorporate richer data into existing information systems. Yet they also serve another, perhaps even more important, function: fostering communication.

In schools, communication is always a challenge. A single principal, working a ten-hour day, and responsible for a vast number of other tasks, is charged with aggregating the knowledge and perspectives of dozens of teachers. Teachers, who are similarly outnumbered and overburdened, are each tasked with hearing and seeing dozens of students.

Other factors complicate the effort to communicate. Power distorts messages—between students and teachers, between teachers and administrators, and between administrators and policymakers. The loudest voices are often not representative of the greater whole. Time is always limited. And many members of a school community—particularly the children in it—are often not even sure what they should be considering with regard to the quality of their schools.

Yet communication is essential. What are our goals as a school community? How well are we doing in pursuit of those goals? Where are we weakest? Where are we the strongest? Educators inside a school often have a sense of these things, but they are rarely on the exact same page with regard to priorities and concerns, or with regard to the progress they are making. And they are often unaware of what is going on in other teachers' classrooms.

Additionally, those outside the school want answers to these questions. Parents want to know how the school is doing, as do prospective parents. Although parents are familiar with the experiences of their own children, they often are unsure of how those experiences match those of others. Policymakers, too, want to be able to track the progress of a school.

Currently, a great deal of detailed, specific, and accurate information about schools can be gathered. But most of it doesn't travel very easily or very cleanly. Instead, it is trafficked via word of mouth, which also happens to be the conduit for a great deal of unreliable information. Savvy parents and educators can often sort this out for themselves. Others, however, cannot. There is, of course, the data collected by the state—test score reports, for instance, that often determine a school's rating. But as earlier chapters have discussed, that information can also be misleading.

The trick here is to capture and package a core of information that matches reality.

Each day, the barriers to building a reliable system of communication—one built around a broader and more nuanced set of data—are shrinking. And what is today the leading edge of school quality assessment will soon be standard practice. In the next decade, for instance, it is not beyond the realm of possibility that every school will have a texting platform, a system for collecting student phone numbers, a policy for rewarding students who participate, and a batch of free phones to give to students who lack their own. Similarly, it is not beyond imagining performance tasks replacing standardized tests, relegating multiple choice to the dustbin of history. Combined with more effective district data collection procedures, we might gather a set of information that truly represents the work being done inside our schools. And we might share it with everyone involved in the process, bringing everyone into the same clearly defined and well-evidenced conversation.

5

An Information Superhighway:
Making Data Usable

WHAT IF A DISTRICT or state were to gather all this new data? Let's imagine that perception surveys, performance tasks, school site observations, and daily recordkeeping have all been deployed, and we have reams of rich information about school quality coming in. What then?

It's probably safe to say that if this new information is simply dumped into a spreadsheet and posted online, few people will access it. And those who *do* access it will likely struggle to interpret it. District analysts and self-professed data geeks would gain access to some new tools, but it is hard to picture parents, community members, or even educators becoming more empowered in such a scenario.

Everyone, whatever their level of expertise, has a right to know how the schools are doing. They should be able to easily access information about a school, and they should be supported in their efforts to make sense of it—both through clear presentations of data and through teaching tools that help users learn how to interpret them. So, believing this, our team brought on two web developers to build something new. We envisioned an online portal that would visualize the new data in a straightforward and user-friendly manner, giving all parties equal access to the same information.

Putting data on the web has an obvious limitation. While the vast majority of Americans have Internet access, rates of access are lower among particular demographic subgroups. Rates of Internet access among families with limited fluency in English, families headed by individuals without a high school diploma, and low-income families all hover around 50 percent. Still, rates of access are rapidly expanding, and increasing numbers of those without computer-based Internet access are now on the web through their mobile phones.[1]

Perhaps the most obvious advantage of a web tool over print material is that it can be interactive—allowing designers to shepherd users through data in a way that is impossible through print media. Many users do not have expertise in educational research. Consequently, they can struggle to interpret data, or even to know what they should be looking for when faced with a vast array of statistics. A well-designed website, however, can ease users into the process, help them navigate, and even serve an educative function. We might imagine, for example, a design that identifies users' levels of expertise and offers multiple pathways to move them through the site—each customized to a different level of background knowledge. Or we might imagine clickable tabs offering definitions of terminology, user-friendly explanations, and short animations. It is even possible to imagine a social networking component to the web tool, allowing users to connect with each other, with school leaders, and with state and district administrators.

The web can also allow users to input something about themselves, making their information-gathering experiences more relevant. The web tool we designed for the *Boston Globe,* for instance, asked users to weight six different variables according to their values. Because not all people value all aspects of schools in the same way, it seems to make sense that the data portrait they receive would align with their actual priorities and concerns. Alternatively, a web tool might allow users to input the demographic characteristics of their own children, in order to produce a more detailed picture of how students like theirs are doing in a school. This isn't to say that parents are, or should be, unconcerned with the welfare of other students. Rather, the point is merely that some information is more relevant to some people, at some times, than other information.

Information on the web is also easily updated. All states and many districts currently update their data systems on an annual basis. But as it becomes possible to collect data more frequently—through tools like cellphone-based surveys and student performance assessments—state and district leaders will need to think creatively about what to do with a larger number of snapshots. A well-designed website could automatically update itself each time new information was available. Equally important, it could provide different ways of viewing that information. Imagine looking at data by the day of the week, for instance, to see how Mondays differed from Fridays. Or imagine looking at data over the course of a school year, tracking shifts in school culture, or student engagement, or mental health. Such information might be particularly useful to educators and administrators, though it would also be of interest to parents seeking to understand how one day differs from another in the life of a school.

A web-based system can also be easily modified. In our efforts in Somerville, we were often forced to choose between the ideal and the achievable, and we landed consistently on the side of the latter. Creating explanatory animations for each subcategory, for instance, was an exciting idea that we simply did not have the capacity to pursue. Yet these decisions need not be seen as final. Schools, districts, and states that build relatively basic systems today can add more layers of complexity in the future. Thus, future systems in Somerville might include virtual tours of schools, messages from school principals, links to school improvement plans, and much more.

Some might argue that all of this would be nice to have but is not absolutely necessary. Yet, if we want parents to make good choices and to advocate for their children, if we want educators to use evidence to inform their decisions, if we want administrators and policy leaders to support the full range of values in education, and if we want to begin having better conversations about what constitutes a "good" school, then it is time to take seriously the construction of better data systems. Such systems might provide us with the information we want about our schools, and might give all of us, regardless of training and prior knowledge, the same level of access. Seeing how our schools are actually doing, and drawing on a common evidence base to structure our conversations, we might better work together to support a set of shared aims.

What Does "Success" Look Like?

The web tool we developed was not designed to take advantage of every opportunity provided by the Internet. It did not allow users to input information about themselves. Nor was it designed to automatically update. It did, however, offer a number of clear improvements over current district- and state-level data systems.

The first improvement is the visual representation of a school's performance. On the home page of our site, each school has its own icon. Upon clicking that icon, users are taken to a school-specific page displaying the five major categories of the Somerville school quality framework. Each category is accompanied by a brief description and a color-coded "data interpretation." We wanted to keep things as simple as possible after that first click—giving people an immediate visual sense of school performance. But we also wanted to emphasize that school success is multifaceted and that no school is uniformly good or bad. As a result, that first page was designed to strike a balance—offering a simple yet nuanced view of school quality.

Color coding is a standard way to help users understand performance—a way of translating scores into something easier to comprehend. Otherwise our users would be in a position where they would have to determine for themselves what particular statistics mean. The public, of course, is quite capable of doing such work. Consider how baseball fans engage with statistics such as batting average or earned run average—figures that the typical fan can immediately translate into an assessment of player performance. But building that capacity takes time. Consequently, we wanted to offer a clear, and perhaps temporary, benchmark against which to compare performance—the equivalent to saying that a .280 batting average for a baseball player is good, and a .300 batting average very good.

Establishing benchmarks is not a particularly novel approach, and most educational data systems offer an interpretation of statistics for users. In Massachusetts, for instance, schools are given "level" ratings of 1–5. But these systems are generally plagued by two problems. The first is labeling. Identifying a school by a rank, or an A–F grade, as many states do, implies that its quality is fixed. This is exacerbated by the fact that schools are given single ratings, as if they are uniformly good or bad—a move that disregards the fact that schools may be successful in some ways but not others. We addressed the latter issue—the implication of uniform quality—by interpreting each of the five major categories for users rather than offering one single data interpretation for the whole school. And we addressed the former issue—the implication of fixed quality—by leveraging the concept of growth. We hypothesized that by emphasizing the *time* it might take for a school to reach its goals—its projected growth time line—rather than merely including the *distance* between current performance and those goals, it might be possible to present an honest picture of unsatisfactory performance while also recognizing that schools are always changing.

The second problem with current approaches to interpreting data has to do with the way that benchmarks are determined. The easiest approach is to compare schools against each other, ranking them by quartile—top 25 percent, second 25 percent, third 25 percent, and bottom 25 percent—or by quintile—top 20 percent, second 20 percent, third 20 percent, fourth 20 percent, and bottom 20 percent. In Massachusetts, schools are divvied into tiers this way. Such an approach, however, is flawed insofar as schools may not naturally sort into quartiles or quintiles. If most schools are good, then rank-ordering them makes the lowest-scoring of the "good" schools appear to be far worse than they actually are. Conversely, if most schools are bad, the top-scoring "bad" school is going to look far better than it should.

The fix for this problem is conceptually simple but practically quite challenging: to generate performance targets. On the face of it, this might not seem so challenging. After all, targets are set all the time, most frequently in the form of "cut" scores on standardized tests. These predetermined boundaries help translate the points a student has earned on a test into something easier to understand. In classroom grading, for instance, the standard cut score separating a B− from a C+ is 80. On a state standardized test a score of 260 may be "Advanced," whereas a score of 259 may be "Proficient."

Designating which scores align with a particular category of performance, however, is a notoriously difficult process. Even when working with only a single metric such as standardized test scores, those seeking to interpret scores are often forced to make relatively arbitrary judgments. As a report commissioned by the governing board of the National Assessment of Educational Progress noted: "Performance at the

Proficient level [is not] synonymous with 'proficiency' in the subject. That is, students who may be considered proficient in a subject, given the common usage of the term, might not satisfy the requirements for performance at the [Proficient] achievement level."[2] In short, the process is hardly as scientific as it may seem.

Generating benchmarks is even more complicated when it comes to the quality of an entire school. What combination of scores and results, for instance, makes a school an "A" school rather than a "B" school? In Florida, which uses an A–F rating system to measure school quality, an "A" school is one that earns 62 percent or more of all possible points on the state's scorecard—producing high raw test scores as well as high levels of test score growth among particular subgroups. Schools earning 61 percent of points earn "B" ratings. In Oklahoma, which also issues A–F grades, the cutoff for an "A" school is 93—the same cutoff point frequently used by teachers in grading student work—and schools can earn "bonus points" for achieving established criteria in attendance, advanced coursework, graduation, and college entrance exams. The guidelines for each state are quite clear, but however straightforward they may seem, these cutoff points raise questions. One is left wondering: What are these grades actually telling us? Are different grades reflecting actual differences between schools?

The work of creating benchmarks does not become any easier when it comes to other kinds of data—data not derived from standardized tests. In Illinois, for instance, the state employs the Five Essentials framework, developed by the University of Chicago's Consortium on School Research. The state board of education, in its rationale for using the Five Essentials, notes that "test scores alone do not provide a full picture of teaching and learning in any one school," adding that the survey is intended to inform school administrators, teachers, parents, and the general public.[3] In taking such action, Illinois is miles ahead of most other states. Still, they are faced with the same challenge: translating results into some kind of meaningful narrative. And their strategy has been to use statewide averages to determine quality benchmarks. Schools that come in significantly above the average get higher marks; schools that come in below the average get lower marks. But what if most schools are doing poorly? Or what if most are doing well?

Another challenge arises when multiple scores, in various kinds of units, need to be squeezed together into a single composite. Many of our data in Somerville, for instance, came from surveys and were scored on a 1–5 scale. But many of our data were in the form of figures from the state or the district—the percentage of students taking Advanced Placement tests, for instance, or the ratio of arts classes to students in a school. We needed to combine these kinds of figures with our survey data. Consequently, before we could try to generate a benchmark, we had to figure out how to combine apples with oranges. How do you combine an average score of 3.3 on a survey scale with a .08 teacher turnover rate? Certainly not by adding them together.

We decided to convert our nonsurvey data into a 1–5 scale, allowing us to combine different items in composites. For instance, we could take survey responses from teachers and students about the well-roundedness of the school curriculum and combine those data with figures from the district on the number of arts classes per student and the number of health and PE classes per student.

To convert figures like dollar amounts or class ratios into scores with ranges of 1–5, we used two methods. The first method was to create z-scores—a statistical technique used to indicate how far from "normal" a particular result is. Imagine that the average teacher turnover rate for the state is 7 percent, and that schools with higher and lower turnover rates are distributed in the shape of a bell curve. For the sake of this example, we'll assume that the standard deviation—a statistic that measures distance from the mean—is 2 percent. That means that in this scenario, most schools would have teacher turnover rates within two percentage points of that 7 percent mean—a range of 5 to 9 percent. Roughly one-third of schools would have a turnover rate of 7 to 9 percent, and roughly one-third of schools would have a turn-over rate of 5 to 7 percent. In a normal distribution, about 15 percent of schools would have a turnover rate that was an additional standard deviation away from the mean—a rate of 9 to 11 percent. And another 15 percent would have a turnover rate of 3 to 5 percent. Very few schools would have turnover rates of more than 11 percent or less than 3 percent.

If a school in this scenario has a teacher turnover rate of 5 percent, it is one standard deviation below the mean. So its z-score is −1. If a school has a teacher turnover rate of 3 percent, it is two standard deviations below the mean. Its z-score is −2. Most schools will have z-scores of −2, −1, 0, 1, or 2.

One of our methods was to create z-scores, drawing on state and national averages or the recommendations of scholars and professional organizations. We then shifted those scores a few places over on the number line, to align with our 1–5 scale. And, in cases like teacher turnover rates, where a low score—indicating low turnover—was a good thing, we reversed the order of the numbers.

This approach is better than divvying schools into quintiles. After all, it presumes that most schools are somewhere near the middle on performance, with a small number of very high-performing and very low-performing outliers. Dividing all schools into four groups, on the other hand, presumes that a whopping 25 percent of schools are at the very lowest level. However, insofar as it still relies on averages, the use of z-scores is hardly ideal. Theoretically, we might want experts—

scholars and practitioners—to determine targets for each of these variables, and then we would want to track figures over time, to see how accurately they align with what stakeholders feel to be high or low performance.

Once we had all of our data in the same format, it was time to translate scores into something easier to understand—something like A–F grades, 1–5 levels, or, in our case, colors. Colors, it seemed, had less baggage than many alternatives, and seemed more fluid. Using colors would also allow us to craft a more nuanced visual representation— using different shades, for example, or multiple colors at once.

But what would the boundary lines for particular color zones be? And what would those zones be called?

A Performance Spectrum

We wanted to establish a clear benchmark for each of our five major categories—a level of performance indicating that a school had met community standards. And our strategy for establishing this cutoff was simple: we would ask stakeholders about their expectations.

We drafted a survey that would define the core elements of each category and help participants think through what each particular measure meant, then we distributed it to teachers, principals, administrators, and parents.

The survey was five pages long, and on each page we asked a different version of the same question—one for each major category of the framework. For Teachers and the Teaching Environment, for instance, we stated that an impossibly perfect school would have a rating of 100, based on results from student perception surveys, teacher perception surveys, state data, and district data. We then offered an explanation of what that score would reflect:

This means:

> 100 percent of teachers at this school employ effective teaching practices.
>
> 100 percent of teachers display a strong interest in students.
>
> 100 percent of teachers feel supported in their growth as professionals.
>
> 100 percent of teachers feel that the school has effective leadership.

We then instructed stakeholders to think about one particular school—perhaps the school they work at or send their children to—and asked them to answer two specific questions:

> **Question 1:** What is the *lowest* score for this category that would *still be acceptable*?
>
> **Question 2:** What is the most *ambitious* score the school *might achieve by next year*?

After gathering responses to the survey, we began to organize a series of focus groups. Our aim there was to dig deeper. Primarily, we did that by talking through what each category meant and by describing general trends from survey responses. Participants had opportunities to ask clarifying questions, to listen to each other, and to make suggestions.

Through this work we were able to establish a draft district-wide benchmark for each of our five categories. We began referring to this as the "approval zone," because it ostensibly reflected a level of performance that parents, teachers, principals, and district leaders would be satisfied with. Though our initial draft would only be an approximation, we believed that we could continue refining our benchmarks over the next several years.

We selected dark green for the approval zone and described it in the following way: "Schools falling in this range earned scores between 'acceptable' and 'ideal.' This zone, established by teachers, principals, parents, and district administrators, is the target that all schools should be striving to hit. Scoring in this range does not mean that a school is perfect; but it does mean that it is meeting or exceeding community-wide expectations in a particular category."

We felt relatively confident that we were closing in on a benchmark for success. But what came after the approval zone? Certainly there wasn't simply a binary between approval and disapproval.

We envisioned the next region as the "growth zone." After all, schools just missing the approval zone were probably within striking distance of their target. With a bit of focus, they would likely get there, meaning that placing them in a "disapproval zone" would not only distort reality but also potentially inhibit that school's growth.

We also wanted to emphasize the concept of growth because schools are not static entities. They hire new teachers and staff, implement new policies and practices, adopt new curricula. Students cycle through; parents exhibit different levels of engagement; principals establish new priorities. Schools, then, are dynamic systems that can change. Furthermore, particularly if the school community is focused on a shared goal, they can improve.

With this in mind, we created draft language for the growth zone: "Schools falling in this range earned scores just below 'acceptable.' Yet these schools are close enough to the Approval Zone that they might reasonably reach it within two years. As established by teachers, principals, parents, and district administrators, this zone is an acceptable place for schools to be *if* they have the leadership, focus, and resources to improve their work in a particular area."

Seeking to establish this zone, which we planned to color-code light green, we included questions about growth in both our surveys and our focus groups. First, we asked what an appropriate window of time was for growth. Parents generally said one year. That makes sense;

their children are a priority for them, and they want schools to improve as swiftly as possible. Teachers and administrators, on the other hand, generally said three years. That, too, made sense, since it takes schools time to improve, and few things can generally be accomplished by a large organization in a single year. We split the difference and set two years as a target for growth.

Next, we needed to figure out how much a school might reasonably grow in two years, that is, if it were focused on improving performance in a particular area. In both our surveys and our focus groups, we asked stakeholders—primarily teachers, principals, and district administrators—what a reasonable but ambitious amount of growth would be for two years. Their consensus was around 15 percent. If a school focused on a particular category—school culture, say—it might improve its rating by 15 percent over two years.

That might not seem particularly ambitious; but consider a specific survey question such as "How much do students at this school care about each other?" It is unlikely that student responses would dramatically change, even over two years. If the average response is "not at all" (1 out of 5), it may take a decade to turn things completely around. Nevertheless, we might imagine the average response moving from "somewhat" (3 out of 5) to "a good amount" (4 out of 5), particularly if the school invested time and resources into building a stronger sense of community.

It is worth noting here that only time will really tell. Can a single school improve performance in a particular area by 15 percent? Certainly. Can most schools? It simply isn't clear. It sounds reasonable, but determining how realistic this proposition is will require tracking progress over a period of several years—to see what schools actually achieve with some degree of consistency.

So, despite the fact that our growth figure might change, we continued to use it as a mechanism for determining zones. Working with that two-year maximum shift of 15 percent, we calculated the next band in our rating framework, which we called the "watch zone." Our language for the watch zone, which we color-coded yellow, stated that "schools falling in this range are three or four years away from reaching community-wide targets. This zone, established by teachers, principals, parents, and district administrators, is not an ideal place for schools to be. But it does not mean that the school is failing. Instead, it means that the school needs to place particular emphasis on improving its work in this area."

Finally, we established what we called the "warning zone." Again using the 15 percent growth figure, we moved one more step away from the approval zone. The language we used for this zone was: "Schools that fall in this range are five or more years away from reaching community-wide targets. Consequently, this zone, as established by teachers, principals, parents, and district administrators, indicates that a school is in significant need of improvement. If the school is not in the Warning Zone in other areas, it may be a relatively successful school overall. Still, it must immediately develop a plan for addressing its shortcomings."

We colored the warning zone orange. Our goal was to be fair and not to scare people. Insofar as that was the case, we could have chosen cool colors like blue or purple to mark our "watch" and "warning" zones. But it was also a priority to be clear and honest, and insofar as orange signals "slow down and pay attention," it seemed like a reasonable, if contestable, choice. A school that is five or more years away from reaching community-wide targets is not in a good place, at least with regard to whatever aspect of school quality is being measured. Such performance merits the attention of all stakeholders.

Because we were creating something entirely new, these zones were educated guesses. Consequently, we continued to refine them. Returning to this work in the 2015–16 school year, we conducted a revised series of focus groups in which we followed three basic steps. First, we presented background information to people—defining the various components of the category, sharing recommendations from professional societies, and providing national, state, and district averages. Then we presented school performance data from the previous year, which we had manipulated to align roughly with the approval and growth zones, seeking to home in on the line separating the two. Finally, we asked questions about how satisfactory the performance of the school was for that category or subcategory. We used this information to continue revising our zones.

Again, it will take time to establish reasonable benchmarks. Growth targets, for instance, may be realized faster than we currently imagine to be possible. Alternatively, we may discover that no school is able to move across zones, even within a single category, in a two-year period.

One way to expedite that process would be through the creation of a consortium of districts, or perhaps by working statewide, to share information, thereby generating more data to analyze. In moving forward along these lines, though, it will be important to determine where we want accountability to live—at the school, district, or state level. Standards may differ across each community of stakeholders, and whoever has the power to control the process will decide which standards are used.

Visualizing Data

Once we had data for each school and were able to translate that data for the public—letting them know how schools were performing with regard to community benchmarks—it was time to build a website.

Our primary goal was to make the website user-friendly. Plenty of information currently goes unused on district and state websites because it is difficult to find, and, once found, information about school quality is often impenetrable or overwhelming to laypeople. Perhaps as a result of this, state data portals often receive far less traffic than websites offering simple interpretations of state data. According to the Massachusetts Department of Elementary and Secondary Education, total page views for the online school profiles clocked in at roughly 7.5 million for 2015. The *Boston Globe* Dreamschool Finder, by contrast, received roughly that many views in the first two weeks after its launch.[4]

Consequently, we decided that our main landing page for each school would simply offer the five main categories of the framework, as well as color-coded visualizations of each. We included a short description of each category's meaning and importance and offered a key for understanding the color-coding scheme.

We also wanted to make it possible for users to get more information. Plenty would never move past the main landing page, but plenty more, we reasoned, would want to dive deeper. We designed the site so that when users click on one of the categories, they are taken to a more detailed view—a view that includes visualized data for each subcategory. Those interested in learning more about School Culture, for instance, could click on it to see each subcategory—Safety, Relationships, and Academic Orientation—accompanied by a definition. Interested users could then click on each of those subcategories to dive down even further—to the level of particular measures. Someone interested in the Relationships subcategory, for example, might advance to a page with breakdowns for Student Sense of Belonging and Student-Teacher Relationships.

Nesting information in the web tool would allow all users to have a meaningful experience at whatever level they chose to engage the data. Additionally, it allowed us to build an educational component into the tool. Experts could rapidly click down to whatever particular measure they were interested in seeing, but novices could stay at the simplest level and still engage with the same corpus of data. Or, if they chose to drill down further, they could do so with the support of accompanying descriptions and clarifications.

One of the major potential benefits of this project was giving stakeholders a common language for discussing school quality. If parents could articulate their interests and concerns in language understood by policymakers, they might gain a more powerful voice. Currently, parent voice is inhibited by the fact that parents often describe the same phenomena in many different ways, struggling to move past relatively vague conceptualizations. If instead they could collectively articulate the same clearly defined vision, in language used by policymakers themselves, they might have substantially more influence. Of course, the benefits of such communication are not limited to parents. All stakeholders—educators, administrators, policy leaders, parents, and community members—stand to benefit from clearer and more consistently defined goals. They might not always agree; but at least they would be on the same page. Insofar as that was a priority for our team, we sought to create a single tool that all users would be able to share.

The data for each school, by design, were sortable only by school. That is, our system did not allow users to create a rank-ordered list of schools for each category or subcategory. Now, it is certainly possible for users to do this themselves. There is no way to prevent that. In fact, such users may end up assembling well-rounded pictures of each school as they sort through particular categories. Yet we believe this information makes the most sense when it is presented as a collective whole—like a human body. We could rank people by their eyesight, for instance, or by arm length; but ultimately, what matters most is how all of those pieces work together to create a healthy and functional human being. That does not mean that differences are unimportant; it just means they need to be understood in context.

We also avoided ranking schools by particular traits because we did not wish to foster the methodologically dubious idea that very slight quantitative differences between schools necessarily reflect *real* differences that might be felt by stakeholders. First, there is a degree of error in all measurement, meaning that slight differences in the data may reflect error. Second, even if the measurements are accurate, it is quite possible that schools with different scores on a metric such as Student Sense of Belonging might be totally indistinguishable to anyone inside either school.

Ultimately, the tool we produced was both easy to use and multi-faceted. It required no training or expertise to engage with, at least at a basic level, and it offered a more comprehensive and nuanced portrait of school quality.

Even so, it was far from perfect, and our wish list remained long, even after we updated the beta version of our web tool. We wanted the site to be even more visual, using animations and other images to clearly convey what each category and subcategory was all about. We wanted the site to be easily translated—through the click of a button—into the other primary languages spoken in Somerville: Spanish, Portuguese, and Haitian Creole. We wanted to include a way for principals, teachers, parents, and students to share insights about their schools. We also wanted to include buttons that would allow users to easily contact adult members of the school community—administrators, teachers, and parents—in order to ask questions raised by the data. Perhaps if we could show proof of concept, we reasoned, we might make a case for hiring a team of web developers to work full time on the project.

But Does It Work? Testing the System

At the end of our first year collecting data and importing it into the online school information portal, we wanted to test the system. One concern was that all of this new information might not make much of a difference to parents. They might, in other words, feel just as informed by standardized test scores and other data currently collected and disseminated by the state.

Another concern was that this additional information might actually damage perceptions of the schools. We felt quite confident in the picture we assembled for each school, but we were also working closely with the district and the city, and we believed we owed them an honest assessment of what public reaction to the tool might be. Certainly, we worried that the city would pull the plug on the project if we were to tell them that more data made the schools look worse. At the same time we also worried that we might be encouraging Somerville to invest in something that would, at least in the short run, have a detrimental impact on the city's educational system.

Thus, with support from city hall, we began designing an experiment—in the form of a modified deliberative poll.[5] Deliberative polling usually entails taking a representative sample of citizens, providing them with balanced information, and then encouraging them to discuss and deliberate on the chosen topic. The goal is to uncover what public opinion would be if people had time, background knowledge, and support to truly deliberate.[6]

In our experiment, the structure of the polling procedure was modified slightly. Our poll took place over one afternoon, as opposed to multiple days, and participants were exposed to only one of two data sets—a treatment set and a control set—rather than multiple sources of competing information and presentations from experts. Nonetheless, we maintained many of the most important elements of traditional deliberative polling, with opportunities for people to engage with evidence as well as with each other.

But first we needed participants. After two weeks of recruiting through online, print, and face-to-face efforts, we selected fifty individuals representing racial, gender, age, income, and school-connection subgroups. In short, we tried to piece together a representative sample of the city's population, while also recruiting a mix of parents and nonparents, as well as a group of parents with children in the public schools. On the day of the poll, forty-five participants arrived for a half-day of data viewing, discussion, and polling.

Once inside the building, participants were randomly divided into one of two groups. One group worked with existing data, available through the Massachusetts Department of Elementary and Secondary Education website. Through that site, they could access information about student and teacher demographics, attendance and dropout rates, and, of course, test scores. Most of the information on the site, in fact, was related to standardized testing.

The other group worked with the web tool developed through our project.

Each group was asked to select a school with which they were familiar. Then they were randomly assigned an additional school to work with. The aim in this approach was twofold. First, it would allow us to determine whether data would affect those two groups—people familiar with a school, and people unfamiliar with a school—in the same way. Second, it would allow us to see if either data system could produce, among those unfamiliar with a school, the same kinds of perceptions held by those with higher levels of familiarity. In short, could data give the uninitiated an *insider's* view of the school?

Participants were polled four times—upon arrival, after initial data viewing, after small-group conversations, and after mixed-group conversations—about a range of questions. What we found out surprised us.[7]

Improving User Knowledge

We believed that users of the new data system would value the information they gathered from it. More specifically, we predicted that they would issue higher ratings to the new system than to the state system. And that turned out to be true. As shown in Figure 5.1, on questions about how much they learned, how confident they were in their knowledge, and how useful the information was, the new data system outperformed the state system by 15 to 25 percent.

If users actually learned more from the new data system, then presumably they would be able to answer more-specific questions about the schools. To examine this, we gave participants a series of surveys in which we asked them to rate schools on a number of different variables, such as teacher effectiveness, school culture, and preparing students for the future. The surveys were given at the beginning of the poll, before participants had looked at any data. They were given again after participants viewed data by themselves, working with either the new data system or the state data system, depending on the group to

	State Data	New Data	Improvement
"How much did you learn from this information about the two schools that was new to you?"	3.0	3.6	20%
"How confident are you in how much you know about these two schools?"	2.5	2.9	16%
"How useful was this information in allowing you to form an opinion of these schools?"	2.7	3.4	26%

Figure 5.1. New data system versus state data system on questions related to user knowledge

which they had been assigned. The surveys were given a third time after participants were given a chance to talk with each other in small groups. Then they were given a final time after we created mixed groups—of people assigned to treatment and control conditions—for another discussion.

Before looking at data, many people simply didn't have enough information to weigh in, particularly when randomly assigned to rate an unfamiliar school. Not surprisingly, many of them selected the "I don't know" option for questions about the school. However, we were curious: How many would still be clicking "I don't know" after they looked at one of the two data systems?

Users of the state data system and the new data tool started out with relatively similar percentages of "I don't know" responses across all questions. The treatment group, using the new data system, responded "I don't know" 121 times. The control group, using the state data system, responded that way 130 times.[8]

As the two groups viewed data and had small-group discussions, however, the numbers began to diverge. Among users of the new data tool, "I don't know" responses decreased 80 to 100 percent for all questions, leaving only ten such responses by the final survey. By contrast, users of the state data system still clicked "I don't know" fifty-seven times in the final survey.

In sum, it appears that users of the new data system—the system we designed for Somerville—not only valued the information more highly but also felt that they had enough knowledge to answer most of questions posed to them about school quality.

Improving Perceptions of Quality

In addition to thinking that the new data tool would better inform people, we hypothesized that it would have a positive influence on their perceptions of school quality. That turned out to be true. Somewhat surprisingly, though, it only appeared to affect ratings of schools with which users were not already familiar.

Interestingly, opinions about the quality of familiar schools appear to be fairly durable. Participants in both groups issued similar ratings to their familiar schools, from the first rating before viewing any data, to later ratings after data viewing and group discussions. One potential explanation for this is that those who feel they know a school are not likely to be influenced much by data. That makes sense. If someone showed me positive data for my daughter's school, which we are all quite happy with, the data would have little impact on my perception—I'm already quite satisfied. If someone showed me negative data about the school, I would be skeptical, perhaps even dismissing them. In short, data are unlikely to significantly sway someone's overall impression of a school if he or she knows it well.

That said, it is important to remember that many of the participants in our poll could not answer specific questions about the schools familiar to them. They may have had strong *general* views about school quality; but they were less clear about specific components such as school culture or teacher effectiveness. Thus, we might conclude that although more holistic information about school quality may be put to use differently by different groups—parents of students in a school, prospective parents, educators, policymakers—it might nevertheless be useful to all of them, even if they have established opinions.

Additionally, it is worth noting that overall ratings of familiar schools did go *down* slightly after poll participants viewed data. Their ratings did not go down by much—less than 10 percent, but it does indicate that participants were not merely issuing high ratings to their familiar schools. They appeared to be working hard to give a rating that reflected reality.

The story was quite different, however, when it came to the randomly assigned *unfamiliar* schools. In the case of these schools, the data our participants were viewing had a substantial impact on their perceptions of quality. Generally speaking, when participants used the state data system to learn about unfamiliar schools, they assigned them significantly lower scores than they had assigned to their familiar schools.

This was not true among users of the new data system. Participants rating randomly assigned schools, and relying on the new data system for their information, issued substantially higher scores than those relying on the state data system. In fact, their scores were almost perfectly in line with those issued by familiar raters. After initial data viewing, the average overall rating given to familiar schools, in both the treatment group and the control group, was 3.4 out of 5. Participants rating randomly assigned schools, and using the state data system, gave an average score of 2.9. Participants using the new data system to rate randomly assigned schools issued an average rating of 3.3.

After issuing these ratings, participants were then given the opportunity to have brief group discussions. Users of the new data system talked with other users of the new data system, and users of the state data system talked with other users of the state data system. They were then asked to go back and complete the survey again. After these discussions, ratings stayed mostly the same, though they did go up slightly for users of the new data system, to 3.5, and down slightly for users of the state data, to 2.8. One potential explanation for that modest uptick is that the new data were a bit more complicated to navigate, offering information that people are not accustomed to having. Whatever the case, though, the ratings issued to unfamiliar schools by users of the new data system, as Figure 5.2 indicates, continued to closely match those issued to familiar schools.

	Familiar School	Random School
New Data Group	3.4	3.5
State Data Group	3.5	2.8

Figure 5.2. Average ratings of school quality after viewing and discussing data

Why should it matter that ratings issued by users of the new data system closely matched those given to familiar schools? Well, consider: Which participants are most likely to have accurate views of the schools, those familiar with a school, or those randomly assigned to rate it? Probably those familiar with the school. Also, recall that when it came to rating their familiar schools, participants in both the treatment and control conditions *lowered* their ratings, if only slightly, after viewing data. Their ratings after group discussion reflect the information they had previously gathered about the school *and* the knowledge that could be gained from data—knowledge that had changed their ratings.

Of course, it is still possible that people rating familiar schools may simply be biased in their favor. This possibility is raised every year when the annual Phi Delta Kappa / Gallup poll is released. Consistently, the poll has found that Americans rate the schools they know best—those attended by their own children—far more favorably than they rate the nation's schools as a whole. In the 2015 edition of the poll, 51 percent of public school parents gave their own schools a grade of either A or B, while just 21 percent of them gave the nation's schools that rating.[9]

Again, however, it is worth asking: Which schools are Americans likely to know well enough to rate—the schools attended by their children, or the 98,000 other public schools in the United States? And though it is possible that parents may be psychologically inclined to say that their children are enrolled in good schools, it is equally true that they will have higher standards when it comes to their own children than when it comes to the children of strangers.

When we design information systems in education, we have an ethical obligation to get it right. We know that data produced by such systems are going to be used by the public to make decisions about where to live and where to send their children to school. Furthermore, we know that policymakers are going to use the data to hold schools accountable.

But what does it mean to "get it right"? Researchers can assess the validity and reliability of measures and can analyze the relationships between those measures and particular valued outcomes. These kinds of tests can and should be run. Another kind of test, however—one that is not currently discussed in many circles—concerns the extent to which information about a school matches what well-informed insiders know. Imagine handing over a set of data to a school's principal, a cross-section of teachers, and a group of parents, all sitting in a room together. If the data are accurate, wouldn't they have some sense of it? Shouldn't that be one of our goals—to capture some of what they feel?

Improving Word of Mouth

Our third research question for the deliberative poll was about how discussions would shape the way participants rated schools. After all, people don't develop their opinions about schools in a vacuum. They talk with friends and neighbors, sharing insights with each other. Consequently, we sought to simulate that by putting people into small-group discussions. Again, what we found was surprising.

After viewing data on their own, participants completed a second-round survey—designed to capture any impact of engaging with data. Then participants were placed in small groups and asked to discuss what they had just reviewed. After those discussions, they completed a third-round survey. Finally, we placed them in heterogeneous groups, mixing new data viewers and state data viewers together, and asking them to complete one last survey. The purpose of mixing the

	Before Mixed Groups	After Mixed Groups	Difference
New Data Group			
Familiar School	3.36	3.32	-.04
Random School	3.48	3.43	-.05
State Data Group			
Familiar School	3.55	3.68	+.13
Random School	2.78	3.11	+.33

Figure 5.3. Changes in overall impression of school quality after "cross-talk" discussion

groups was to see if engagement with either data set would have a spillover effect. For instance, would talking with someone from the new data group change the opinions of a participant from the state data group, even if he or she had not interacted directly with that set of data?

As Figure 5.3 indicates, these conversations did not appear to have a large effect on ratings issued by users of the new data system; their ratings declined only trivially after talking to users of the state data system. These conversations had only a slightly stronger effect on those users of the state data system who were rating familiar schools. But for users of the state data system rating *unfamiliar* schools, the impact was substantial. After talking with users of the new data system, they issued ratings that were, on average, over 10 percent higher.

So what does this reveal? It seems that word of mouth can have a powerful effect on how people view school quality—at least when it comes to schools they do not already know well.

In our poll, word of mouth appeared to have a stronger impact on how participants viewed their randomly assigned schools than on how they viewed their familiar schools. And it appeared to have a stronger effect on those working with the state data system than on those working with the new data system. In each case, it might be argued that low levels of knowledge—from unfamiliarity, or from a narrow set of data—made participants more likely to change their ratings.

From one perspective, this seems an encouraging finding. Perhaps, via the mechanism of unstructured conversation, less-informed opinions will give way to more-informed ones. From another perspective, however, it is a bit more unsettling, for it may be that the data currently being used to structure understandings of unfamiliar schools—and most schools are unfamiliar to most people—are creating unjustly negative perceptions of school quality, at least in some places. In other words, people are sharing information that may be narrow or inaccurate, but that is nevertheless casting many schools in an unflattering light.

Now, it is important to note that our deliberative poll was a very small-scale experiment that included only forty-five participants. Though we were careful to design the event in a methodologically rigorous way, we cannot say for certain that it perfectly reflects reality. We may have had an exceptional group of participants who, for one reason or another, are not like most Americans. Or our findings may be in some significant way the product of chance.

On the whole, however, we believe that we can reasonably make a few claims about our new data system.

First, it seems that the new system is more useful than a typical state data system like the one that exists in Massachusetts. We have some evidence from our poll to support this claim; but it also squares with common sense, as our new data system simply provided much more information than the existing state system.

Second, it seems that a more robust data system will not harm perceptions of school quality, at least in districts where standardized test scores are not hugely impressive. This is not to deny that there are bad schools. Rather, it is to say that many schools with lower standardized test scores may, in fact, be high-quality schools. It may simply be that such schools *appear* to be ineffective due to variables outside of their control. In the case of schools with top standardized test scores, the story might be different: perceptions of quality might end up being depressed by a broader range of data. Yet insofar as our framework aligns with what the public values, as well as with what research indicates to be important, we should want that information. Only by knowing the true state of reality can we go about changing it.

Finally, it seems that a high-quality information system might change the nature of our conversations about school quality. It might expand opportunities to learn about school performance while also providing a clear and standard basis for communication. It might nudge out less reliable forms of evidence in our discussions about schools. And it might start shifting us away from a culture of testing, as schools would be evaluated in many different ways.

Can All Schools Be Good?

Would more robust data lead to all communities feeling more confident in the quality of their schools? Possibly. It may be the case that schools with low standardized test results are better than they are often imagined to be—possessing strengths that don't show up in test scores. And it may be that schools presumed to be good because of their test scores would rate highly for other reasons as well—for levels of student engagement, for instance, or the strength of the teaching staff.

So, perhaps our schools are simply better than we give them credit for. After all, Americans are generally satisfied with the schools attended by their children. Though they issue low overall ratings to the nation's schools, this may be the result of a perception gap—a gap driven by polarizing rhetoric and incomplete data. A more robust set of data, it seems, would do quite a bit to close the distance between perception and reality, at least when it comes to unfamiliar schools.[10]

Of course, this is not a claim that all schools are strong. Some schools do have significant weaknesses, and data systems should identify them. The underlying priority in the creation of educational data systems, after all, should be to inform and empower engaged stakeholders, not to market schools to unwitting consumers.

It is also worth noting that improved data systems might continue to misidentify schools. Despite efforts to create measures that are fair and comprehensive, such systems may continue to portray schools with high percentages of low-income and minority students as weaker than they actually are. Though this may be the case, our analyses indicate that test scores tend to correlate more strongly with demographic variables than do other school quality metrics. In short, we can at the very least do much better than we are currently doing.

It is also possible that schools with dazzling reputations would appear somewhat less lustrous in a system that incorporated more than standardized test scores. Insofar as such schools may not be as thoroughly superior as they are imagined to be, more information might theoretically present the schools more negatively than people currently view them. Yet results from our deliberative poll indicate, as does common sense, that data will not likely change the views of those familiar with a school. Parents, students, teachers, and administrators who are already members of a school community will likely not be surprised by what a more robust set of data indicates. And even if it reveals a less than perfect picture of the school, such information may lead to clearer communication and more rigorous decision making. The net outcome appears positive.

It may be possible that those unfamiliar with a high-status school, when looking beyond test scores, would make different decisions—about where to live or where to enroll their children. Still, it is hard to make the case that this represents harm. Schools with high standardized test scores are, by and large, schools with more privileged populations. Additionally, these schools are often relatively homogeneous with regard to socioeconomic composition. Thus, if families with this profile were to seek out other schools, it is unlikely that demographic sorting would be exacerbated, either at the schools they choose or the schools they leave behind; in fact, it might lead to higher levels of integration. It is also unlikely that the schools they leave behind would face increased accountability consequences, at least as state-level accountability is currently designed.[11]

Are all schools good? No—but it may be the case that most of them are. It at least seems likely that many American schools are much better than they are presumed to be—by parents, policymakers, and the public. The perception gap has very real consequences for schools, and particularly for schools serving the most vulnerable members of our society. Insofar as that is the case, addressing the perception gap is a matter of social justice.

When we measure only a particular feature of what we want schools to do, when we do so in a way that inherently advantages schools with particular kinds of student populations, and when we present the results in a manner that suggests a clear hierarchy—of top schools, average schools, and bottom schools—we are doing grievous harm. These distortions, we must remember, are not merely academic. They affect the spirit of a school and the faith of a community. They shape the decisions people make about where they live and where they send their children to school. And they play a critical role in policy, often leading directly to penalties and sanctions.

Are some schools better than others? Certainly—at particular things, depending in large part on what the school's mission is and who it serves. A school may be better at fostering the arts, for instance, or at cultivating a caring community. This is ranking, certainly, but this kind of ranking is far less problematic than the ranking of schools by test scores.

In the end, of course, it may be that schools are not really that different from one another. Though that might be frustrating for those with the resources and inclination to shop for the best school, it would induce a sigh of relief for many others. Knowing that so much depends on the unpredictable—on individual children, on the friends they make, on the teachers they click with, on the passions they develop over time—many of us want something fairly simple from our schools. Our aim is not to create perfect schools, which simply do not exist. Instead, it is to cultivate a national network of schools that are safe, caring, challenging environments that offer many different kinds of opportunities for young people. As a society, we can guarantee that aim, and we should be doing everything we can to realize it.

Getting Better All the Time

Our work in Somerville has been well received, at least so far, by parents, educators, administrators, and civic leaders, and results from our deliberative poll were encouraging. Still, it is important to remember that this is hardly a complete and replicable model. This project is simply too big, and the work too important, for a single research team—much less a small team with a modest budget—to reach anything resembling a definitive conclusion.

Therefore, this book is designed less as an instruction manual than as a field guide. Its aim is not to give readers a set of rules to follow, but rather to help them see the environment—in this case, an educational environment—with deeper understanding and a clearer sense of what to look for.

The kind of data system described in this chapter can be built in any state or district. Though that may seem intimidating, it should not be. We will not arrive at a perfect system through the dissemination of a single model. Rather, we should engage in multiple projects simultaneously—experimenting, tracking progress, constantly tinkering, and sharing information. The first goal in this work should be to immediately replace inadequate information systems. The second should be simply to get better, all the time.

6

A New Accountability: Making Data Matter

IMAGINE BEING a parent in Los Angeles or Cleveland or Richmond, or in one of countless other cities, and opening the paper—seemingly every day—to read coverage of failing schools. Picture yourself flipping to a *Boston Globe* piece titled "Six More Schools 'Underperforming,'" reading a declaration by the Nashville *Tennessean* that "failing schools demand board response," or clicking on a Rochester CBS television news story, "City to Address Failing Schools."[1]

It can be both discouraging and disempowering. The schools are in decline, these stories tell us; and it isn't clear there are any strengths to build on, any reasons to doubt the narrative of failure, or anything we can do to slow the deterioration.

Not surprisingly, public faith in K–12 schools, which had been eroding for several decades, reached a nadir during the NCLB era. In 2002, the year NCLB was signed into law, 24 percent of respondents in the annual Phi Delta Kappa / Gallup poll gave the nation's public schools an A or a B grade. Sixty percent gave them a C or a D. A decade later, after ten years under the standardized testing regime, views of the nation's schools reached an all-time low. Only 18 percent gave the nation's schools an A or a B grade. Seventy-two percent gave them a C or a D.[2]

Some might argue that these responses reflect a clearer sense of reality. NCLB, they might contend, helped show Americans that their schools were much worse than they had realized.

Yet, when Americans in that 2013 poll were asked to rate the quality of the schools attended by their own children, 71 percent gave them an A or a B—the same percentage that had done so ten years earlier. Only 27 percent assigned grades of C and D.

Some have explained this phenomenon by likening it to the way people rate Congress: on average, voters rate the representatives of their own districts much more highly than they rate Congress as a whole. This analogy seems misleading, though. The way voters align with political parties, for instance—making it possible to have, say, a Democratic congresswoman even when there is a Republican majority in the House of Representatives—does not appear to have a parallel in the world of education. Also, whereas voters have relatively equal levels of information about local and national politics, parents have far more information about their own children's schools than they do about the nation's schools.[3]

Another explanation for this divide in ratings is that the public suffers from a "Lake Wobegon effect," mistakenly believing that local children are above average. Yet research has not substantiated this hypothesis. In fact, a recent Harvard study found that Americans have surprisingly accurate perceptions of the level of student achievement in their local school districts. As its author, Martin West, concluded: "citizens are quite well-informed about the level of student performance in American schools."[4]

What this likely means is that our schools haven't actually declined in quality. They are hardly perfect, certainly, and that is particularly true with regard to inequities across demographic groups. But on almost every measure, including the National Assessment of Educational Progress—a nationally representative assessment of student learning, often referred to as "the nation's report card"—American schools are doing better today, on average, than at any previous time.[5] Instead of capturing a real decline in quality, then, it may be that the data available to us since 2002 have merely exacerbated the rhetoric of crisis, which has become increasingly pervasive over the past several decades. Such rhetoric is politically useful insofar as it generates momentum for specific candidates or particular proposals; crisis, after all, calls for action. Because this rhetoric does not appear to be closely tethered to reality, though, it has fostered a gap between actual performance and perceived performance.[6]

This perception gap is of significant consequence. After all, if we believe that our schools are in crisis, we are far more likely to support aggressive and disruptive reform efforts such as high-stakes accountability policies. To turn an aphorism on its head, if it's broken, fix it. But if our schools are *not* in crisis, we may be fostering the wrong kinds of policies—policies that intrude and distract.[7]

Many of the most harmful effects of our current approach to educational measurement have been felt in urban schools. Educating a larger share of students from demographic strata that predict lower test score performance—low-income students, non–native English speakers, and students of color—urban schools have been subject to more policy intervention and reputational slander than their suburban counterparts.

Yet we might remember that insufficient measures of school quality affect everyone. High test scores may provide the cover for some schools to ignore important but unmeasured goals, and, believing that there is such a thing as a generic and uniformly "good school," parents can overlook the importance of fit, making sacrifices to place their children in schools that may not best serve their needs and interests.

So why not quit cold turkey? Particularly when our data systems have had other problematic consequences, such as a narrowing curriculum, why not turn back the clock entirely? Why not simply dump measurement once and for all?

The answer is that not all of the impacts of educational data usage have been troubling. NCLB, for instance, did lead to more transparency. Tests do measure something, and NCLB mandated the universal and public reporting of test scores. Particularly useful was the disaggregation of student test data by subgroups. That meant that schools needed to report the scores not just for the student body as a whole, but for particular racial and economic groups whose scores had often been concealed in averages. Even in high-scoring schools, achievement gaps between student subgroups were often alarming.

Additionally, it is important to remember that even if the state were to retreat from the work of measuring school quality, information about school performance would not go away. Parents and the public have long engaged in the informal exchange of information about school quality, and though the rise of modern educational measurement may have accelerated that trend, it did not create it. Moreover, with the advent of privately run school rating companies like GreatSchools .org, it is hard to justify a public retreat from such work. If districts or states abandon efforts to measure school quality, they will leave the field to those who may not have the resources or incentives to do it right.

The challenge, it seems, is to *fix* our data systems rather than to dump them. After all, district, state, and federal leaders should be able to create thoughtful and supportive accountability systems. Parents should be able to engage in informed advocacy and make rational choices. Educators should be able to carefully and consistently track progress. And we should all be able to communicate clearly with each other about the strengths and weaknesses of our schools.

How to Construct State and Federal Accountability

State and federal accountability structures currently prioritize raw student standardized test scores in math and English. They do so with little acknowledgment of the connection between demography and test scores and with little regard for other factors of school quality. Thus, even if formal sanctions have eased somewhat with the transition from NCLB to ESSA, accountability systems remain problematic.

If fixing these systems were to become a priority for federal and state policymakers, however, there are several immediate steps that they might take.

The first would be to expand the number of factors by which schools are measured. Certainly it would help to use more of the information about schools that is already commonly collected—attendance and graduation data, for instance, or student growth scores. Many states are on this path, and the new Every Student Succeeds Act is a step in the right direction. It would be far better, however, to create school quality frameworks that actually align with the things stakeholders care about.

One potential concern here is about the level of effort such a shift would require. States would need to establish new frameworks, develop measures aligned with those frameworks, and support districts as they learned to deploy those measures. If state and federal leaders are actually interested in accountability for funding, however, they must begin to look not merely at student standardized test scores, but at the full range of characteristics that make a school successful. Failing to do so, they will continue distorting our common definition of what a good school is. In short, whatever the effort, it is worth our time and energy.

Another potential concern is about all that can go wrong in overhauling an accountability structure. What if a state includes factors outside the control of schools? Or what if it adopts measures that produce an inaccurate picture of reality? Might this not be just as bad as the current test-based accountability model?

Perhaps the most obvious and immediate way of addressing such questions is to decouple educational data from punishments and sanctions, taking a page from the no-stakes National Assessment of Educational Progress. Political accountability, after all, is the product of two different kinds of instruments—those that provide information and those that offer a means of enforcement. These systems, we might recall, need not always be yoked together. In fact, "tight coupling" might be viewed as an indicator of mistrust in the deliberative capacities of citizens and their representatives. In a functional democratic system governed by elections and the rule of law, information can promote accountability without being paired with predetermined sanctions, at least outside some minimum standard. And insofar as measurement will always represent only an approximation of reality—even in the case of measures that extend beyond test scores—it may be worth considering how sensible it is to craft policies that mechanically punish schools for a data-based picture of performance.[8]

Another important move in mitigating problems associated with a broader sort of accountability would be to establish an embargo period for research and development. If particular kinds of outcomes tend to align with race, ethnicity, income, or other demographic factors, for instance, they will need to be adjusted. Thus, we might provisionally adopt newer measures, even if they are imperfect, provided there is adequate time for field testing and revision. If current state accountability frameworks were to remain in place without the kind of changes described above, it would also be wise to forestall any enforcement mechanisms. By establishing a period of time in which schools and districts would be held harmless for performance—say two years—state and federal policy leaders would do a great deal to stave off potential pitfalls.

A third way of improving accountability would be to give localities more of a voice in the accountability process—allowing them to co-determine the factors used to measure performance. Doing so, state and federal authorities might mitigate distorting effects of data systems, drawing on local knowledge and expertise.[9] Additionally, state and federal policymakers might work with districts to establish reasonable benchmarks for performance. This, of course, would create different standards for different places, opening up questions about unequal expectations. It is important, however, to distinguish the process of setting short-term standards, which might be revised annually or biennially, from the process of establishing long-term expectations. In the short term, we simply cannot expect that all schools will be the same; policy must acknowledge that. Thus, we might maintain our focus on the long-term goal of equity while recognizing the constraints of present reality.[10]

Such shifts in how accountability is structured might produce higher levels of uncertainty than state and federal leaders are comfortable with. Yet anxious policymakers might recall that most current systems in place are highly flawed. Insofar as that is the case, the standard for amending or replacing them need not be particularly strict. Rather than seeking flawless systems, which simply cannot be designed in the laboratory, we should seek systems that represent an improvement over what exists. This does not mean that we should accept weakly theorized replacements. Rather, it means that we need not be paralyzed by the fear that a perfect accountability system cannot be designed without making adjustments along the way.

So let's imagine that every state, perhaps with encouragement from the U.S. Department of Education, were to rethink its accountability system. What might that process look like?

The first step would be to develop a broader framework for school quality—a framework like that presented in this book. Such work might be piloted at the district level, among consortia of districts, or even at the state level. With feedback from key stakeholders, they might, at relatively low cost, determine what, exactly, is worth measuring.

The second step would be to locate any currently available tools that align with the goals of their chosen frameworks. Borrowing tools that are already in use, or piloting new tools, it would be possible to track the effectiveness of various measures and adjust them over time. Such work would be painstaking and time-consuming were it to be done on a school-by-school basis—but that need not happen. Schools, districts, and states, working in conjunction with scholars and researchers—like the Chicago Consortium on School Research, California's CORE districts, or the Massachusetts Consortium for Innovative Education Assessment—might discover a great deal by sharing information with each other, accelerating progress along the learning curve.

The third and final step would be to determine what levels of performance schools would be held accountable for.[11] One approach would be to allow districts and consortia to establish performance targets in consultation with the state. Looking at current levels of performance, and then tracking growth for a period of time, they collectively might establish realistic short-term benchmarks. Next, by looking at performance across schools and districts, and tracking levels of stakeholder satisfaction with those outcomes, the state might establish longer-term benchmarks for all schools. Were long-term benchmarks to be the same across schools, the state would need to accept responsibility for ensuring school capacity to meet those benchmarks—a system of what might be called "reciprocal accountability."

Alternatively, the state might act on its own to determine reasonable performance benchmarks, creating two separate sets of targets: minimum targets and model targets. Minimum targets would apply to all schools, across categories—establishing a performance floor. Model targets, on the other hand, which would set significantly higher standards for performance, would only apply to particular categories determined by districts. Such a system would allow for state-level standards and for local control. For schools and districts performing below minimum thresholds, the state might mandate particular levels of growth, for which it could provide targeted support.

To be clear: this is merely a rough sketch of how policy leaders might revise their accountability systems. The purpose of this discussion, after all, is not to map out in great detail a stronger state or federal accountability system. Rather, the point is to outline the basic moves that state or federal authorities would need to make and to show that, although such a shift would not be easy, it would certainly be possible.

Whether or not such a shift *will* happen, on the other hand, is another matter entirely. The strongest advocates of federal and state accountability have little faith in local control. As a consequence, they might express concern about various aspects of a proposal like this. And perhaps chiefly, they might worry that a broader set of measures would lead to schools having too diffuse a focus. What if schools take their eyes off the prize of academic achievement and we produce a generation of kids who are happy, well-rounded, and academically weak? For such concerns it is worth offering two separate responses.

The first response is rooted in scholarship. No significant body of research indicates that the multiple aims of schools are mutually exclusive. Focus on the arts, for instance, does not undermine student learning in the sciences. Attention to citizenship preparation does not weaken a student's ability to comprehend a reading passage. Additionally, longitudinal research does not appear to suggest that the acquisition of content knowledge plays a more essential role in shaping personal or societal outcomes than other aims do. Even if that were the case, however, it would be hard to argue that various kinds of skills do not overlap with and strengthen each other.[12]

The second response is philosophical. The schools in this country belong to the people. They are democratic institutions that should reflect democratic values. So, while it may be the case that leaders in business and government want the schools to prepare workers with basic skills for the purpose of economic productivity, citizens may not want their children to be defined exclusively as future labor. If the American people want their schools to pursue a range of aims— preparing young people to lead rich, full, happy lives, for instance— then that is what the schools should do.

Advocates of state and federal accountability might also worry about the degree to which a broader set of measures might be easy to game; that is, they might believe that it is easier to produce inaccurate reports of school culture than to produce inaccurate reports of student learning. This concern also might be met with two replies. The first is that our current measures of student learning—standardized test scores in math and English—*do* offer an inaccurate picture of student learning. For many reasons discussed in Chapter 1 of this book, test scores are hardly a clear window into what schools have helped students learn. Second, given that current accountability systems focus primarily on a single set of measures—test scores—they may be easier to game, even if those measures appear more objective than student and teacher self-reports. Consequently, a broader set of measures, even if seemingly "softer," might actually prevent schools from gaming accountability systems—doing so by increasing the burden on would-be cheaters, as well as by establishing more measures that might be corroborated with each other.[13]

To return to an earlier point, however, the most important step to take in assuring information accuracy is to reduce the incentive to cheat. In a high-stakes accountability system, even the most carefully crafted measures will be distorted by pressure to produce "right answers." Consequently, if policy leaders are serious about getting accurate information, they must wrestle with the possibility of scaling back the sanctions associated with low performance. Accurate information, even without associated punishments, can empower stakeholders and foster communication. It can lead to more informed decision making, and insofar as it identifies gaps between schools, it can promote fairer and more intelligent allocation of resources.

What State and Federal Leaders Can Do to Strengthen Schools

State and federal leaders might take a number of bold steps with regard to improving educational accountability systems, including moves that would radically redefine the very nature of accountability. Yet, though revising these systems might devolve significant power to the local level, it would not require a retreat from state and federal involvement. Instead, it would require a shift in purpose, with state and federal leaders using data not to punish, but to support. With a clearer sense of what a school's strengths and weaknesses are, state and federal leaders could go well beyond setting reasonable expectations; they could actually help schools and districts *meet* expectations, focusing primarily on more fairly and effectively directing resources.

This is not to say that a more robust school quality framework would lead inevitably to the creation of new resources. It would not. It would, however, allow for the creation of more targeted support— addressing specific needs, as identified through more effective measurement systems—as well as for more efficient allocation of resources to those with greatest need.

Currently, states offer their most robust support to schools only when taking them over. This practice undermines the effectiveness of intervention by stripping a community of its autonomy. It is further hindered by the fact that it is usually triggered by low test scores, which many stakeholders may not recognize as a valid measure of school quality. As a result, state takeover can be fiercely resisted by educators and families, which only further erodes any potential upside of the intervention.[14]

The most common form of state aid is financial support for specific programming, delivered to schools through a motley assortment of grant programs. In Massachusetts, for instance, there are grants for building standards-aligned curricula, improving school security, extending the school day, expanding vocational education, and more. But such programs generally reflect best guesses about what is needed. Additionally, they do not align with any particular framework for school quality. Consequently, such programs can appear to educators somewhat arbitrary and can be difficult to measure in terms of impact.

The same is true at the federal level. The Teaching American History (TAH) grants program, for instance, dispersed roughly a billion dollars prior to its wind-down in 2011. Yet beyond being a passion project of the late West Virginia senator Robert Byrd, it is not particularly clear why the TAH program was created. Social studies is not among tested subjects, so student achievement scores did not drive its creation, and no coalition of educators ever demanded such a program.

TAH grants went to districts, which partnered with colleges or nonprofit organizations to develop workshops, seminars, and field trips for K–12 history teachers. Because there was not a clear vision of what those grants were supposed to accomplish, though, it was hard to track progress. According to the U.S. Department of Education, the program was supposed to "improve instruction and raise student achievement."[15] But were teachers supposed to design different kinds of lessons? Were they supposed to engage in different instructional practices? Would students achieve more because they would be more engaged? Would they achieve more in all subjects, or just history?

This is not to say that TAH grants were a bad idea. Rather, the point is that too many unknowns surrounded the program. It wasn't clear, for instance, that schools needed TAH programming, and it was never clear what the impact of these grants was.[16]

State and federal leaders, if they were to have a clearer sense of what schools are working to accomplish, and if they were to possess sensible measures associated with those goals, might develop programs with a stronger sense of purpose. This would not only foster greater levels of focus and relevance but also allow schools and districts to make more effective choices. By choosing from a clearly labeled menu of options, schools and districts might seek resources aligned with their aims, rather than merely chasing available pots of money.

Additionally, such an approach would allow state and federal funders to direct resources more equitably. Currently, state and federal grants that go through a competitive process are often awarded on the basis of a well-written and well-organized grant proposal as much as on any other criteria. That may not change; but if our priority is directing resources to where they are most needed, we must invest in making it possible for schools and districts to clearly demonstrate their needs.

State and federal offices of education might use more robust information to support schools in other ways, too. Though grants are perhaps the most common way to build capacity, they are not the only way. The CORE districts in California, for instance, are piloting an effort in which they are pairing higher- and lower-performing schools for the purpose of coaching and capacity building—something that can be done effectively only if a school's performance on particular measures is clear.

Finally, it is worth noting that research would benefit tremendously from a more robust picture of school quality. The more information we gather—about which outcomes can be influenced though schooling, about what kinds of outcomes are possible, about programmatic effectiveness, and so on—the more state and federal leaders will be able to craft thoughtful and effective policies. Certainly there will always be an ideological dimension to policymaking, as well as an element of guesswork; but we can, and should, do much more to collect the kinds of information that will support rigorous decision making.

What Local Leaders Can Do to Strengthen Schools

State and federal leaders are not the only ones who might use better data systems to support schools. Many key decisions about school policies and practices are made at the local level—by school boards, district administrators, and school principals. And though local leaders have more direct knowledge of the schools, they are still limited in terms of the data they have available for identifying specific problems and tracking results.

Consider the case of the district-wide goals that the Somerville school committee set in 2014. Seeking to move beyond what one member called "top-down state policy, emphasizing math and English test scores at the expense of play and character building," the school committee articulated a wide range of ambitious goals for the schools:

Goal 1: Support the "Whole Child" by working with stakeholders to increase and improve activities that develop the intellectual, physical, and emotional potential of all students.

Goal 2: Improve Student Achievement.

Goal 3: Establish and begin implementation of a plan for Universal Kindergarten Readiness and grade-level literacy.

Goal 4: Promote a culture of Innovation and Collaboration.

Goal 5: Improve Communication.

Taken together, these goals cover a broad range of educational aims. Also, it is quite telling that the committee's first priority, even ahead of improving student achievement, was to develop the whole child, not just the part of the child that takes standardized achievement tests. Scratch beneath the surface, though, and the limitations of available data become quite clear.

For Goal 1, the Somerville school committee listed three targets for the schools to meet:

Maintain and expand access to co-curricular and extra-curricular activities for all students.

Develop an analysis of activities that support the "Whole Child."

Decrease chronic absenteeism and tardiness by 10 percent.

Tellingly, the only specific aim here pertains to the reduction of chronic absenteeism and tardiness. Expanding access to cocurricular and extracurricular activities could presumably be measured, though no specific goal is articulated. And there is no specific target aligned with physical, social, or emotional outcomes, despite the committee's mention of those in its general goal.

Now consider the specific targets for Goal 2: Improve Student Achievement:

> Each school will meet or exceed the State Performance and Progress Index (PPI) targets for each school.[17]
>
> The District will meet or exceed the State Performance and Progress Index target for the District.
>
> Achieve a minimum District-wide student growth percentile (SGP) average of 60 and implement intervention measures for any student who does not meet this standard.
>
> Reduce the achievement gap by 10 percent.
>
> Increase the number of students ranking Proficient or Advanced on MCAS by 10 percent in all subgroups.[18]
>
> Increase the number of students ranking Proficient or Advanced on Science MCAS by 10 percent.
>
> Improve the four year and five year graduation rates by 10 percent.

Tapping into nearly all of the available metrics—state-calculated PPI, SGP, gaps between subgroups, MCAS levels, and graduation rates—the committee articulated a remarkably specific set of targets. Are they ideal measures of student achievement? Hardly. All but graduation rates rely heavily on test scores. Also, for reasons discussed in Chapter 1, standardized tests present a highly incomplete picture of learning.

Although the school committee's goals are laudable, the limits of available data mean that those goals will have varying degrees of impact on classroom practice. District and school leaders, for instance, might believe strongly in educating the "whole child," but may arrive at different understandings of what it means to do so. Student achievement, by contrast, is defined in highly concrete terms. Thus, it is not hard to guess which issues will become priorities when seven specific aims are articulated for one goal, and three relatively nebulous aims are articulated for the other. Goal 1, despite its primacy on the list, seems destined to be subverted.

The good news, however, is that change isn't hard. In Somerville, the school committee was ready to integrate new data into their work as soon as they had access to it. This may not be true everywhere—in other places, there may be ideological disagreements to work through, or resistance to change—but it is hard to imagine that members of local school boards would react much differently than they did in Somerville. Specifically, they articulated a desire to put the new data to use as well as to continue expanding the quality indicators available to them.

Another similar example can be found in the work done by committees within individual schools. In the state of Massachusetts, schools are required to form school councils, which are made up of parents, teachers, and community members. Their task is to work with principals in reviewing the school budget, developing school goals, and formulating a school improvement plan. In Somerville, those school improvement plans have tended, at least for the past few years, to articulate a range of aims reflective of the many facets of school quality.

Still, these school improvement plans have tended to be vague and seemingly ad hoc in nature. One, for instance, called for a new robotics program, a professional development workshop for teachers on managing student behavior, and increased funding for student clubs. Not surprisingly, the plan was rejected. Why? Because the requests seemed arbitrary and disparate. Furthermore, there was no tangible evidence that such additions were necessary, nor were there any mechanisms for tracking the effectiveness of new programming.

Imagine, however, if the council had started with a set of core values and a set of rich data that allowed them to systematically identify particular strengths and weaknesses. Looking directly at such targets, they might have made different choices, or they might have made the same choices, but with a more compelling rationale for their proposal—a case that might have included a whole slate of programs and policies designed to address each weakness. Were their proposal accepted, they might have had tools at their disposal to track progress.

Again, stakeholders in Somerville were ready and willing to integrate new tools. In August 2016, school improvement councils were given the new data system to work with. After looking at the new data for the first time, one council member bubbled over with excitement. "I'm really interested in the student sense of belonging stuff," he said. "Our lowest score was on feeling connected to adults at the school; that's really interesting; I want to figure out what's going on there." To get the whole story, he'd have to do more than look at data; but he had a new question to ask, a new way to communicate, and a new way to track progress over time.

These kinds of data systems could also be used for other purposes. School and district teams, for instance, might better plan teacher professional development, which often fails because it does not relate directly to the specific issues that are of concern to educators.[19] They might communicate more clearly with parents, community members, and prospective parents—helping them navigate the schools and become better advocates. Or they might use such systems as the basis for planning extracurricular and after-school activities in a more rigorous and evidence-oriented manner, making selections for the purpose of supplementing and enhancing the school's overall program. Whatever the case, it is clear that school and district leaders would benefit from a more broadly defined, measurable framework for school quality. As Somerville superintendent Mary Skipper put it, districts don't simply need *more* data; they need *better* data—"useful information that we can act upon and solve educational problems with."

A Few Rules for Accountability

This book is primarily focused on measuring school quality. Insofar as measurement systems often end up tied to accountability structures, though, it is important to go beyond a general discussion of accountability, to offer a few rules—rules that policy leaders at various levels might keep in mind if they want educational data to have a powerful and positive impact. In service of that aim, here are nine broad guidelines for establishing a fair and effective accountability system:[20]

1. Empower communities in the improvement of schools. State education agencies should extend greater responsibility and ownership to districts by working to strengthen local accountability systems. Effective data systems empower local leaders to make decisions that fit the needs of their schools and communities. The state can offer an important resource by providing common guidelines, support, and comprehensive data.

2. Create a system of reciprocal accountability. In present accountability systems, schools are responsible for demonstrating responsible use of resources. Yet it is the responsibility of state and local agencies to ensure that resources delivered to schools are sufficient. In a reciprocal accountability system, data should be used not only to measure school performance but also to measure state and local support for schools.

3. Use multiple measures to assess and report on school quality. Using and reporting on multiple measures of school quality, rather than a single standardized test, provides a more robust picture of student achievement, student engagement, and school progress. To realize their full potential, these measures must not be reduced to a

single composite score, which prevents educators and parents from understanding the nuances of areas in which a school may be doing well and others that may need improvement.

4. Capture what communities want to know. Accountability systems are designed not only to inform policymakers but also to inform community constituencies. Insofar as that is the case, community members should have a role in determining the measures that are most important to know about student learning and school quality.

5. Establish performance benchmarks for schools based upon the characteristics of a high-quality school. Theoretically, it is possible that all schools are doing good work, even if some are outperforming others. By measuring how schools are performing relative to target thresholds, we can learn more about where to direct attention and assistance. In such a system, we can eliminate leveling and ranking schools relative to each other, which sends a confusing message to the public about school quality and unfairly stigmatizes those at the bottom of distributions.

6. Place greater weight on growth than on absolute scores. Due to the influence of socioeconomic factors such as parental education and family income, students enter formal schooling at different starting points. Consequently, absolute scores reflect as much about families and neighborhoods as they do about schools. Thus, while an effective accountability system should continue to track absolute performance, student growth is ultimately a more informative indicator.

7. Emphasize support rather than punishment. Information leads to improvement when involved parties act to address gaps. When low performance is met with punishment, it triggers responses such as data suppression or quick fixes designed to raise test scores without necessarily improving student learning. Effective accountability systems use evidence to direct relevant support to schools, building capacity for improvement.

8. Capture a reality that members of the school community will be familiar with. Right now, educational data are presumed to be valid even if they send a message that conflicts with what parents, teachers, principals, and students know about their schools. Accountability systems, insofar as they seek to present a condensed version of reality, should produce impressions that at least roughly match what those inside schools know about their organizations. If they do not, a healthy dose of skepticism may be in order.

9. Remain an unfinished product. No accountability system is ever perfect; there is always an opportunity to learn about how our information systems are working. Thus, as daunting as it may seem, such systems must be understood as works in progress if they are going to realize their full potential.

Using Data to Choose a School

All parents get to choose which schools their children attend. The problem is that, given most public school zoning policies, many are choosing before their children are even born, or before they have started school.

This is a less than ideal state of affairs because it requires all schools to develop relatively generic identities. A school cannot reasonably emphasize the creative and performing arts, for instance, or math and science education, if it is serving students who have been assigned to attend rather than those who have opted in. Some, certainly, will thrive, but what about those who lack talent and interest? No wonder schools are often so similar to one another.

In this imperfect system, parents still want to optimize their selections. If all schools have relatively standard identities, then many people will naturally seek to find the best among them. In this quest, a large subset currently turns to test score reports, taps into social networks, heads to the Internet, or relies on common wisdom for information about school quality. The information parents get from these sources, however, is often inaccurate and almost always incomplete.

In a more perfect world, districts would cultivate unique identities for schools and use better data systems to promote the idea of fit—guiding families to schools that match their values and interests. This would require some form of school choice, which most families do not currently have access to. But it is important to note that choice alone is *not* a panacea, whatever the claims of free market ideologues. Unless schools possess different strengths and distinct visions, choice plans are likely to pit families against each other in a winner-take-all competition for the one "best school." Additionally, unless a broader set of data exists, that object of competition is likely to be the "best" only in a very narrowly defined sense. Thus, while choice does matter, we must first work to create new data systems that can recognize different kinds of strengths, and we must overhaul our account-ability systems so that they make room for different kinds of school identities.[21]

Of course, the vast majority of students continue to be assigned to schools based on where they live. Consequently, most schools will re-main relatively similar in scope and function; schools that "fit" will remain an elusive ideal. Therefore, what do parents need to know about choosing a school? What basic steps should they be taking when trying to determine where to live?

First, parents should look at inputs: teachers, school culture, and resources. Why? Inputs may be a more useful indicator of school quality because of the tremendous influence that out-of-school factors have on student-level outcomes. Thus, parents should seek to guar-antee that a school's teaching staff and teaching environment, school culture, and resources are adequate. If they aren't, it may be very hard for a child to reach his or her full potential at that school. To be clear: this does not mean that more is necessarily better. A school with a very low teacher turnover rate, for example, may be no different, or possibly *better,* than a school with no turnover at all. But a school that replaces a quarter of its teachers each year has issues. The point here is merely that minimal thresholds must be met.

Of course, outcomes matter, too, and outcome measures can be collected and presented in a manner that makes them useful for gauging school quality. Measures such as raw test scores, of course, will tell you more about student background variables than about the work being done inside a school. Many outcomes—even if they differ across populations—are under sufficient control of the school to warrant inclusion. Additionally, it is increasingly possible to track student growth on outcome measures, creating a fairer apples-to-apples comparison than looking at raw results.

Another way that parents can interpret outcome data is by seeing how students who are most similar to their own children perform. In other words, they need to account for demographic differences by examining data that have been disaggregated by subgroup. If parents want to know how a school is doing in general, they can and should look at data for the whole school, using growth scores rather than raw scores when possible. If they want to know how children like theirs are faring, however, they should look at the data for children matching their demographic profile rather than for the school as a whole. Those who are building data systems might assist in this effort by allowing users to sort data by race, income, home language, gender, and Special Education status. How are low-income white students doing? How are upper-income African American students doing? How are non-native English speakers doing? Certainly it is possible that a child from one of these groups would be an exception—doing better or worse than his or her demographically similar peers, for any number of reasons. But it is also important to allow parents, as far as possible, to separate out school effects from home effects.

In choosing a school, parents should also consider their family values—their own idiosyncratic set of nonnegotiables. Not all children need access to high-quality Special Education, for instance; but for some, this is a top priority. Other parents may be concerned about walking or driving distance from home, or access to after-school programming. Still others may be concerned with language acquisition programs or the level of diversity at a school. Such priorities and concerns, while essential to some families, will not be essential for *all* families. Consequently, it is important to remember that a school can be generally good, but not right for a particular family.

Finally, parents seeking to understand school quality should step back and try to look at the full picture. Do all of the other factors that make up the school trend toward the positive or the negative? Each one, on its own, may not make much of a difference to a child. But, collectively, do strengths outweigh weaknesses, or are there overwhelming weaknesses despite strengths in particular areas?

Throughout all of this, parents—or, as is often the case, those who plan on *someday* being parents—should remember that a great deal of what can be observed or measured has very little to do with school quality. Do a school's website, the colleges attended by its faculty, or its gleaming exterior matter? Probably not. Other factors, often less visible—and therefore less easily marketed as a sign of superiority—matter a great deal more.

A good data system would give parents all of this information and assist them in making sense of it. Now, the outcome of this might simply be a more intense version of the status quo, with new data systems further empowering data-savvy parents to outcompete their peers in identifying the "best" schools. Troubling as that would be, however, it seems more likely that these systems would do the opposite. That is, rather than intensifying competition, better data might reduce it by expanding the number of schools parents are willing to consider.

Why might that be the case? Well, if we trust what parents say about their children's schools and assume that most schools are generally fine, the most significant impact of better educational data might simply be a clearer presentation of reality. In other words, if most schools are fine, and if better data will more accurately reflect school quality, then parents engaging with data will be presented with a larger pool of acceptable schools. Thus, by dispelling misinformation about schools with diverse populations, and giving people peace of mind that they can live in a particular neighborhood without doing grievous educational harm to their future offspring, we might cultivate even more schools with the kinds of resources—demographic diversity being a key driver of many of those resources—that lead to success.

Ultimately, no information system will be definitive. Plenty of students attend "good" schools that they hate; plenty attend "bad" schools and thrive. Nevertheless, more robust data about our schools might allow parents to more effectively identify schools that would most likely be acceptable; they might even begin to identify schools that have particular strengths that match the interests and abilities of their children. Were this the case, it might help dispel the notion that there is a small number of good public schools in the United States—"good" in some abstract and uniform sense—that we must compete against each other to gain access to.

Getting Organized: Becoming Better Advocates

Better data systems might be important resources for parents in the process of choosing a school. Such systems are equally important for what they might do to empower those already attached to a school—those who have already chosen.

Most parents know how their children are doing in school, and many seek to advocate for their needs. Their advocacy, however, is often viewed as personal, and their evidence interpreted as anecdotal. Each parent, if taken seriously by school staff, generally speaks only for his or her own children. This state of affairs is problematic for two reasons. First, parents often lack specific or consistent language to articulate their concerns, making it harder to distill a general consensus, and opening up the possibility for misunderstanding. Second, not all parents have the time, the energy, or the capital to get involved. Thus, however inclusive a school's most engaged parents seek to be, the voices of others will inevitably be lost in the process.

Better information about school quality might change this. Imagine if parents could look at a robust schoolwide report card and match institutional trends with what they are observing in their own children. It would be far more powerful, for instance, to say that the school as a whole has a bullying problem, and that it is playing out in a particular way for one's own child, than to say merely that one's child is being bullied.

A more comprehensive public data system might also make it easier for parents to engage in strategic planning rather than merely reacting to problems. Getting organized is a challenge, not simply because parents are pressed for time but also because they have different priorities and concerns. If clear and specific data were available, parents might form work groups or task forces to make improvements in particular areas—areas of particular importance or interest to them. One can envision affinity groups, made up of various stakeholders, forming around specific facets of school quality. If a school were providing insufficient access to the arts, for instance, parents attentive to that issue might band together to voice their concerns, to start after-school programming, and to collect materials. Another work group, looking at school facilities, might help school leaders think outside the box about the design of play spaces, engage in beautification projects, or help locate new resources. This kind of organization, it is worth noting, might also help advocates conduct more effective school fund-raising. If community members had a clear understanding not only of what funds would be used for but also of the demonstrated need for such a project, they might be more inclined to support a school financially.

Perhaps most importantly, a more robust data system—a multifaceted framework for school quality, with easy-to-interpret indicators of school progress for each facet—might more effectively engage families in the life of a school. As one critic of a typical state data system noted: "I think that a lot of times school staff get frustrated because families aren't involved, but this is not a tool that would engage a family. Most people would look at this and they wouldn't even know where to start, in terms of asking a question."[22] Better information systems, then, would help parents and community members generate questions—for schools, for school leaders, for children, and for each other. Such systems, in other words, might be a starting point for a range of essential conversations.

If Students Matter: The Nonprofit Sector

American public education is full of nonprofit organizations seeking to advocate for students and families, and particularly for the least advantaged. These groups have names like Students Matter, Students-First, and the Partnership for Educational Justice, and they spend millions of dollars annually on advertising, political lobbying efforts, legal challenges, and direct action. Additionally, organizations such as the NAACP, though not exclusively focused on education reform, do a great deal of advocacy for school improvement.

On the surface, this would seem a very good thing, yet the efforts of these organizations are often controversial. In fact, they are often directly opposed by educators. How can that be?

Certainly it is true that, despite near-universal support for education, ideological differences exist. Some groups, for instance, view market-oriented solutions—charter schools and voucher plans—as essential for school improvement. Others are opposed to the inflexibility imposed by most collective bargaining contracts between teachers and districts.

Still, much of this divide is driven by the fact that we do not possess a set of school quality measures about which all parties can agree. Advocates outside of schools frequently use student standardized test scores as indicators of school and teacher quality. After all, that is the evidence they have to work with. As a 2015 press release from twelve civil rights organizations put it, "Data obtained through some standardized tests are particularly important to the civil rights community because they are the only available, consistent, and objective source of data about disparities in education outcomes." Such data, they continued, "are used to advocate for greater resource equity in schools and more fair treatment for students of color, low-income students, students with disabilities, and English learners."[23]

Teachers, however, have pushed back against the notion that test scores measure educator or school effectiveness. As an October 2014 press release from the American Federation of Teachers put it: "The fixation on high-stakes testing hasn't moved the needle on student achievement. Testing should help inform instruction, not drive instruction. We need to get back to focusing on the whole child— teaching our kids how to build relationships, how to be resilient and how to think critically. We need to celebrate improvement and the joy of learning, not sanction based on high-stakes standardized tests."[24]

Consequently, these advocacy groups, which might do so much to strengthen the work of teachers and administrators, are often at odds with them. Students Matter, for example, which claims to fight "for education equality in the court of law and in the court of public opinion," funded a high-profile lawsuit in Los Angeles—*Vergara v. California*—which was strongly opposed by teachers. The case sought to strike down teacher permanent status, commonly referred to as tenure, as well as statutes regulating teacher dismissal. As the group claimed, these regulations denied the right of California children to an equal education by keeping ineffective educators in the classroom. Yet, when making their case about teacher ineffectiveness, the Students Matter legal team relied for evidence on student standardized test scores. Consequently, when the case was decided in favor of the plaintiffs, it was immediately appealed by teachers and their allies, who viewed the lawsuit and the decision as a poorly informed attack on their profession. Relying on different sources of evidence, each side vowed to fight on.[25]

Despite such conflicts, it is important to recall that these two sides—advocacy organizations and educators—are not necessarily in pursuit of different aims. The NAACP, Students Matter, and others want evidence of student progress and of teacher effectiveness. Nevertheless, it is not beyond the realm of possibility that, were new forms of evidence to emerge, they might be adopted in place of the limited tools currently available. If broader measures of school quality existed, and if they were perceived by all parties as fair and legitimate, data might do a great deal to bring current opponents onto the same side.

Good data systems would also allow outside organizations to advocate for children in a smarter and more effective way. Currently, for instance, civil rights organizations use student standardized test scores to guide their pursuit of equal educational opportunities. However, as discussed earlier in this book, this approach often places undue responsibility at the feet of educators. Schools alone do not determine test scores, and when we pretend that they do, we are setting them up to fail. Just as problematically, when we look only at outcomes, rather than at the whole slate of factors that led to those outcomes, we overlook the many things schools *can* do to better serve the young people in their care.

Perhaps the most troubling consequence of test score–based advocacy is the way that it narrows our understanding of what all children deserve. As a group, children from low-income and minority families do score lower on standardized achievement tests. We should be troubled by that fact, and we should take action to address it, inside and outside our schools. But poverty and racism limit opportunity in all senses—denying young people equal time, resources, and exposure to discover their interests, foster their passions, and expand their outlooks. Over the past decade, well-intended policymakers, relying primarily on standardized test scores as indicators of school quality, have overlooked most of what good schools do. Worse, their pursuit of high-stakes testing has even further curtailed the broader mission of schools. At many high-poverty schools, the curriculum has narrowed. Testing and practice for test taking consume an inordinate amount of time, taking away from history, the arts, and free play. And "no excuses" discipline practices adopted in many schools have promoted regimented and controlling learning environments. As one scholar concluded, this model "produces test results yet limits the development of students' higher-level skills."[26]

Even if we assumed that such practices would get students better jobs—a huge assumption—we should be skeptical merely of the fact that high-poverty schools have never looked less like the schools where elite policymakers send their own children. Barack Obama, we might recall, chose to send his daughters to private Sidwell Friends

School, which recently built a multimillion-dollar performing arts complex, and which doesn't bombard its students with high-stakes standardized tests. That is his right and his privilege, and he should not be criticized for wanting the best for his children. Still, we might remember that, in a fairer world, we would want for all children whatever we want for our own. We should want it, particularly, for our most vulnerable.

Reframing Accountability

In recent years, accountability has become a dirty word. After two decades of high-stakes testing, educators have become frustrated with a system that has failed to recognize much of their good work, and that has all too often punished their schools for outcomes beyond their control. Parents, too, have grown tired of a system that values the bottom line of test scores over other aims. In 2015, more than half a million students refused to take standardized tests.[27]

Despite occasional, and mostly fruitless, efforts to end high-stakes testing, accountability systems remain largely unchanged. Why? For many reasons, certainly, but perhaps chiefly because accountability, at least in theory, is not a bad thing. Schools should be accountable to taxpayers. They should be accountable to parents and community members, and they should be accountable to themselves—to the teachers and students who make up the school. Thus, when critics of high-stakes testing suggest an end to the current accountability system, they are often met with a simple question: What would you replace it with?

Accountability does not need to be abolished. It needs to be reframed. Specifically, it needs to shift away from an ethos of testing and punishment and toward one of transparency and support. Parents, community members, district administrators, civic leaders, state and federal policymakers, nonprofit organizations, and research institutions can all strengthen schools. In order to do that, however, they need a set of shared goals, clear language for communication, and accurate information that they all recognize as valid. Perhaps most importantly, they need to work in an environment that emphasizes capacity building and assistance over threats and sanctions.

In short, accountability can work, but only if it provides stakeholders with accurate information, and only if all of those involved in the system—including policymakers themselves—are accountable for ensuring that schools have what they need to succeed.

Conclusion

UNLIKE GOLD OR SILVER, good schools are not limited natural resources. They are not created independently of human processes; they are not confined to particular regions; and their quantity is not fixed.

Instead, good schools are successful communities. They are places where stakeholders bring their varied resources to bear on a collective good. Perhaps chief among those resources is a shared sense of purpose. Insofar as that is the case, supporting good schools means learning how to communicate more clearly—about what our goals are and about how we are progressing toward those goals.

It is certainly possible that better data on school quality would allow various stakeholders to operate with greater effectiveness on their own, without working together. Policymakers, for instance, might use better information about schools to gauge where assistance is needed, as well as to improve accountability systems so that schools are not simply punished for their demography. School and district administrators might use better information to track progress and make evidence-based decisions. Teachers might use better information to learn more about their students as well as about the larger school community. Parents, for their part, might use better information to make rational choices as well as to engage in more-adept advocacy.

But though better information on school quality might empower each group separately, it might do a great deal more if it were consciously used as a mechanism for facilitating communication. Pursuing common aims with a common language and a common set of data, stakeholders might break out of their silos and stop working at cross-purposes. Together, they might achieve great things.

Better information alone, however, is not enough to realize this vision. To support good schools, we must first do something even more fundamental: we must restore a fuller view of the purpose of education. And this means challenging two currently dominant and deeply entrenched conceptions of schooling.

In the first of those problematic conceptions, the quest for good schools is a competitive act of consumption—one in which the primary purpose of education is to secure an advantage over others. School quality, from this vantage point, is a positional good, valued in relation to what others have rather than in relation to some core benchmark or value. Parents scramble to find the "right" schools, obsess over test scores and rankings, and lean heavily on demography as an indicator of quality. The actual inner workings of a school are not particularly consequential. Getting ahead is what matters, not getting an education.

We must remember, however, that schools can give students an advantage without actually doing what is best for them. Parents can choose high-status schools with glaring weaknesses or that are a poor fit for their children. Policymakers can promote practices that raise a school's prestige—through higher test scores, perhaps—but that do little for overall student well-being. And perfectly good schools can suffer merely because they do not confer privilege, whether or not they have any control over the matter. Perhaps most troubling of all, if getting ahead is what matters, then only a small number of schools can succeed; the rest are destined to fail, and they will be populated largely by those who lacked privilege in the first place.[1]

Good schools do so much more than secure advantage for students. When successful, education is a process that helps young people lead good lives. It plays a critical role in helping them develop their full human potential. Insofar as that is the case, cultivating good schools requires a particular kind of civic participation.

Rather than participating in the educational system as consumers shopping for a commodity, we must engage as members of a community nurturing a public good. Schools, after all, are not products. They are places where we make the future—for our own children as well as for our society. If we remember this truth, we might concern ourselves less with the status of schools and more with what actually happens *inside* them. By seeking quality over credentials, we might create better schools that help students lead better lives—and we might do so for everyone, not just those best positioned to win.

Even if we were to orient ourselves away from competition-oriented consumerism, however, we would still need to tackle another equally troubling conception of schooling—one that prioritizes returns to the state without particular consideration for the individuals who constitute it.

Specifically, schooling is often framed as a mechanism for promoting economic growth. As such, budgetary expenditures on education are worthwhile only if they will produce calculable returns. While this approach may benefit the state as an abstract entity, it can end up harming a majority of the individuals residing within it. Policymakers pursuing this narrow understanding of the purpose of school, for instance, have used standardized tests to hold schools accountable for performance, and in doing so have punished schools working with nondominant populations while encouraging practices that run counter to what we should want for children.

To be clear: many underserved students are in desperate need of basic skills, and there is a simple justice in the promotion of literacy and numeracy. Our most vulnerable young people need to be able to read, write, and compute, and assessment is an appropriate practice to ensure that this happens.

Nevertheless, we should also want so much more, not just for our own children, but for every young person. We should want all children to read critically, write clearly, and reason fluidly. We should want them to paint and dance and learn an instrument. We should want them to laugh, to play, to explore. We should want them to seek out challenge, to brush themselves off after failure, and to chase down ambitious goals. We should want them to discover their passions and their talents. Yet low-income students, particularly if they are members of racial or linguistic minorities, are so often denied this full conception of a good school. According to the state, their schools are success stories only if they produce high standardized test scores.

Schools, of course, are not to blame for the problem of poverty. Liability rests with our entire society, and we are all implicated in the problem. But education has a powerful role to play in combating poverty and its various manifestations—not just by exposing children to career-advancing skills that might be measured by tests, but also by exposing them to a full range of potential interests and pursuits, by affording time and resources to discover what they care for and what they are good at, and by supporting creative thinking and creative action. Data systems alone cannot do this; they must be accompanied by a collective commitment to providing a well-rounded education for all children.

Even though all of this may sound like utopian thinking, we might recall that the American educational system was founded not as a consumer or an economic good but as a public good—one designed to foster citizenship in the young republic. Over time, our schools have also been asked to serve many other purposes, and we cannot simply wish those other functions away. But we must not forget that the public school system was designed to make Americans. Across lines of race, class, ethnicity, and language, our best schools have done just that; they have been instruments of alchemy.[2]

Our first step forward in reviving this foundational vision must be to remember what we value and to align our measurement systems with those values. This will require political will and civic energy. It will require leadership and activism. It will require experimentation, trial and error, and missteps. And beyond the first summit is another mountain to climb—the work of acting on that information, of pursuing a broader set of goals for all schools. We are well down a path that has narrowed our view of education and reduced our understanding of what it means to be a good school, and we must not follow it any further.

Measurement, insofar as it explicitly identifies goals and tracks our progress toward those goals, shapes how we think and act. As I hope the preceding chapters have made clear, this is true for schools. It is also generally true for the world beyond schools—from police work to medicine to environmental conservation. When done effectively, measurement can foster engagement, appreciation, care, and support. It can keep us on track. When done poorly, however, it can warp our vision and undermine our ideals. It can lead us astray. Perhaps considering an example from outside education, then, can most clearly bring this point home.[3]

Two years ago a storm ravaged a red maple in our yard. Twelve months later, the electric company nearly hacked it to death, trimming it back from the power lines according to corporate directive.

We considered cutting the tree down, but then we began thinking about what it would cost to save it, what it would cost to replace it, and what the tree itself was worth. As I calculated it, our maple would produce roughly 300 board feet of quality lumber. That's about $150 in salable hardwood—a nice, concrete measure of our tree's value. To value the tree solely for its lumber, though, would be like valuing a school only on the basis of its test scores; it would miss almost the whole story of what makes a tree a tree.

So I flipped the paper over and began a new calculation.

We love our maple because each fall it turns gold, the color of the sun, a few weeks before it goes deep crimson. We love it because at the end of winter we tap it for syrup, right in the middle of the most densely populated city in New England. And in the summer we sit beneath its shade. I built a swing for my daughter and hung it from that tree. I use the tree as a landmark when I give directions. I regularly find myself staring out the window at it, lost in thought.

By the measure of board feet, it isn't a particularly good tree. Log buyers usually measure tree height from the ground to the first major defect, such as a large branch or fork. Part of what makes our tree good for climbing is that it splits in several directions at roughly five feet. It's also full of knots and healed wounds, which I think give it character, but which are otherwise classified as defects in the wood.

So by one measure, our tree isn't worth a tremendous amount—about the cost of an expensive dinner. If we valued board feet, we would sell our maple for its lumber and invest the proceeds in something that grows taller, faster, and smoother.

Yet that hardly captures the value of our tree. To act on such a calculation would be a terrible mistake.

Ultimately, schools are ecosystems. And because a healthy ecosystem will find its own distinct balance and become its own unique place, there is no perfect measure to deploy—no one set of standards to put in place. As the ecologist Aldo Leopold sagely put it: "A thing is right when it tends to preserve the integrity, stability, and beauty of the biotic community. It is wrong when it tends otherwise."[4]

Whatever our progress in measuring school quality, then, it is essential that we keep this simple truth in mind, because without such an ethos we will create an educational future that is narrow, homogeneous, and uninspiring, however advanced our information systems. Measurement, after all, is merely a means to an end. The deeper purpose of education is the pursuit of goodness, truth, beauty, and justice. However we try get there, we must not forget where we are trying to go.

Postscript

IN 2014, I had coffee with my state senator, Pat Jehlen, who represents Somerville, Cambridge, and Winchester in the Massachusetts state legislature. Pat is a strong supporter of public education, as is her husband, Alain, who is a board member of Citizens for Public Schools. Pat and I were writing an op-ed in the *Boston Globe* outlining our opposition to the state's method for identifying "low-performing" schools. It didn't seem fair to us that, given the relationship between socioeconomic status and test scores, the schools with the largest share of low-income and minority students were the most likely to be branded as failures.

The state could easily change its calculation, we argued, by looking at test score growth rather than raw test scores. Doing so would create a more level playing field across lines of race and class. That isn't to say that we thought that growth scores fully measured school quality; but we saw it as a simple and straightforward improvement. As we wrote: "Neither of us has much confidence in the exclusive or near-exclusive reliance on test scores in any permutation to measure something as complex as school quality. In fact, what we favor is a multi-dimensional model that goes far beyond such narrow measures."[1] Of course, we knew that if we wanted a better system for measuring school quality, we'd have to get the ball rolling ourselves. Test scores had been the coin of the realm in Massachusetts for nearly a quarter-century, and there was little sign of change on the horizon, so we began planning a consortium of districts that would show proof of concept for a new way of assessing school quality.

One big hole in my team's previous work was our lack of expertise in performance assessment. If we truly wanted to get beyond standardized test scores, we would have to establish some kind of alternate assessment system—perhaps via student portfolios—to accompany or replace standardized test results in our Academic Learning category. It so happened that Dan French, of the Center for Collaborative Education (CCE), had a strong working relationship with Pat and Alain and that CCE had just done some very promising work on performance assessment in New Hampshire.[2]

Over the next year, Dan, Pat, Alain, and I talked with district superintendents, school committees, and teachers, gauging interest in a consortium. Our goal was to assemble a large enough and diverse enough group of districts to allow for claims about generalizability—something that might lead the way to state-level change. At the same time, we wanted to keep our group small enough to produce something democratic and of high quality.

Ultimately, six districts came on board: Attleboro, Boston, Lowell, Revere, Somerville, and Winchester. The newly created Massachusetts Consortium for Innovative Education Assessment would be governed jointly by superintendents and teacher union presidents from member districts. And it would seek funding from both public and private sources, beginning with $350,000 from the state legislature.

The going wasn't easy. Union leaders, for instance, had questions about how much teachers would be asked to do on top of their substantial existing workloads. Three districts that had originally expressed interest in the consortium eventually decided not to join. Limited funding necessitated some creative thinking about day-to-day operations.[3] Nevertheless, the group began to move forward, and did so by taking the same first step we had taken in Somerville: figuring out what was worth measuring. So we got to work, conducting focus groups with students, teachers, administrators, parents, and community members in all member districts—incorporating their feedback into our evolving school quality framework.

Meanwhile, because Somerville was already two years ahead of the curve, our team continued working there to pilot practices that might be adopted by the rest of the consortium. We planned a parent survey, which would be built into the district's new online school registration system. We began designing a short form of our student survey—with perhaps twenty to twenty-five questions—for third and fourth graders. We set about building a feature into our web tool that would allow teachers to text message responses to questions from their principals. We also worked with the district to begin rolling the new data out to the public. As superintendent Mary Skipper put it: "We didn't cooperate on this project so we could keep it on a shelf. Let's put it out there and see how it does."

In short: we continue moving forward. We still don't have all the answers. But the ground beneath our feet is firm.

Although the future of this work is unwritten, it is hardly uncertain. There is mounting desire among parents and educators for better information about how our schools are doing. And there is increasing acceptance among policymakers that the era of test scores is coming to a close. That doesn't mean that we will create perfect replacement systems overnight. It has, however, created the space to begin moving slowly toward our goal. New tools are coming off the shelf—we'll see how they do.

Notes

Acknowledgments

Index

Notes

Introduction

1. See, for instance, the annual survey of public attitudes toward education conducted by Phi Delta Kappa and Gallup. See also the Gallup Poll Social Series: Work and Education; polling from 2005 to 2010 indicates that roughly 80 percent of respondents are "completely satisfied" or "somewhat satisfied" with their children's schools. Later chapters discuss small-scale polling in Somerville.
2. I am referring here to average scores, by grade level, on the Massachusetts Comprehensive Assessment System (MCAS).
3. The connection between test scores and family background is discussed in much greater detail in Chapters 2 and 3.
4. See, for instance, Micere Keels, Julia Burdick-Will, and Sara Keene, "The Effects of Gentrification on Neighborhood Public Schools," *City and Community* 12, no. 3 (2013): 238–259; David R. Garcia, "The Impact of School Choice on Racial Segregation in Charter Schools," *Educational Policy* 22 (2008): 805–829.
5. Jesse Rothstein, "College Performance Predictions and the SAT," *Journal of Econometrics* 121, nos. 1–2 (2004): 297–317; Donald C. Orlich and Glenn

Gifford, "The Relationship of Poverty to Test Scores," *Leadership Informa-tion* 4, no. 3 (2005): 34–38; Catherine Rampell, "SAT Scores and Family Income," *New York Times,* August 27, 2009, http://economix.blogs.nytimes .com/2009/08/27/sat-scores-and-family-income/?_r=0.

6. It is worth noting here that the Educational Testing Service is revamping the SAT to remain relevant.

7. The practice is so standard that Microsoft offers a Microsoft Office Business Scorecard Manager with Balanced Scorecard Templates. For more, see Robert S. Kaplan and David P. Norton, *The Balanced Scorecard: Translating Strategy into Action* (Cambridge, MA: Harvard Business School Press, 1996).

8. See, for instance, David Scharfenberg, "Boston's Struggle with Income Segregation," *Boston Globe,* March 6, 2016, https://www.bostonglobe.com /metro/2016/03/05/segregation/NiQBy000TZsGgLnAT0tHsL/story.html.

9. Thomas Dee, Brian A. Jacob, and Nathaniel Schwartz, "The Effects of NCLB on School Resources and Practices," *Educational Evaluation and Policy Analysis* 35, no. 2 (2013): 252–279; Dana Markow, Lara Macia, and Helen Lee, *MetLife Survey of the American Teacher*: Challenges for School Leadership (New York: Metropolitan Life Insurance Company, 2013).

10. Amy S. Finn, Matthew A. Kraft, Martin R. West, Julia A. Leonard, Crystal E. Bish, Rebecca E. Martin, Margaret A. Sheridan, Christo-pher F. O. Gabrieli, and John D. E. Gabrieli, "Cognitive Skills, Student Achievement Tests, and Schools," *Psychological Science* 25, no. 3 (2014): 736–744.

11. Massachusetts Department of Elementary and Secondary Education, "Indicators of School Quality or Student Access," http://www.doe.mass .edu/boe/docs/FY2017/2016–09/item3-ESSASuggestedIndicators.pdf.

12. Hunter is now at the University of California, Santa Barbara.

13. As later discussion in the book reveals, generating support for this work once we had results to show was quite easy. The Massachusetts Consor-tium for Innovative Education Assessment came together in a matter of months, despite the need to coordinate across multiple districts. Neverthe-less, with little to show for ourselves other than theoretical knowledge and civic commitment, it isn't hard to imagine that other cities would not have been particularly inclined to partner with us.

14. These racial categories are taken from the U.S. Census.

15. National Center for Education Statistics, "Characteristics of Public and Private Elementary and Secondary Schools in the United States: Results from the 2011–12 Schools and Staffing Survey," August 2013, http://nces .ed.gov/pubs2013/2013312.pdf; National Center for Education Statistics, "Racial / Ethnic Enrollment in Public Schools," http://nces.ed.gov /programs/coe/indicator_cge.asp.

16. It is important to note here that Somerville represents a case study rather than a "sample." As Robert K. Yin has argued, case studies are generalizable to theoretical propositions rather than to populations. So although Somerville's demographics do roughly match those of the United States as a whole, we must still treat the city as a site for expanding and generalizing theories rather than as one for generating more statistical generalizations.

17. Focus groups conducted between 2014 and 2016 included meetings with all school principals, all district administrators, parent liaisons for each school, and roughly 10 percent of teachers in the district. Additional focus groups, organized and facilitated with the help of the Somerville Family Learning Collaborative and the Welcome Project, elicited the feedback of over thirty parents whose native languages include Spanish, Portuguese, Haitian Creole, and Arabic. Surveys were also conducted in Somerville— with all principals and administrators, with roughly 100 community members, and with roughly 400 parents. As discussed in detail in Chapter 5, a deliberative poll was also conducted with forty-five parents and community members.

Chapter 1 Wrong Answer

1. For those unfamiliar, "English Language Arts" is simply another way of describing what was once simply called "English." MCAS results can be accessed electronically through the state Department of Elementary and Secondary Education "School and District Profiles" website: http://profiles .doe.mass.edu/.

2. Pamela E. Davis-Kean, "The Influence of Parent Education and Family Income on Child Achievement: The Indirect Role of Parental Expectations and the Home Environment," *Journal of Family Psychology* 19, no. 2

(2005): 294–304; Sean F. Reardon, "The Widening Academic Achievement Gap between the Rich and the Poor: New Evidence and Possible Explanations," in *Whither Opportunity*, Greg J. Duncan and Richard J. Murnane, eds. (New York: Russell Sage Foundation, 2011), 91–116.

3. Donald J. Hernandez, "Double Jeopardy: How Third-Grade Reading Skills and Poverty Influence High School Graduation," Annie E. Casey Foundation, Baltimore, MD, 2011; Joy Lesnick, Robert Goerge, Cheryl Smithgall, and Julia Gwynne, "Reading on Grade Level in Third Grade: How Is It Related to High School Performance and College Enrollment?," Chapin Hall at the University of Chicago, 2010.

4. Lee Shulman, "Counting and Recounting: Assessment and the Quest for Accountability," *Change* 39, no. 1 (2007): 20–25. Bloom's Taxonomy is a hierarchically-structured device for organizing cognitive acts in education.

5. Morgan S. Polikoff, Andrew C. Porter, and John Smithson, "How Well Aligned Are State Assessments of Student Achievement with State Content Standards?," *American Educational Research Journal* 48, no. 4 (2011): 965–995; Edward Haertel, "Reliability and Validity of Inferences about Teachers Based on Student Test Scores," report based on the 14th William H. Angoff Memorial Lecture at the National Press Club, Educational Testing Service, Princeton, NJ, 2013.

6. Ronald P. Carver, "What Do Standardized Tests of Reading Comprehension Measure in Terms of Efficiency, Accuracy, and Rate?," *Reading Research Quarterly* 27, no. 4 (1992): 346–359; Janice M. Keenan, Rebecca S. Betjemann, and Richard K. Olson, "Reading Comprehension Tests Vary in the Skills They Assess: Differential Dependence on Decoding and Oral Comprehension," *Scientific Studies of Reading* 12, no. 3 (2008): 281–300.

7. Nel Noddings, "Identifying and Responding to Needs in Education," *Cambridge Journal of Education* 35, no. 2 (2005): 147–159; Theresa Perry and Lisa D. Delpit, *The Real Ebonics Debate: Power, Language, and the Education of African-American Children* (Boston: Beacon Press, 1998).

8. For a good primer on psychometrics, see John Rust and Susan Golombok, *Modern Psychometrics: The Science of Psychological Assessment* (London: Routledge, 2014).

9. Robin B. Howse, Garrett Lange, Dale C. Farran, and Carolyn D. Boyles, "Motivation and Self-Regulation as Predictors of Achievement in Economically Disadvantaged Young Children," *Journal of Experimental Education* 71, no. 2 (2003): 151–174; Greg J. Duncan, Chantelle J. Dowsett, Amy Claessens, Katherine Magnuson, Aletha C. Huston, Pamela Klebanov, Linda S. Pagani, et al., "School Readiness and Later Achievement," *Developmental Psychology* 43, no. 6 (2007): 1428.

10. See, for example, Claude Steele, *Whistling Vivaldi: How Stereotypes Affect Us and What We Can Do* (New York: W. W. Norton, 2011). Steele's book provides an overview of his extensive work in this area.

11. Reardon, "The Widening Academic Achievement Gap," 91–116; Jeanne Brooks-Gunn and Greg J. Duncan, "The Effects of Poverty on Children," in *Consequences of Growing Up Poor*, ed. Greg J. Duncan and Jeanne Brooks-Gunn (New York: Russell Sage Foundation), 596–610; Karl L. Alexander, Doris R. Entwisle, and Samuel D. Bedinger, "When Expectations Work: Race and Socioeconomic Differences in School Performance," *Social Psychology Quarterly* 57, no. 4 (1994): 283–299; Valerie E. Lee and Robert G. Croninger, "The Relative Importance of Home and School in the Development of Literacy Skills for Middle-Grade Students," *American Journal of Education* 102, no. 3 (1994): 286–329.

12. Betty Hart and Todd R. Risley, "The Early Catastrophe: The 30 Million Word Gap by Age 3," *American Educator* 27, no. 1 (2003): 4–9. For more on the relationship between family income and child development, see Robert Haveman and Barbara Wolfe, "The Determinants of Children's Attainments: A Review of Methods and Findings," *Journal of Economic Literature* 33, no. 4 (1995): 1829–1878; Jean W. Yeung, Miriam R. Linver, and Jeanne Brooks-Gunn, "How Money Matters for Young Children's Development: Parental Investment and Family Processes," *Child Development* 73, no. 6 (2002): 1861–1879; Mark M. Kishiyama, W. Thomas Boyce, Amy M. Jimenez, Lee M. Perry, and Robert T. Knight, "Socioeconomic Disparities Affect Prefrontal Function in Children," *Journal of Cognitive Neuroscience* 21, no. 6 (2009): 1106–1115.

13. For a much more thorough account of what standardized tests do and don't tell us, see Daniel Koretz, *Measuring Up: What Educational Testing Really Tells Us* (Cambridge, MA: Harvard University Press, 2009).

14. For more, see Jason L. Endacott and Christian Z. Goering, "Assigning Letter Grades to Public Schools? The Danger of the Single Performance Indicator," *Teachers College Record,* December 11, 2015, http://www .tcrecord.org/Content.asp?ContentID=18834.

15. In compliance with No Child Left Behind, states began administering science tests at three grade levels in the 2007–8 school year. No stakes were attached to these, however.

16. For more on the role of history, see David Tyack and Larry Cuban, *Tinkering toward Utopia: A Century of Public School Reform* (Cambridge, MA: Harvard University Press, 1995); Jack Schneider and Ethan Hutt, "Making the Grade: A History of the A–F Marking Scheme," *Journal of Curriculum Studies* 46, no. 2 (2014): 201–224.

17. Much of the following history of standardized testing was researched in partnership with my colleague Ethan Hutt.

18. William J. Reese, *Testing Wars in the Public Schools: A Forgotten History* (Cambridge, MA: Harvard University Press, 2013).

19. "Blame Regents Test for Faulty Teaching," *New York Times,* November 14, 1927, 14.

20. "Linville Assails Tests by Regents," *New York Times,* February 26, 1930, 19.

21. Educational Policies Commission, *The Purposes of Education in American Democracy* (Washington, DC: National Education Association of the United States and the American Association of School Administrators, 1938).

22. Ibid.

23. For more on the thinking behind this initiative, see Wilford M. Aikin, *The Story of the Eight-Year Study* (New York: Harper and Brothers, 1942).

24. For a history of meritocracy, see Joseph F. Kett, *Merit: The History of a Founding Ideal from the American Revolution to the Twenty-First Century* (Ithaca, NY: Cornell University Press, 2012).

25. See, for instance, Lawrence Cremin, *The Republic and the School: Horace Mann on the Education of Free Men* (New York: Teachers College Press, 1957).

26. J. B. Canning, "The Meaning of Student Marks," *School Review* 24, no. 3 (1916): 196.

27. Denton L. Geyer, *Introduction to the Use of Standardized Tests* (Chicago: Plymouth Press, 1922), 8.

28. "Need Better School Test, Says Bachman," *New York Times,* November 22, 1912, 8.

29. William K. Stevens, "Once-Feared Regents Tests Face Hazy Future," *New York Times,* June 18, 1971, 41.

30. James C. Scott, *Seeing Like a State* (New Haven, CT: Yale University Press, 1999).

31. Leonard Buder, "Educators Split on Regents Tests," *New York Times,* September 28, 1954, 31.

32. Glenn R. Snider, "The Secondary School and Testing Programs," *Teachers College Record* 65, no. 1 (1963): 57–67.

33. *New York State Pupil Evaluation Program: School Administrator's Manual* (Albany: New York State Education Department, 1970), 10.

34. Stephen Jay Gould, *The Mismeasure of Man* (New York: W. W. Norton, 1981).

35. Philander P. Claxton, "Army Psychologists for City Public School Work," *School and Society* 9, no. 216 (1919): 203–204.

36. Burdette Ross Buckingham, *Bureau of Educational Research Announcement, 1918–1919* (Urbana: University of Illinois Press), 46.

37. Joan Cook, "Unrelenting Pressure on Students Brings Varied Assessment of Tests for Intelligence and Ability," *New York Times,* September 24, 1964, 51.

38. See, for instance, Valerie Strauss, "Big Education Firms Spend Millions Lobbying for Pro-Testing Policies," *Washington Post,* March 30, 2015, https://www.washingtonpost.com/news/answer-sheet/wp/2015/03/30/report-big-education-firms-spend-millions-lobbying-for-pro-testing-policies/.

39. Harlan C. Hines, "Measuring the Achievement of School Pupils," *American School Board Journal* 65, (1922): 37.

40. Michael Capuano, "With Test Resistance Rising Nationwide, What's Next for Federal Education Policy?," Citizens for Public Schools Forum, Tufts University, Medford, MA, October 6, 2014.

41. Ethan Hutt, "Certain Standards: How Efforts to Establish and Enforce Minimum Educational Standards Transformed American Schooling (1870–1980)" (doctoral diss., Stanford University, 2013); Walter Haney, George Madaus, and Robert Lyons, *The Fractured Marketplace for Standardized Testing* (Boston: Kluwer, 1993).

42. For evidence of this constancy, see Larry Cuban, *How Teachers Taught: Constancy and Change in American Classrooms, 1890–1990* (New York: Teachers College Press, 1993).

43. Marshall Smith and Jennifer O'Day, "Systemic School Reform," in *The Politics of Curriculum and Testing*, ed. Susan Fuhrman and Betty Malen (Bristol, PA: Falmer, 1991).

44. National Commission on Excellence in Education, *A Nation at Risk: The Imperative for Educational Reform* (Washington, DC: Government Printing Office, 1983).

45. Committee for Economic Development, *Investing in Our Children: Business and the Public Schools* (New York: Committee for Economic Development, 1985), 2.

46. National Governors' Association, *Time for Results: The Governors' 1991 Report on Education* (Washington, DC: National Governors' Association, 1986).

47. Reagan Walker, "Bush: Capturing the 'Education' Moment?," *Education Week,* October 19, 1988.

48. H.R. 1804, Goals 2000: Educate America Act, 103rd Congress of the United States of America, January 25, 1994, http://www2.ed.gov /legislation/GOALS2000/TheAct/index.html.

49. Ethan Bronner, "Texas School Turnaround: How Much Bush Credit?," *New York Times,* May 28, 1999.

50. Ibid.

51. For a good primer on school funding, see Bruce D. Baker, David G. Sciarra, and Danielle Farrie, *Is School Funding Fair? A National Report Card* (Newark, NJ: Rutgers University Education Law Center, 2014).

52. Marga Mikulecky and Kathy Christie, *Rating States, Grading Schools: What Parents and Experts Say States Should Consider to Make School Accountability Systems Meaningful* (Washington, DC: Education Commission of the States, 2014).

53. According to a U.S. Department of Education report, funding increased roughly 10 percent between 1998–99 and 2001–2, when adjusted for inflation: U.S. Department of Education, "10 Facts about K–12 Education Funding," http://www2.ed.gov/about/overview/fed/10facts/index.html ?exp; for an excellent analysis of NCLB and the tutoring industry, see Jill

Koyama, *Making Failure Pay: For-Profit Tutoring, High-Stakes Testing, and Public Schools* (Chicago: University of Chicago Press, 2010).

54. See, for instance, Kris Axtman, "When Tests' Cheaters Are the Teachers," *Christian Science Monitor,* January 11, 2005, http://www.csmonitor.com /2005/0111/p01s03-ussc.html.

55. Kathryn A. McDermott, "Incentives, Capacity, and Implementation: Evidence from Massachusetts Education Reform," *Journal of Public Administration Research and Theory* 16, no. 1 (2006): 45–65.

56. Some states had done this already, as a part of their Race to the Top proposals.

57. Thomas Ahn and Jacob Vigdor, *Were All Those Standardized Tests for Nothing?* (Washington, DC: American Enterprise Institute, 2013); Jaekyung Lee and Todd Reeves, "Revisiting the Impact of NCLB High-Stakes School Accountability, Capacity, and Resources: State NAEP 1990–2009 Reading and Math Achievement Gaps and Trends," *Educational Evaluation and Policy Analysis* 34, no. 2 (2012): 209–231; Sean F. Reardon, Erica H. Greenberg, Demetra Kalogrides, Kenneth A. Shores, and Rachel A. Valentino, *Left Behind? The Effect of No Child Left Behind on Academic Achievement Gaps* (Stanford, CA: Center for Education Policy Analysis, 2013).

58. Lee and Reeves, "Revisiting the Impact of NCLB," 209–231; Jennifer L. Jennings and Jonathan Marc Bearak, "'Teaching to the Test' in the NCLB Era: How Test Predictability Affects Our Understanding of Student Performance," *Educational Researcher* 43, no. 8 (2014): 381–389.

59. U.S. Department of Education, "Every Student Succeeds Act (ESSA)," http://www.ed.gov/essa.

60. Melissa Lazrin, *Testing Overload in America's Schools* (Washington, DC: Center for American Progress, 2014).

61. For a more detailed history of the SAT, see Nicholas Lemann, *The Big Test: The Secret History of the American Meritocracy* (New York: Farrar, Straus and Giroux, 1999).

62. Maria V. Santelices and Mark Wilson, "Unfair Treatment? The Case of Freedle, the SAT, and the Standardization Approach to Differential Item Functioning," *Harvard Educational Review* 80, no. 1 (2010): 106–134; Josh Zumbrun, "SAT Scores and Income Inequality," *Wall Street Journal,*

October 7, 2014, http://blogs.wsj.com/economics/2014/10/07/sat-scores -and-income-inequality-how-wealthier-kids-rank-higher/.

63. Although the College Board claims that coaching raises scores by only fifteen to twenty points on the verbal section and twenty to thirty points on the math section, evidence suggests that effective coaching can have an impact two to three times as great. See, for instance, Derek C. Briggs, "Evaluating SAT Coaching: Gains, Effects, and Self-Selection," in *Rethinking the SAT: The Future of Standardized Testing in University Admissions*, ed. Rebecca Zwick (New York: Routledge, 2004): 217–233; and Jack Kaplan, "An SAT Coaching Program That Works," *Chance* 15, no. 1 (2002): 12–22.

64. William W. Turnbull, *Student Change, Program Change: Why the SAT Scores Kept Falling*, College Board Report no. 85-2 (New York: ETS, 1985).

65. "The ACT: Biased, Inaccurate, and Misused," National Center for Fair and Open Testing, August 20, 2007, http://www.fairtest.org/act-biased -inaccurate-and-misused.

66. Education Commission of the States, "High School Exit Exams," http://www.ecs.org/html/issue.asp?issueid=108&subIssueID=159; Thomas S. Dee and Brian A. Jacob, "Do High School Exit Exams Influence Educational Attainment or Labor Market Performance?," NBER Working Paper 12199, National Bureau of Economic Research, Cambridge, MA, May 2006; Nanette Asimov, "Judge Says California Exit Exam Is Unfair," *San Francisco Chronicle*, May 9, 2006.

67. "Why Other Countries Teach Better," *New York Times*, December 17, 2013, http://www.nytimes.com/2013/12/18/opinion/why-students-do -better-overseas.html?_r=2&.

68. Stefan Thomas Hopmann, Gertrude Brinek, and Martin Retzl, *PISA according to PISA* (New Brunswick, NJ: Transaction, 2007), http://www .univie.ac.at/pisaaccordingtopisa/pisazufolgepisa.pdf; Daniel Tröhler, Heinz-Dieter Meyer, David F. Labaree, and Ethan L. Hutt, "Accountability: Antecedents, Power, and Processes," *Teachers College Record* 116, no. 9 (2014): 1–12.

69. Russell W. Rumberger and Gregory J. Palardy, "Test Scores, Dropout Rates, and Transfer Rates as Alternative Indicators of High School Performance," *American Educational Research Journal* 42, no. 1 (2005):

3–42; Stephen B. Billings, David J. Deming, and Jonah E. Rockoff, *School Segregation, Educational Attainment and Crime: Evidence from the End of Busing in Charlotte-Mecklenburg,* no. w18487 (Cambridge, MA: National Bureau of Economic Research, 2012).

70. Michael B. Henderson, Paul E. Peterson, and Martin R. West, "The 2015 EdNext Poll on School Reform," *Education Next* 16, no. 1 (2016), 8–20, http://educationnext.org/2015-ednext-poll-school-reform-opt-out -common-core-unions/; 47th Annual PDK / Gallup Poll of the Public's Attitudes toward the Public School, September 2015, http:// pdkpoll2015.pdkintl.org/wp-content/uploads/2015/08/pdkpoll47_2015 .pdf.

71. Kwame Anthony Appiah, "Do We Have to Send Our Kid to a Bad Public School?," The Ethicist, *New York Times Magazine,* January 6, 2016, http://www.nytimes.com/2016/01/10/magazine/do-we-have-to-send-our -kid-to-a-bad-public-school.html?_r=0.

Chapter 2 Through a Glass Darkly

1. Christine Armario, "82 Percent of U.S. Schools May Be Labeled 'Failing,'" *Washington Post,* March 9, 2011, http://www.washingtonpost.com/wp-dyn /content/article/2011/03/09/AR2011030903226.html.

2. Marga Mikulecky and Kathy Christie, *Rating States, Grading Schools: What Parents and Experts Say States Should Consider to Make School Accountability Systems Meaningful* (Washington, DC: Education Commission of the States, 2014).

3. California Office to Reform Education, Local Educational Agencies' Request for Waivers under Section 9401 of the Elementary and Secondary Education Act of 1965 (2013), https://www2.ed.gov/policy/eseaflex /approved-requests/corerequestfullredacted.pdf.

4. Quoted in Joy Resmovits, "These California Districts Are Measuring Schools in a New Way," *Los Angeles Times,* December 4, 2015, http://www .latimes.com/local/education/standardized-testing/la-me-edu-core -districts-new-accountability-index-nclb-waiver-20151203-story.html.

5. Quoted in Joy Resmovits, "California Schools Won't Be Judged Only by Their Test Scores, School Board Votes," *Los Angeles Times,* September 8,

2016, http://www.latimes.com/local/education/la-me-california-school
-accountability-20160908-snap-story.html.

6. "ESEA Flexibility," U.S. Department of Education, http://www2.ed.gov
   /policy/elsec/guid/esea-flexibility/index.html; Sarah Reckhow and Megan
   Tompkins-Stange, " 'Singing from the Same Hymnbook': Education Policy
   Advocacy at Gates and Broad," American Enterprise Institute, February 5,
   2015, http://www.aei.org/publication/singing-hymnbook-education
   -policy-advocacy-gates-broad/.

7. Eileen Lai Horng, Daniel Klasik, and Susanna Loeb, "Principal's Time Use
   and School Effectiveness," American Journal of Education 116, no. 4
   (2010): 491–523.

8. Linda Darling-Hammond, "What Matters Most: A Competent Teacher for
   Every Child," Phi Delta Kappan 78, no. 3 (1996): 193–200; Donald L.
   Haefele, "Evaluating Teachers: A Call for Change," Journal of Personnel
   Evaluation in Education 7, no. 1 (1993): 21–31; New Teacher Project,
   Teacher Hiring, Assignment, and Transfer in Chicago Public Schools
   (Brooklyn, NY: New Teacher Project, 2007).

9. Lauren Sartain, Sara Ray Stoelinga, and Eric R. Brown, Rethinking Teacher
   Evaluation in Chicago, Consortium on Chicago School Research, Univer-
   sity of Chicago (2011), http://www.joycefdn.org/assets/1/7/Teacher-Eval
   -Report-FINAL1.pdf.

10. Readers interested in thorough treatment of value-added measures of
    teacher quality should read Douglas Harris, Value-Added Measures in
    Education: What Every Educator Needs to Know (Cambridge, MA:
    Harvard Education Press, 2011).

11. Noelle A. Paufler and Audrey Amrein-Beardsley, "The Random
    Assignment of Students into Elementary Classrooms: Implications for
    Value-Added Analyses and Interpretations," American Educational
    Research Journal 51, no. 2 (2014): 328–362; Kun Yuan, "A Value-Added
    Study of Teacher Spillover Effects across Four Core Subjects in Middle
    Schools," Educational Policy Analysis Archives 23, no. 38 (2015): 1–24;
    Edward Haertel, "Reliability and Validity of Inferences about Teachers
    Based on Student Test Scores," report based on the 14th William H.
    Angoff Memorial Lecture at the National Press Club, Educational
    Testing Service, Princeton, NJ, 2013; Derek Briggs and Ben Domingue,

Due Diligence and the Evaluation of Teachers (Boulder, CO: National Education Policy Center, 2011), http://nepc.colorado.edu/files/NEPC -RB-LAT-VAM_0.pdf; Eva L. Baker, Paul E. Barton, Linda Darling-Hammond, Edward Haertel, Helen F. Ladd, Robert L. Linn, Diane Ravitch, Richard Rothstein, Richard J. Shavelson, and Lorrie A. Shepard, *Problems with the Use of Student Test Scores to Evaluate Teachers*, EPI Briefing Paper 278 (Washington, DC: Economic Policy Institute, 2010).

12. Valerie Strauss, "Master Teacher Suing New York State over 'Ineffective' Rating Is Going to Court," *Washington Post,* August 9, 2015, https://www.washingtonpost.com/news/answer-sheet/wp/2015/08/09 /master-teacher-suing-new-york-state-over-ineffective-rating-is-going -to-court/.

13. One example of this, and one of the earliest of these models, is the IMPACT system in use in Washington, DC. For an overview of IMPACT, see Susan Headden, *Inside IMPACT: DC's Model Teacher Evaluation System* (Washington, DC: Education Sector, 2011).

14. Susanna Loeb, "How Can Value-Added Measures Be Used for Teacher Improvement?," Carnegie Foundation for the Advancement of Teaching, 2013, https://cepa.stanford.edu/sites/default/files/CKN-Loeb_Teacher -Improvement.pdf; Haertel, "Reliability and Validity of Inferences about Teachers."

15. David Shenk, *Data Smog: Surviving the Information Glut* (San Francisco: HarperCollins, 1997).

16. Mikulecky and Christie, *Rating States, Grading Schools.*

17. To say *U.S. News* is the leader in this practice is not to say it does it well. For criticism, see Nicholas A. Bowman and Michael N. Bastedo, "Getting on the Front Page: Organizational Reputation, Status Signals, and the Impact of *U.S. News and World Report* on Student Decisions," *Research in Higher Education* 50, no. 5 (2009): 415–436; Michael N. Bastedo and Nicholas A. Bowman, "*U.S. News and World* Report College Rankings: Modeling Institutional Effects on Organizational Reputation," *American Journal of Education* 116, no. 2 (2010): 163–183.

18. As one Boston Latin parent remarked to me: "It's a good school. But my daughter is stressed out all the time. And all she does is study for tests."

19. Zillow.com, "Zillow Now Exclusive Real Estate Search Partner of Great-Schools," http://www.zillow.com/blog/zillow-now-exclusive-real-estate-search-partner-of-greatschools-126514/, accessed February 18, 2016.

20. Separately, polling has found that 51 percent of parents report utilizing websites that rate and compare schools. See, for instance, Trevor Tompson, Jennifer Benz, and Jennifer Agiesta, "Parents' Attitudes on the Quality of Education in the United States," Associated Press–NORC Center for Public Affairs Research, 2013, http://www.apnorc.org/PDFs/Parent%20 Attitudes/AP_NORC_Parents%20Attitudes%20on%20the%20Quality%20 of%20Education%20in%20the%20US_FINAL_2.pdf

21. Dan A. Black and Jeffrey A. Smith, "How Robust Is the Evidence on the Effects of College Quality? Evidence from Matching," *Journal of Econometrics* 121, no. 1 (2004): 99–124; Stacy Berg Dale and Alan B. Krueger, "Estimating the Payoff to Attending a More Selective College: An Application of Selection on Observables and Unobservables," NBER Working Paper No. 7322 (Cambridge, MA: National Bureau of Economic Research, 1999).

22. ACT, "College Enrollment by Student Background and School Location," information brief, 2014–2015, http://www.act.org/research/researchers /briefs/pdf/2014–15.pdf.

23. Justine S. Hastings, Thomas J. Kane, and Douglas O. Staiger, "Parental Preferences and School Competition: Evidence from a Public School Choice Program," NBER Working Paper 11805, National Bureau of Economic Research, 2005; Carol Ascher, *Hard Lessons: Public Schools and Privatization* (New York: Twentieth Century Fund Press, 1996); Jeffrey R. Henig, *Rethinking School Choice: Limits of the Market Metaphor* (Princeton, NJ: Princeton University Press, 1995); Jeffrey Henig, "Race and Choice in Montgomery County, Maryland, Magnet Schools," *Teachers College Record* 96, no. 4 (1995): 729–734; Jack Dougherty, Jeffrey Harrelson, Laura Maloney, Drew Murphy, Russell Smith, Michael Snow, and Diane Zannoni, "School Choice in Suburbia: Test Scores, Race, and Housing Markets," *American Journal of Education* 115, no. 4 (2009): 523–548; Courtney A. Bell, "Space and Place: Urban Parents' Geographical Preferences for Schools," *Urban Review* 39, no. 4 (2007): 375–404.

24. Hastings, Kane, and Staiger, *Parental Preferences and School Competition;*
Courtney Bell, "Geography in Parental Choice," *American Journal of
Education* 115, no. 4 (2009): 493–521.

25. Carl Bagley, Philip A. Woods, and Ron Glatter, "Rejecting Schools:
Towards a Fuller Understanding of the Process of Parental Choice," *School
Leadership and Management* 21, no. 3 (2001): 309–325; Ernest Boyer,
School Choice (Princeton, NJ: Carnegie Foundation, 1992); Jennifer
Jellison Holme, "Buying Homes, Buying Schools: School Choice and the
Social Construction of School Quality," *Harvard Educational Review* 72,
no. 2 (2002): 177–206.

26. Holme, "Buying Homes, Buying Schools"; Mark Schneider, Paul Teske,
Christine Roch, and Melissa Marschall, "Networks to Nowhere: Segregation
and Stratification in Networks of Information about Schools," *American
Journal of Political Science* 41, no. 4 (1997): 1201–1223; Arne Duncan,
"Remarks at the Statehouse Convention Center in Little Rock, Arkansas,"
U.S. Department of Education, August 25, 2010, http://www.ed.gov/news
/speeches/secretary-arne-duncans-remarks-statehouse-convention-center
-little-rock-arkansas.

27. Tiffany A. Ito, Jeff T. Larson, N. Kyle Smith, and John T. Cacioppo,
"Negative Information Weighs More Heavily on the Brain: The
Negativity Bias in Evaluative Categorization," *Journal of Personality
and Social Psychology* 75, no. 4 (1998): 887–900; Daniel Kahneman, *Thinking Fast and Slow* (New York: Farrar, Straus and Giroux,
2013).

28. Miller McPherson, Lynn Smith-Lovin, and James Cook, "Birds of a
Feather: Homophily in Social Networks," *Annual Review of Sociology* 27,
no. 1 (2001): 420; Peter V. Marsden, "Core Discussion Networks of
Americans," *American Sociological Review* 52, no. 1 (1987): 122–131;
Miller McPherson, Lynn Smith-Lovin, and James M. Cook, "Birds of a
Feather: Homophily in Social Networks," *Annual Review of Sociology* 27,
no. 1 (2001): 415–444.

29. Stephen J. Ball, Richard Bowe, and Sharon Gewirtz, "Circuits of Schooling:
A Sociological Exploration of Parental Choice of School in Social Class
Contexts," *Sociological Review* 43, no. 1 (1995): 52–78; Mark Schneider,
Paul Teske, and Melissa Marschall, *Choosing Schools: Consumer Choice*

and the Quality of American Schools (Princeton, NJ: Princeton University Press, 2000), 133.

30. Schneider, Teske, Roch, and Marschall, "Networks to Nowhere," 1220; Peter Rich and Jennifer Jennings, "Choice, Information, and Constrained Options: School Transfers in a Stratified Educational System," *American Sociological Review* 80, no.5 (2015): 1069–1098.

31. Jeffrey Henig, "Race and Choice in Montgomery County, Maryland, Magnet Schools," *Teachers College Record* 96, no. 4 (1995): 729–734; Salvatore Saporito and Annette Lareau, "School Selection as a Process: The Multiple Dimensions of Race in Framing Educational Choice," *Social Problems* 46 (1999): 418–435.

32. David Sikkink and Michael O. Emerson, "School Choice and Racial Segregation in US Schools: The Role of Parents' Education," *Ethnic and Racial Studies* 31, no. 2 (2008): 267–293; Saporito and Lareau, "School Selection as a Process"; Ryan Holeywell, "The Troubling Ways Wealthy Parents Pick Schools," Kinder Institute, July 30, 2015, http://urbanedge .blogs.rice.edu/2015/12/24/the-troubling-ways-wealthy-parents-pick -schools/#.VuBUrvkrJD8.

33. Schneider, Teske, and Marschall, *Choosing Schools.*

34. For a much more thorough discussion of how such heuristics are developed, see Kahnemann, *Thinking Fast and Slow.*

35. Jon Hurwitz and Mark Peffley, "Public Perceptions of Race and Crime: The Role of Racial Stereotypes," *American Journal of Political Science* 41, no. 2 (1997): 375–401; Patricia G. Devine and Andrew J. Elliot, "Are Racial Stereotypes Really Fading? The Princeton Trilogy Revisited," *Personality and Social Psychology Bulletin* 21, no. 11 (1995): 1139–1150; Lincoln Quillian and Devah Pager, "Black Neighbors, Higher Crime? The Role of Racial Stereotypes in Evaluations of Neighborhood Crime," *American Journal of Sociology* 107, no. 3 (2001): 717–767; Mahzarin R. Banaji and Anthony G. Greenwald, *Blindspot: Hidden Biases of Good People* (New York: Delacorte Press, 2013).

36. Ann Owens, "Inequality in Children's Contexts: Income Segregation of Households with and without Children," *American Sociological Review* 81, no. 3 (2016): 549–574. It is also worth noting here that segregation by race is also higher among households with children than among other households.

37. Douglas Lee Lauen and S. Michael Gaddis, "Exposure to Classroom Poverty and Test Score Achievement: Contextual Effects or Selection?," *American Journal of Sociology* 118, no. 4 (2013): 943–979; Robert A. Garda, "The White Interest in School Integration," *Florida Law Review* 63 (2011): 605–660; Aprile D. Benner and Robert Crosnoe, "The Racial / Ethnic Composition of Elementary Schools and Young Children's Academic and Socioemotional Functioning," *American Educational Research Journal* 48, no. 3 (2011): 621–646; National Center for Education Statistics, *School Composition and the Black-White Achievement Gap* (Washington, DC: U.S. Department of Education, 2015).

38. For a good discussion of the relationship between fictional narrative in film and reality in schools, see Marshall Gregory, "Real Teaching and Real Learning vs. Narrative Myths about Education," *Arts and Humanities in Higher Education* 6, no. 1 (2007): 7–27.

39. Linda Darling-Hammond, "Third Annual Brown Lecture in Education Research: The Flat Earth and Education; How America's Commitment to Equity Will Determine Our Future," *Educational Researcher* 36, no. 6 (2007): 318–334; Matthew Ronfeldt, Susanna Loeb, and James Wyckoff, "How Teacher Turnover Harms Student Achievement," *American Educational Research Journal* 50, no. 1 (2013): 4–36; Christopher Jencks and Meredith Phillips, eds., *The Black-White Test Score Gap* (Washington, DC: Brookings Institution Press, 2011); Russell J. Skiba, Robert H. Horner, Choong-Geun Chung, M. Karega Rausch, Seth L. May, and Tary Tobin, "Race Is Not Neutral: A National Investigation of African American and Latino Disproportionality in School Discipline," *School Psychology Review* 40, no. 1 (2011): 85.

40. It is worth noting that there are clear and powerful exceptions to this, where ethnic or racial pride infuse a school with an ethos of community.

41. Zillow.com, "Zillow Now Exclusive Real Estate Search Partner of GreatSchools."

42. Ryan Dezember, "Blackstone Gains from Banks' Financial-Crisis Pain," *Wall Street Journal,* January 21, 2016, http://www.wsj.com/articles /blackstone-gains-from-banks-financial-crisis-pain-1453408139.

43. In most intradistrict choice plans, preference is given to students who live within a short walk of the school, as well as to students with siblings at the

school. If more students wish to attend a school than there are spots available, students are usually admitted via a lottery. This might seem to present a complicated scenario for a district, but parental preference for proximity usually ensures that schools are not underenrolled.

44. Allison Roda and Amy Stuart Wells, "School Choice Policies and Racial Segregation: Where White Parents' Good Intentions, Anxiety, and Privilege Collide," *American Journal of Education* 119, no. 2 (2013): 261–293.

45. See, for instance, Christopher A. Lubienski and Sarah Theule Lubienski, *The Public School Advantage: Why Public Schools Outperform Private Schools* (Chicago: University of Chicago Press, 2013).

46. Those with greater financial resources are best positioned to consider multiple places for their homes. Still, polling indicates that the connection between schools and home selection is fairly common. See, for instance, Editorial Projects in Education, *Accountability for All: What Voters Want from Education Candidates,* January 2002, from the iPOLL Databank, Roper Center for Public Opinion Research, University of Connecticut, retrieved June 9, 2014, http://files.eric.ed.gov/fulltext /ED464190.pdf.

47. Rhema Thompson, "Poll: School Grades Important but Not Understood," *WJCT 89.9 News,* December 11, 2014.

48. Saporito and Lareau, "School Selection as a Process."

49. Gallup, "In U.S., Private Schools Get Top Marks for Educating Children," August 29, 2012, http://www.gallup.com/poll/156974/private-schools-top -marks-educating-children.aspx.

50. Groton Matriculations, https://www.groton.org/page/academics/college -counseling/matriculations.

51. Jed Kolko, "Where Private School Enrollment Is Highest and Lowest across the U.S.," *CityLab,* August 13, 2012, http://www.citylab.com /housing/2014/08/where-private-school-enrollment-is-highest-and-lowest -across-the-us/375993/.

52. National Center for Education Statistics, *Digest of Education Statistics* (Washington, DC: NCES, IES, U.S. Department of Education, 2016), table 302.30: Percentage of Recent High School Completers Enrolled in 2-Year and 4-Year Colleges, by Income Level: 1975 through 2013.

53. Simone Robers, Anlan Zhang, Rachel E. Morgan, and Lauren Musu-Gillette, *Indicators of School Crime and Safety: 2014* (Washington, DC: U.S. Department of Education and U.S. Department of Justice Office of Justice Programs, 2015); U.S. Department of Education, National Center for Education Statistics, Schools and Staffing Survey (SASS), "Private School Teacher Data File," 2007–8; U.S. Department of Education, National Center for Education Statistics, Schools and Staffing Survey (SASS), "Public School Teacher Data File," 2007–8.

54. Douglas Lee Lauen, Bruce Fuller, and Luke Dauter, "Positioning Charter Schools in Los Angeles: Diversity of Form and Homogeneity of Effects," *American Journal of Education* 121, no. 2 (2015): 213–239; Christina Clark Tuttle, Bing-ru Teh, Ira Nichols-Barrer, Brian P. Gill, and Philip Gleason, *Student Characteristics and Achievement in 22 KIPP Middle Schools: Final Report* (Washington, DC: Mathematica Policy Research, 2010); CREDO, National Charter School Study, 2013, http://credo.stanford.edu /documents/NCSS%202013%20Final%20Draft.pdf; Devora H. Davis and Margaret E. Raymond, "Choices for Studying Choice: Assessing Charter School Effectiveness Using Two Quasi-Experimental Methods," *Economics of Education Review* 31, no. 2 (2012): 225–236; Caroline M. Hoxby and Sonali Murarka, "Charter Schools in New York City: Who Enrolls and How They Affect Their Students' Achievement," NBER Working Paper No. 14852, National Bureau of Economic Research, Cambridge, MA, 2009; Lauen, Fuller, and Dauter, "Positioning Charter Schools in Los Angeles," 213–239; RAND, *Charter School Operations and Performance: Evidence from California* (2003), http://www.rand.org/pubs/monograph _reports/MR1700.html.

55. Ron Zimmer, Brian Gill, Kevin Booker, Stéphane Lavertu, and John Witte, "Examining Charter Student Achievement Effects across Seven States," *Economics of Education Review* 31, no. 2 (2012): 213–224.

56. Stephen Worchel, Jerry Lee, and Akanbi Adewole, "Effects of Supply and Demand on Ratings of Object Value," *Journal of Personality and Social Psychology* 32, no. 5 (1975): 906–914.

57. Ashley Morris and Brittany Landsberger, "Charter School Operators Use Key Words to Entice Families away from Public Schools," *Akron Beacon Journal,* May 27, 2014, http://www.ohio.com/news/local/charter-school

-operators-use-key-words-to-entice-families-away-from-public-schools-1
.491420; Nora Kern and Wentana Gebru, "Waiting Lists to Attend Charter
Schools Top One Million Names," National Alliance for Public Charter
Schools, May 2014, http://www.publiccharters.org/wp-content/uploads
/2014/05/NAPCS-2014-Wait-List-Report.pdf.

58. Edith K. McArthur, Kelly Colopy, and Beth Schlaine, *Use of School Choice,*
NCES 95–742R (Washington, DC: U.S. Department of Education,
National Center for Educational Statistics, 1995); Simona Botti, "The Dark
Side of Choice: When Choice Impairs Social Welfare," *Journal of Public
Policy and Marketing* 25, no. 1 (2006), http://www.columbia.edu/~ss957
/articles/dark_side_of_choice.pdf.

59. Research has raised questions about the accuracy of these calculations for
very-high-achieving and very-low-achieving students, due to scaling
issues. For a concise discussion of this, see Haertel, "Reliability and
Validity of Inferences about Teachers."

60. Basmat Parsad and Maura Spiegelman, *A Snapshot of Arts Education in
Public Elementary and Secondary Schools: 2009–10* (Washington, DC: U.S.
Department of Education, 2011).

61. Robert Balfanz and Vaughan Byrnes, *The Importance of Being There: A
Report on Absenteeism in the Nation's Public Schools* (Baltimore, MD:
Johns Hopkins University School of Education, Everyone Graduates
Center, 2012).

62. Kathryn R. Wentzel and Kathryn Caldwell, "Friendships, Peer
Acceptance, and Group Membership: Relations to Academic Achievement in Middle School," *Child Development* 68, no. 6 (1997): 1198–
1209; Kathryn R. Wentzel, Carolyn McNamara Barry, and Kathryn A.
Caldwell, "Friendships in Middle School: Influences on Motivation
and School Adjustment," *Journal of Educational Psychology* 96, no. 2
(2004): 195–203; Thomas J. Berndt, Ann E. Laychak, and Keunho
Park, "Friends' Influence on Adolescents' Academic Achievement
Motivation: An Experimental Study," *Journal of Educational Psychology*
82, no. 4 (1990): 664; Allison M. Ryan, "Peer Groups as a Context for
the Socialization of Adolescents' Motivation, Engagement, and
Achievement in School," *Educational Psychologist* 35, no. 2 (2000):
101–111.

63. Mary A. Burke and Tim R. Sass, "Classroom Peer Effects and Student Achievement," *Journal of Labor Economics* 31, no. 1 (2013): 51–82; Caroline Hoxby, *Peer Effects in the Classroom: Learning from Gender and Race Variation,* NBER Working Paper No. w7867, National Bureau of Economic Research, 2000; Michael A. Gottfried and Jennifer Graves, "Peer Effects and Policy: The Relationship between Classroom Gender Composition and Student Achievement in Early Elementary School," *BE Journal of Economic Analysis and Policy* 14, no. 3 (2014): 937–977; Michael A. Gottfried, "Peer Effects in Urban Schools: Assessing the Impact of Classroom Composition," *Educational Policy* 28, no. 5 (2014): 607–647; Caroline M. Hoxby and Gretchen Weingarth, "Taking Race out of the Equation: School Reassignment and the Structure of Peer Effects," working paper, 2005, http://isites.harvard.edu/fs/docs/icb.topic185351 .files/hoxby_weingarth_taking_race.pdf; Eric A. Hanushek, John F. Kain, and Steven G. Rivkin, *New Evidence about Brown v. Board of Education: The Complex Effects of School Racial Composition on Achievement,* NBER Working Paper No. w8741, National Bureau of Economic Research, 2002; Roslyn Arlin Mickelson, Martha Cecilia Bottia, and Richard Lambert, "Effects of School Racial Composition on K–12 Mathematics Outcomes: A Metaregression Analysis," *Review of Educational Research* 83, no. 1 (2013): 121–158; Michael A. Gottfried, "The Positive Peer Effects of Classroom Diversity: Exploring the Relationship between English Language Learner Classmates and Socioemotional Skills in Early Elementary School," *Elementary School Journal* 115, no. 1 (2014): 22–48.

64. It is important to note here that adverse peer effects can manifest in many different ways, and in every kind of school. Issues such as bullying or drug use are hardly confined to schools with low levels of academic achievement, despite popular perceptions.

65. Dan D. Goldhader, Dominic J. Brewer, and Deborah J. Anderson, "A Three-Way Error Components Analysis of Educational Productivity," *Education Economics* 7, no. 3 (1999): 199–208; Barbara Nye, Spyros Konstantopoulos, and Larry V. Hedges, "How Large Are Teacher Effects?," *Educational Evaluation and Policy Analysis* 26, no. 3 (2004): 237–257; Steven G. Rivkin, Eric A. Hanushek, and John F. Kain, "Teachers, Schools, and Academic Achievement," *Econometrica* 73, no. 2 (2005): 417–458;

Brian Rowan, Brian, Richard Correnti, and Robert Miller, "What Large-Scale Survey Research Tells Us about Teacher Effects on Student Achievement: Insights from the Prospects Study of Elementary Schools," *Teachers College Record* 104, no. 8 (2002): 1525–1567.

66. Jennifer Glass, Vern L. Bengtson, and Charlotte Chorn Dunham, "Attitude Similarity in Three-Generation Families: Socialization, Status Inheritance, or Reciprocal Influence?," *American Sociological Review* 51, no. 5 (1986): 685–698.

67. Betty Hart and Todd R. Risley, *Meaningful Differences in the Everyday Experience of Young People* (Baltimore, MD: Paul H. Brookes, 1995); Carol Sue Fromboluti, Diane Magarity, and Natalie Rinck, *Early Childhood: Where Learning Begins; Mathematics: Mathematical Activities for Parents and Their 2- to 5-Year-Old Children* (Washington, DC: U.S. Department of Education, Office of Educational Research and Improvement, 1999).

68. Kara S. Finnigan and Betheny Gross, "Do Accountability Policy Sanctions Influence Teacher Motivation? Lessons from Chicago's Low-Performing Schools," *American Educational Research Journal* 44, no. 3 (2007): 594–630.

69. Sandra E. Black and Stephen J. Machin, "Housing Valuations of School Performance," *Handbook of Economics of Education* 3 (2011): 485–516; Steve Bogira, "Three Families Tell Us Why They Ditched CPS," *Chicago Reader,* September 24, 2013; Rebecca Jacobsen, Andrew Saulz, and Jeffrey W. Snyder, "When Accountability Strategies Collide: Do Policy Changes That Raise Accountability Standards Also Erode Public Satisfaction?," *Educational Policy* 27, no. 6 (2013): 360–389.

Chapter 3 What Really Matters

1. Philip W. Jackson, Robert E. Boostrom, and David T. Hanson, *The Moral Life of Schools* (San Francisco: Jossey-Bass, 1993), xii.

2. Blue Three, Comment on Anya Kamenetz's "To Measure What Tests Can't, Some Turn to Surveys," NPR, December 2, 2015, http://www.npr.org /sections/ed/2015/12/02/457281686/how-schools-are-using-surveys-to -measure-what-tests-can-t.

3. Richard Rothstein, Rebecca Jacobsen, and Tamara Wilder, *Grading Education: Getting Accountability Right* (Washington, DC: Economic Policy Institute, 2008).

4. For more on these efforts, see discussion of the Massachusetts Consortium for Innovative Education Assessment in this book's postscript.

5. George A. Miller, "The Magical Number Seven, Plus or Minus Two: Some Limits on Our Capacity for Processing Information," *Psychological Review* 63, no. 2 (1956): 81–97; Alan Baddeley, "Working Memory," *Science* 255, no. 5044 (1992): 556–559; Nelson Cowan, "Metatheory of Storage Capacity Limits," *Behavioral and Brain Sciences* 24, no. 1 (2001): 154–176.

6. Thirty-nine teachers and support staff participated in four focus groups; they were recruited through e-mails sent by district administrators and were offered stipends to attend; teachers from all schools in the district were represented. Five additional teachers participated in a separate Special Education focus group, which was conducted to learn more about the particular issues of importance to teachers working with that student population. All principals and key district administrators participated in focus groups organized by the district. Thirty-three parents attended two open focus groups; recruitment for these was conducted via e-mails sent by the principals of each K–8 school and the high school. A separate focus group was conducted with the eight community liaisons who have been contracted by the Somerville Family Learning Collaborative (SFLC) to reach out to families at each of the city's schools—particularly members of racial and ethnic minorities; two staff from the SFLC also participated in this focus group, which was designed to elicit feedback around traditionally underserved communities. Thirty non-English-speaking parents attended focus groups facilitated with the help of the SFLC and Somerville's Welcome Project. We conducted one focus group with high school students, recruited with assistance from the district. Generally speaking, participants in focus groups were introduced to the project with the following statement: "The goal of this study is to better understand the way people think about issues of school quality and evaluation. In thinking beyond standardized test scores as the only way to judge school performance, we've identified some major categories of inputs and outputs that people might think about in evaluating schools. We're hoping to

receive feedback about these categories. In general, we would like to hear your thoughts on whether our categories and sub-categories make sense and measure the right things. We'll talk briefly about each of the main categories until we have discussed all of them. Are there any questions before we begin?" The basic categories for these discussions were established by our team's review of polling data and educational research. In discussing the various major categories, participants were asked whether particular draft subcategories seemed more important than others, whether anything was missing, and whether anything seemed unclear. Our team also solicited feedback about values and priorities that might not fit into the major categories that were used to guide the discussion.

7. Memo from David Casalaspi, October 1, 2014.

8. After analysis of year one data, we found positive between-category Pearson correlation coefficients, with magnitudes varying from 0.18 to 0.70. Overall, these findings suggest that categories used to construct the framework exhibit meaningful associations while not being deterministically related. We believe that this lends support to their combined use as more valid representation of school quality.

9. Matthew A. Kraft, William H. Marinell, and Darrick Yee, *Schools as Organizations: Examining School Climate, Turnover, and Student Achievement in New York City* (New York: Research Alliance for New York City Schools, 2016); Matthew A. Kraft and Sarah Grace, "Teaching for Tomorrow's Economy? Teacher Effects on Complex Cognitive Skills and Social-Emotional Competencies" (working paper, Brown University, 2016), http://scholar.harvard.edu/files/mkraft/files/teaching_for _tomorrows_economy_-_final_public.pdf.

10. This is not to say that parental engagement is entirely outside the control of schools. Research does, however, suggest that the way parents engage—with their children and with schools—is mediated by factors such as social class. See, for instance, Annette Lareau, "Invisible Inequality: Social Class and Childrearing in Black Families and White Families," *American Sociological Review* 67, no. 5 (2002): 747–776.

11. This would not necessarily invalidate the measures. Instead, it would suggest that the measures are telling users something that they already know, which they can learn simply by examining the school's demography.

12. Philip Elliott and Jennifer Agiesta, "AP-NORC Poll: Parents Back High-Stakes Testing," August 17, 2013, http://www.apnorc.org/news-media/Pages/News+Media/ap-norc-poll-parents-back-high-stakes-testing.aspx.

13. Eric A. Hanushek, "The Economic Value of Higher Teacher Quality," *Economics of Education Review* 30, no. 3 (2011): 466–479. See also Steven G. Rivkin, Eric A. Hanushek, and John F. Kain, "Teachers, Schools, and Academic Achievement," *Econometrica* 73, no. 2 (2005): 417–458; Linda Darling-Hammond, "Teacher Quality and Student Achievement," *Education Policy Analysis Archives* 8 (2000): 1.

14. Mark Schneider, Paul Teske, and Melissa Marschall, *Choosing Schools: Consumer Choice and the Quality of American Schools* (Princeton, NJ: Princeton University Press, 2000), 108.

15. Jack Jennings and Diane Stark Rentner, "Ten Big Effects of the No Child Left Behind Act on Public Schools," *Phi Delta Kappan* 88, no. 2 (2006): 110; Leslie S. Kaplan and William A. Owings, "No Child Left Behind: The Politics of Teacher Quality," *Phi Delta Kappan* 84, no. 9 (2003): 687; Laura Goe, "The Link between Teacher Quality and Student Outcomes: A Research Synthesis," National Comprehensive Center for Teacher Quality, 2007, http://files.eric.ed.gov/fulltext/ED521219.pdf; Joshua D. Angrist and Jonathan Guryan, "Does Teacher Testing Raise Teacher Quality? Evidence from State Certification Requirements," *Economics of Education Review* 27, no. 5 (2008): 483–503.

16. Suzanne M. Wilson, Robert E. Floden, and Joan Ferrini-Mundy, "Teacher Preparation Research: An Insider's View from the Outside," *Journal of Teacher Education* 53, no. 3 (2002): 190–204; Thomas J. Kane, Jonah E. Rockoff, and Douglas O. Staiger, "What Does Certification Tell Us about Teacher Effectiveness? Evidence from New York City," *Economics of Education Review* 27, no. 6 (2008): 615–631; Richard Buddin and Gema Zamarro, "Teacher Qualifications and Student Achievement in Urban Elementary Schools," *Journal of Urban Economics* 66, no. 2 (2009): 103–115; Andrew J. Wayne and Peter Youngs, "Teacher Characteristics and Student Achievement Gains: A Review," *Review of Educational Research* 73, no. 1 (2003): 89–122; Charles T. Clotfelter, Helen F. Ladd, and Jacob L. Vigdor, "Teacher Credentials and Student Achievement: Longitudinal Analysis with Student Fixed Effects," *Economics of Education Review*

26, no. 6 (2007): 673–682; Douglas N. Harris and Tim R. Sass, "Teacher Training, Teacher Quality and Student Achievement," *Journal of Public Economics* 95, no. 7 (2011): 798–812.

17. Daniel D. Goldhaber and Dominic J. Brewer, "Does Teacher Certification Matter? High School Teacher Certification Status and Student Achievement," *Educational Evaluation and Policy Analysis* 22, no. 2 (2000): 129–146; Daniel D. Goldhaber and Dominic J. Brewer, "Why Don't Schools and Teachers Seem to Matter? Assessing the Impact of Unobservables on Educational Productivity," *Journal of Human Resources* 32, no. 3 (1997): 505–523; David H. Monk and Jennifer A. King, "Multilevel Teacher Resource Effects in Pupil Performance in Secondary Mathematics and Science: The Case of Teacher Subject Matter Preparation," in *Choices and Consequences: Contemporary Policy Issues in Education,* ed. R. G. Ehrenberg (Ithaca, NY: ILR Press, 1994); Jacob M. Marszalek, Arthur L. Odom, Steven M. LaNasa, and Susan A. Adler, "Distortion or Clarification: Defining Highly Qualified Teachers and the Relationship between Certification and Achievement," *Education Policy Analysis Archives* 18, no. 27 (2010).

18. Charlotte Danielson and Thomas L. McGreal, *Teacher Evaluation to Enhance Professional Practice* (Alexandria, VA: ASCD, 2000); Linda Darling-Hammond, *Getting Teacher Evaluation Right: What Really Matters for Effectiveness and Improvement* (New York: Teachers College Press, 2013); Helen Ladd and Susanna Loeb, "The Challenges of Measuring School Quality: Implications for Educational Equity," in *Education, Justice, and Democracy*, Danielle Allen and Rob Reich, eds. (University of Chicago Press, 2013), 18–42; Heather Hill and Pam Grossman, "Learning from Teacher Observations: Challenges and Opportunities Posed by New Teacher Evaluation Systems," *Harvard Educational Review* 83, no. 2 (2013): 371–384.

19. For more on the development of survey questions and scales, see Chapter 4.

20. Jason J. Teven, "Teacher Temperament: Correlates with Teacher Caring, Burnout, and Organizational Outcomes," *Communication Education* 56, no. 3 (2007): 382–400; Kathleen Buss, James Gingles, and Jay Price, "Parent-Teacher Temperament Ratings and Student Success in Reading,"

Reading Psychology: An International Quarterly 14, no. 4 (1993): 311–323; Jason J. Teven and James C. McCroskey, "The Relationship of Perceived Teacher Caring with Student Learning and Teacher Evaluation," *Communication Education* 46, no. 1 (1997): 1–9; Nel Noddings, "An Ethic of Caring and Its Implications for Instructional Arrangements," *American Journal of Education* 96, no. 2 (1988): 215–230.

21. Matthew A. Kraft and John P. Papay, "Can Professional Environments in Schools Promote Teacher Development? Explaining Heterogeneity in Returns to Teaching Experience," *Educational Evaluation and Policy Analysis* 36, no. 4 (2014): 476–500; Helen F. Ladd and Lucy C. Sorensen, "Returns to Teacher Experience: Student Achievement and Motivation in Middle School," Working Paper 112, Center for Analysis of Longitudinal Data in Education Research, 2014; Michael Fullan, ed., *Teacher Development and Educational Change* (New York: Routledge, 2014); Andy Hargreaves and Michael Fullan, *Professional Capital: Transforming Teaching in Every School* (New York: Teachers College Press, 2012).

22. Linda Darling-Hammond, "Policy and Professionalism," in *Building a Professional Culture in Schools,* ed. Ann Lieberman (New York: Teachers College Press, 1988), 55–77; Wayne K. Hoy and Megan Tschannen-Moran, "The Conceptualization and Measurement of Faculty Trust in Schools," in *Essential Ideas for the Reform of American Schools,* ed. Wayne K. Hoy and Michael D. Paola (Charlotte, NC: Information Age, 2007), 87–114. Richard Ingersoll, "Teacher Turnover and Teacher Shortages: An Organizational Analysis," *American Educational Research Journal* 38, no. 3 (2001): 499–534; Susanna Loeb, Linda Darling-Hammond, and John Luczac, "How Teaching Conditions Predict Teacher Turnover in California," *Peabody Journal of Education* 80, no. 3 (2005): 44–70; Matthew Ronfeldt, Susanna Loeb, and James Wyckoff, "How Teacher Turnover Harms Student Achievement," *American Educational Research Journal* 50, no. 1 (2013): 4–36.

23. Mike Taylor, Anne Yates, Luanna H. Meyer, and Penny Kinsella, "Teacher Professional Leadership in Support of Teacher Professional Development," *Teaching and Teacher Education* 27, no. 1 (2011): 85–94; Kwang Suk Yoon, Teresa Duncan, Silvia Wen-Yu Lee, Beth Scarloss, and Kathy L. Shapley, "Reviewing the Evidence on How Teacher Professional Development

Affects Student Achievement, " Issues & Answers, REL 2007-No. 033, Regional Educational Laboratory Southwest (NJ1), October 2007, https://ies.ed.gov/ncee/edlabs/regions/southwest/pdf/REL_2007033.pdf; John M. Foster, Eugenia F. Toma, and Suzanne P. Troske, "Does Teacher Professional Development Improve Math and Science Outcomes and Is It Cost Effective?," *Journal of Education Finance* 38, no. 3 (2013): 255–275.

24. Heather E. Price, "Principal-Teacher Interactions: How Affective Relationships Shape Principal and Teacher Attitudes," *Educational Administration Quarterly* 48, no. 1 (2012): 39–85; Philip Hallinger and Ronald H. Heck, "Exploring the Principal's Contribution to School Effectiveness: 1980–1995," *School Effectiveness and School Improvement* 9, no. 2 (1998): 157–191; Anthony S. Bryk, Penny Bender Sebring, Elaine Allensworth, John Q. Easton, and Stuart Luppescu, *Organizing Schools for Improvement: Lessons from Chicago* (Chicago: University of Chicago Press, 2010); Thomas M. Smith and Richard M. Ingersoll, "What Are the Effects of Induction and Mentoring on Beginning Teacher Turnover?," *American Education Research Journal* 41, no. 3 (2004): 681–714; Anthony S. Bryk and Barbara Schneider, *Trust in Schools* (New York: Russell Sage Foundation, 2002).

25. To say that these variables are not dependent on demography is not to say that they are completely independent. Demography shapes almost every aspect of life in schools.

26. In the literature, the research on "school culture" often bleeds together with that on "school climate." I have opted for the phrase "school culture," though I have included many of the perspectives from the work on "school climate." See Education Week Research Center, *Engaging Students for Success: Findings from a National Survey,*2014, http://www.edweek.org /media/ewrc_engagingstudents_2014.pdf; Wayne K. Hoy, John Hannum, and Megan Tschannen-Moran, "Organizational Climate and Student Achievement: A Parsimonious and Longitudinal View," *Journal of School Leadership* 8, no. 4 (1998): 336–359; Talisha Lee, Dewey Cornell, Anne Gregory, and Xitao Fan, "High Suspension Schools and Dropout Rates for Black and White Students," *Education and Treatment of Children* 34, no. 2 (2011): 167–192; Kathleen Fulton, Irene Yoon, and Christine Lee, "Induction into Learning Communities," National Commission on

Teaching and America's Future, 2005; Jessica L. Grayson and Heather K. Alvarez, "School Climate Factors Relating to Teacher Burnout: A Mediator Model," *Teaching and Teacher Education* 24, no. 5 (2008): 1349–1363; Ann Higgins-D'Alessandro, "The Necessity of Teacher Development," *New Directions for Child and Adolescent Development,* no. 98 (2002): 75–84.

27. Grayson and Alvarez, "School Climate Factors Relating to Teacher Burnout"; Bryk et al., *Organizing Schools for Improvement.*

28. Heather P. Libbey, "Measuring Student Relationships to School: Attachment, Bonding, Connectedness, and Engagement," *Journal of School Health* 74, no. 7 (2004): 274–283. For examples of toxic academic culture, see Denise Clark Pope, *Doing School: How We Are Creating a Generation of Stressed Out, Materialistic, and Miseducated Students* (New Haven, CT: Yale University Press, 2001). For examples of toxic social culture, see Jess Bidgood, "Students Say Racial Hostilities Simmered at Historic Boston Latin School," *New York Times,* January 30, 2016, http://www.nytimes.com /2016/01/31/education/students-say-racial-hostilities-simmered-at -historic-boston-latin-school.html?_r=0; and Jeannie Suk, "St. Paul's School and a New Definition of Rape," *New Yorker,* November 3, 2015, http://www.newyorker.com/news/news-desk/st-pauls-school-and-a-new -definition-of-rape.

29. Michael B. Ripski and Anne Gregory, "Unfair, Unsafe, and Unwelcome: Do High School Students' Perceptions of Unfairness, Hostility, and Victimization in School Predict Engagement and Achievement?," *Journal of School Violence* 8, no. 4 (2009): 355–375; Ron Avi Astor, Nancy Guerra, and Richard Van Acker, "How Can We Improve School Safety Research?," *Educational Researcher* 39, no. 1 (2010): 69–78; Jaana Juvonen, Adrienne Nishina, and Sandra Graham, "Ethnic Diversity and Perceptions of Safety in Urban Middle Schools," *Psychological Science* 17, no. 5 (2006): 393–400; Russell Skiba, Ada B. Simmons, Reece Peterson, Janet McKelvey, Susan Forde, and Sarah Gallini, "Beyond Guns, Drugs and Gangs: The Structure of Student Perceptions of School Safety," *Journal of School Violence* 3, nos. 2–3 (2004): 149–171; Lee Shumow and Richard G. Lomax, "Predicting Perceptions of School Safety," *School Community Journal* 11, no. 2 (2001): 93–112.

30. Skiba et al., "Beyond Guns, Drugs and Gangs," 149–171; Salvatore Saporito and Annette Lareau, "School Selection as a Process: The Multiple Dimensions of Race in Framing Educational Choice," *Social Problems* 46 (1999): 418–435; Juvonen, Nichina, and Graham, "Ethnic Diversity," 393–400; Johanna R. Lacoe, "Unequally Safe: The Race Gap in School Safety," *Youth Violence and Juvenile Justice* 13, no. 2 (2015): 143–168.

31. Tonja R. Nansel, Mary Overpeck, Ramani S. Pilla, W. June Ruan, Bruce Simons-Morton, and Peter Scheidt, "Bullying Behaviors among US Youth: Prevalence and Association with Psychosocial Adjustment," *Journal of the American Medical Association* 285, no. 16 (2001): 2094–2100; Ian Rivers, V. Paul Poteat, Nathalie Noret, and Nigel Ashurst, "Observing Bullying at School: The Mental Health Implications of Witness Status," *School Psychology Quarterly* 24, no. 4 (2009): 211.

32. Bryk and Schneider, *Trust in Schools*.

33. Adena M. Klem and James P. Connell, "Relationships Matter: Linking Teacher Support to Student Engagement and Achievement," *Journal of School Health* 74, no. 7 (2004): 262–273; Karen F. Osterman, "Students' Need for Belonging in the School Community," *Review of Educational Research* 70, no. 3 (2000): 323–367; Eric M. Anderman, "School Effects on Psychological Outcomes during Adolescence," *Journal of Educational Psychology* 94, no. 4 (2002): 795; Marti Rice, "Importance of School Connectedness," *Pediatrics for Parents* 25 (2009): 20; Andrea E. Bonny, Maria T. Britto, Brenda K. Klostermann, Richard W. Hornung, and Gail B. Slap, "School Disconnectedness: Identifying Adolescents at Risk," *Pediatrics* 106, no. 5 (2000): 1017–1021; Lyndal Bond, Helen Butler, Lyndal Thomas, John Carlin, Sara Glover, Glenn Bowes, and George Patton, "Social and School Connectedness in Early Secondary School as Predictors of Late Teenage Substance Use, Mental Health, and Academic Outcomes," *Journal of Adolescent Health* 40, no. 4 (2007): 357-e9.

34. Xin Ma, "Sense of Belonging to School: Can Schools Make a Difference?," *Journal of Educational Research* 96, no. 6 (2003): 340–349.

35. Ellen A. Skinner and Michael J. Belmont, "Motivation in the Classroom: Reciprocal Effects of Teacher Behavior and Student Engagement across the School Year," *Journal of Educational Psychology* 85, no. 4 (1993): 571; Theresa M. Akey, *School Context, Student Attitudes and Behavior, and*

Academic Achievement: An Exploratory Analysis (New York: MDRC, 2006); Bronwyn E. Becker and Suniya S. Luthar, "Social-Emotional Factors Affecting Achievement Outcomes among Disadvantaged Students: Closing the Achievement Gap," *Educational Psychologist* 37, no. 4 (2002): 197–214; Anne Gregory and Rhona S. Weinstein, "Connection and Regulation at Home and in School: Predicting Growth in Achievement for Adolescents," *Journal of Adolescent Research* 19, no. 4 (2004): 405–427; Klem and Connell, "Relationships Matter," 262–273.

36. Clea McNeely and Christina Falci, "School Connectedness and the Transition into and out of Health-Risk Behavior among Adolescents: A Comparison of Social Belonging and Teacher Support," *Journal of School Health* 74, no. 7 (2004): 284–292; Stephanie H. Schneider and Lauren Duran, "School Climate in Middle Schools," *Journal of Research in Character Education* 8, no. 2 (2010): 25–37.

37. Education Week Research Center, *Engaging Students for Success;* Nan Marie Astone and Sara S. McLanahan, "Family Structure, Parental Practices and High School Completion," *American Sociological Review* 56, no. 3 (1991): 309–320; Richard J. Murnane, *U.S. High School Graduation Rates: Patterns and Explanations,* NBER Report w18701 (Cambridge, MA: National Bureau of Economic Research, 2013).

38. Wayne K. Hoy, Scott R. Sweetland, and Page A. Smith, "Toward an Organizational Model of Achievement in High Schools: The Significance of Collective Efficacy," *Educational Administration Quarterly* 38, no.1 (2002): 77–77; Valerie Lee, Julia B. Smith, Tamara E. Perry, and Mark A. Smylie, *Social Support, Academic Press, and Student Achievement: A View from the Middle Grades in Chicago* (Chicago: Consortium on Chicago School Research, 1999); Meredith Phillips, "What Makes Schools Effective? A Comparison of the Relationships of Communitarian Climate and Academic Climate to Mathematics Achievement and Attendance during Middle School," *American Educational Research Journal* 34, no. 4 (1997): 633–662.

39. Student standardized test scores can also reveal gaps, but represent less actionable information. Insofar as that is the case, it is critical to measure inputs alongside outcomes, despite a propensity among policymakers to look exclusively at the latter.

40. Per-pupil expenditure can be calculated by taking a school's total spending and dividing by the number of students. These expenditures vary dramatically across states but average out to roughly $12,000 per student nationwide.

41. Howard Blume and Stephen Ceasar, "L.A. Unified's iPad Rollout Marred by Chaos," *Los Angeles Times,* October 1, 2013, http://articles.latimes.com /2013/oct/01/local/la-me-1002-lausd-ipads-20131002; Howard Blume, "L.A. School District Demands iPad Refund from Apple," *Los Angeles Times,* April 16, 2015, http://www.latimes.com/local/lanow/la-me-ln-ipad -curriculum-refund-20150415-story.html. Calculating the additional cost of Special Education students is challenging, given the facts that services differ across populations and price differs across states, but a reasonable estimate is that Special Education students require an addition $10,000 per pupil.

42. Bruce D. Baker, "Revisiting the Age-Old Question: Does Money Matter in Education?," Albert Shanker Institute, 2012, http://www.shankerinstitute .org/resource/does-money-matter-second-edition; Rob Greenwald, Larry V. Hedges, and Richard D. Laine, "The Effect of School Resources on Student Achievement," *Review of Educational Research* 66, no. 3 (1996): 361–396; C. Kirabo Jackson, Rucker C. Johnson, and Claudia Persico, "The Effects of School Spending on Educational and Economic Outcomes: Evidence from School Finance Reforms," *Quarterly Journal of Economics* 131, no. 1 (2015): 157–218.

43. Jack Buckley, Mark Schneider, and Yi Shang, "Fix It and They Might Stay: School Facility Quality and Teacher Retention in Washington, DC," *Teachers College Record* 107, no. 5 (2005): 1107–1123; Cynthia Uline and Megan Tschannen-Moran, "The Walls Speak: The Interplay of Quality Facilities, School Climate, and Student Achievement," *Journal of Educational Administration* 46, no. 1 (2008): 55–73; Valkiria Durán-Narucki, "School Building Condition, School Attendance, and Academic Achievement in New York City Public Schools: A Mediation Model," *Journal of Environmental Psychology* 28, no. 3 (2008): 278–286.

44. Peter Blatchford, Paul Bassett, and Penelope Brown, "Examining the Effect of Class Size on Classroom Engagement and Teacher-Pupil Interaction: Differences in Relation to Pupil Prior Attainment and Primary vs.

Secondary Schools," *Learning and Instruction* 21, no. 6 (2011): 715–730; Diane Whitmore Schanzenbach, *Does Class Size Matter?* (Boulder, CO: National Education Policy Center, 2014).

45. Valerie E. Lee and Ruth B. Ekstrom, "Student Access to Guidance Counseling in High School," *American Educational Research Journal* 24, no. 2 (1987): 287–310; Richard T. Lapan, Norman C. Gysbers, and Yongmin Sun, "The Impact of More Fully Implemented Guidance Programs on the School Experiences of High School Students: A State-wide Evaluation Study," *Journal of Counseling and Development* 75, no. 4 (1997): 292–302; Jenni Jennings, Glen Pearson, and Mark Harris, "Implementing and Maintaining School-Based Mental Health Services in a Large, Urban School District," *Journal of School Health* 70, no. 5 (2000): 201–205; Laura A. Nabors and Matthew W. Reynolds, "Program Evaluation Activities: Outcomes Related to Treatment for Adolescents Receiving School-Based Mental Health Services," *Children's Services: Social Policy, Research, and Practice* 3, no. 3 (2000): 175–189.

46. James Catterall, "The Arts and Achievement in At-Risk Youth: Findings from Four Longitudinal Studies," Research Report no. 55, (Washington, DC: National Endowment for the Arts, 2012; James Catterall, Richard Chapleau, and John Iwanaga, "Involvement in the Arts and Human Development: General Involvement and Intensive Involvement in Music and Theater Arts," in *Champions of Change: The Impact of the Arts on Learning*, Edward B. Fiske, ed. (Washington, DC: President's Committee on the Arts and the Humanities, 1999): 1–18; Kristin D. Conklin, Bridget K. Curran, and Matthew Gandal, *An Action Agenda for Improving America's High Schools. National Education Summit on High Schools* (Washington, DC: National Governors Association, 2005); Michael Chajewski, Krista D. Mattern, and Emily J. Shaw, "Examining the Role of Advanced Placement Exam Participation in 4-Year College Enrollment," *Educational Measurement: Issues and Practice* 30, no. 4 (2011): 16–27; Kristin Klopfenstein and M. Kathleen Thomas, "The Link between Advanced Placement Experience and Early College Success," *Southern Economic Journal* 75, no. 3 (2009): 873–891; Dan Willingham, *Why Don't Students Like School?* (San Francisco: Jossey-Bass, 2010); Thomas Dee, Brian A. Jacob, and Nathaniel Schwartz, "The Effects of NCLB on School

Resources and Practices," *Educational Evaluation and Policy Analysis* 35, no. 2 (2013): 252–279.

47. It is worth noting that this concern was also articulated by focus group participants in other districts in our work through the Massachusetts Consortium for Innovative Education Assessment.

48. For more about core knowledge, see E. D. Hirsch Jr., *Cultural Literacy: What Every American Needs to Know* (New York: Houghton Mifflin, 1987). For culturally responsive curricula, see Lisa Delpit, *Other People's Children: Cultural Conflict in the Classroom* (New York: New Press, 1995); James A. Banks, "A Curriculum for Empowerment, Action, and Change," in *Empowerment through Multicultural Education,* ed. Christine E. Sleeter (Albany: State University of New York Press, 1991); Ana María Villegas and Tamara Lucas, "Preparing Culturally Responsive Teachers: Rethinking the Curriculum," *Journal of Teacher Education* 53, no. 1 (2002): 20–32.

49. Joyce L. Epstein, Mavis G. Sanders, Beth S. Simon, Karen Clark Salinas, Natalie Rodriguez Jansorn, and Frances L. Van Voorhis, *School, Family, and Community Partnerships: Your Handbook for Action* (Thousand Oaks, CA: Corwin Press, 2002); Nancy E. Hill and Lorraine C. Taylor, "Parental School Involvement and Children's Academic Achievement: Pragmatics and Issues," *Current Directions in Psychological Science* 13, no. 4 (2004): 161–164; Robert Pianta and Daniel Walsh, *High-Risk Children in Schools: Constructing Sustaining Relationships* (New York: Routledge, 2014); Anne T. Henderson and Karen L. Mapp, "A New Wave of Evidence: The Impact of School, Family, and Community Connections on Student Achievement; Annual Synthesis 2002," National Center for Family and Community Connections with Schools, 2002, http://files.eric.ed.gov /fulltext/ED474521.pdf.

50. Education Week Research Center, *Engaging Students for Success.*

51. Bryk et al., *Organizing Schools for Improvement;* Henderson and Mapp, "A New Wave of Evidence."

52. Bryk et al., *Organizing Schools for Improvement;* ETS, Ready for the World: *Americans Speak Out on High School Reform* (Princeton, NJ: ETS, 2005), https://www.ets.org/Media/Education_Topics/pdf/2005highschoolreform .pdf; Atelia Melaville, Amy C. Berg, and Martin J. Blank, "Community-Based Learning: Engaging Students for Success and Citizenship," Coalition

for Community Schools, 2006, http://files.eric.ed.gov/fulltext/ED490980
.pdf; Susan Moore Johnson, Matthew A. Kraft, and John P. Papay, "How
Context Matters in High-Need Schools: The Effects of Teachers' Working
Conditions on Their Professional Satisfaction and Their Students'
Achievement," *Teachers College Record* 114, no. 10 (2012): 1–39; Elliot
Washor and Charles Mojkowski, *Leaving to Learn* (Portsmouth, NH:
Heinemann, 2013); Ron Ferguson and Eric Hirsch, "How Working
Conditions Predict Teaching Quality and Student Outcomes," in *Designing
Teacher Evaluation Systems: New Guidance from the Measures of Effective
Teaching Project,* ed. Thomas Kane, Kerri Kerr, and Robert Pianta (San
Francisco: Jossey-Bass, 2014).

53. ETS, *Americans Speak Out;* Richard Rothstein and Rebecca Jacobsen, "The
Goals of Education," *Phi Delta Kappan* 88, no. 4 (2006): 264–272.

54. Doug Shapiro, Afet Dundar, Phoebe K. Wakhungu, Xin Yuan, Angel
Nathan, and Youngsik Hwang, *Completing College: A National View of
Student Attainment Rates—Fall 2008 Cohort,* Signature Report no. 8
(Herndon, VA: National Student Clearinghouse, 2014).

55. Gauging student growth will take a significant amount of research. To be
successful in this enterprise, we must first answer basic questions about
when it is appropriate to take baseline measures, how many years should
pass between baseline and output measures, and how much growth
measures can account for out-of-school factors.

56. Douglas Harris, *Value-Added Measures in Education: What Every Educator
Needs to Know* (Cambridge, MA: Harvard Education Press, 2011).

57. Ray Hart, Michael Casserly, Renata Uzzell, Moses Palacios, Amanda
Corcoran, and Liz Spurgeon, *Student Testing in America's Great City
Schools: An Inventory and Preliminary Analysis* (Washington, DC: Council
of the Great City Schools, 2015).

58. Youb Kim and Lisa Sensale Yazdian, "Portfolio Assessment and Quality
Teaching," *Theory into Practice* 53, no. 3 (2014): 220–227; Betty Mc-
Donald, "Portfolio Assessment: Direct from the Classroom," *Assessment
and Evaluation in Higher Education* 37, no. 3 (2012): 335–347; Elliott Asp,
"Assessment in Education: Where Have We Been? Where Are We
Headed?," Association for Supervision and Curriculum Development
Yearbook (Alexandria, VA: Association for Supervision and Curriculum

Development, 2000), 123–157; Bette S. Bergeron, Sarah Wermuth, and Rebecca C. Hammar, "Initiating Portfolios through Shared Learning: Three Perspectives," *Reading Teacher* 50, no. 7 (1997): 552–562; Judith H. Cohen and Roberta B. Wiener, *Literacy Portfolios: Improving Assessment, Teaching, and Learning* (Merrill, WI: Merrill Publishing, 2003); Kathleen Blake Yancey, "Dialogue, Interplay, and Discovery: Mapping the Role and the Rhetoric of Reflection in Portfolio Assessment," in *Writing Portfolios in the Classroom: Policy, Practice, Promise and Peril,* ed. Robert Calfee and Pamela Perfumo (Mahwah, NJ: Lawrence Erlbaum Associates, 1996), 83–102.

59. Klem and Connell, "Relationships Matter," 262–273. See also: Maria R. Reyes, Marc A. Brackett, Susan E. Rivers, Mark White, and Peter Salovey, "Classroom Emotional Climate, Student Engagement, and Academic Achievement," *Journal of Educational Psychology* 104, no. 3 (2012): 700–712; John Mark Froiland and Emily Oros, "Intrinsic Motivation, Perceived Competence and Classroom Engagement as Longitudinal Predictors of Adolescent Reading Achievement," *Educational Psychology* 34, no. 2 (2014): 119–132; Margaret Beale Spencer, Elizabeth Noll, Jill Stoltzfus, and Vinay Harpalani, "Identity and School Adjustment: Revisiting the 'Acting White' Assumption," *Educational Psychologist* 36, no. 1 (2001): 21–30.

60. Donald J. Hernandez, "Double Jeopardy: How Third-Grade Reading Skills and Poverty Influence High School Graduation," Annie E. Casey Foundation, 2011, http://www.aecf.org/m/resourcedoc/AECF-DoubleJeopardy -2012-Full.pdf; Christine A. Christle, Kristine Jolivette, and C. Michael Nelson, "School Characteristics Related to High School Dropout Rates," *Remedial and Special Education* 28, no. 6 (2007): 325–339; Nan Marie Astone and Sara S. McLanahan, "Family Structure, Parental Practices and High School Completion," *American Sociological Review* (1991): 309–320; Russell W. Rumberger and Gregory J. Palardy, "Test Scores, Dropout Rates, and Transfer Rates as Alternative Indicators of High School Performance," *American Educational Research Journal* 42, no. 1 (2005): 3–42.

61. Rothstein and Jacobsen, "The Goals of Education," 264–272; James Hiebert, Thomas P. Carpenter, Elizabeth Fennema, Karen Fuson, Piet

Human, Hanlie Murray, Alwyn Olivier, and Diana Wearne, "Problem Solving as a Basis for Reform in Curriculum and Instruction: The Case of Mathematics," *Educational Researcher* 25, no. 4 (1996): 12–21.

62. An excellent example of this is "progressive" teaching—an incredibly abstract aim that has primarily impacted the way educators talk about pedagogy. For an in-depth treatment of this, see Larry Cuban, *How Teachers Taught: Constancy and Change in American Classrooms, 1880–1990* (New York: Teachers College Press, 1993).

63. Stephen P. Norris, "Synthesis of Research on Critical Thinking," *Educational Leadership* 42, no. 8 (1985): 40–45.

64. Stephen I. Brown and Marion I. Walter, eds., *Problem Posing: Reflections and Applications* (Mahwah, NJ: Lawrence Erlbaum Associates, 1993); Carolyn N. Hedley, Patricia Antonacci, and Mitchell Rabinowitz, eds., *Thinking and Literacy: The Mind at Work* (New York: Routledge, 2013); Louis Alfieri, Patricia J. Brooks, Naomi J. Aldrich, and Harriet R. Tenenbaum, "Does Discovery-Based Instruction Enhance Learning?," *Journal of Educational Psychology* 103, no. 1 (2011): 1; Timothy R. Elliott, Frank Godshall, John R. Shrout, and Thomas E. Witty, "Problem-Solving Appraisal, Self-Reported Study Habits, and Performance of Academically At-Risk College Students," *Journal of Counseling Psychology* 37, no. 2 (1990): 203; Thomas J. D'Zurilla and Collette F. Sheedy, "The Relation between Social Problem-Solving Ability and Subsequent Level of Academic Competence in College Students," *Cognitive Therapy and Research* 16, no. 5 (1992): 589–599.

65. Susan L. Hersperger, John R. Slate, and Stacey L. Edmonson, "A Review of the Career and Technical Education Research Literature," *Journal of Education Research* 7, no. 3 (2013): 157–179; ACT, Inc., *Ready for College and Ready for Work: Same or Different?* (Iowa City, IA: Act, Inc., 2006); Michael Bangser, *Preparing High School Students for Successful Transitions to Postsecondary Education and Employment* (New York: MDRC, 2008), http://www.mdrc.org/sites/default/files/PreparingHSStudentsforTransition_073108.pdf.

66. Horace Mann, *Twelfth Annual Report to the Secretary of the Massachusetts State Board of Education* (N.p. 1848).

67. "The 48th Annual PDK Poll of the Public's Attitudes toward the Public Schools," *Phi Delta Kappan* 98, no. 1 (2016); NPR / Kaiser Family Foundation / Kennedy School Education Survey, 1999, http://www.npr.org /programs/specials/poll/education/education.results.html.

68. Joseph E. Zins, ed., *Building Academic Success on Social and Emotional Learning: What Does the Research Say?* (New York: Teachers College Press, 2004); James P. Comer, ed., *Rallying the Whole Village: The Comer Process for Reforming Education* (New York: Teachers College Press, 1996); Bryk et al., *Organizing Schools for Improvement*; Higgins-D'Alessandro, "The Necessity of Teacher Development," 75–84.

69. Rothstein and Jacobsen, "The Goals of Education," 264–272.

70. Jack Schneider and Michael Fuerstein, "Thinking Civically," *Social Education,* September, 2013.

71. See, for instance, C. Kirabo Jackson, "Non-cognitive Ability, Test Scores, and Teacher Quality: Evidence from 9th Grade Teachers in North Carolina," NBER Working Paper 18624, National Bureau of Economic Research, December 2012; Jennifer L. Jennings and Thomas A. DiPrete, "Teacher Effects on Social / Behavioral Skills in Early Elementary School," CPRC Working Paper 09–11, Columbia Population Research Center, New York, 2009.

72. Carnegie Corporation of New York and CIRCLE: The Center for Information & Research on Civic Learning and Engagement, *The Civic Mission of Schools* (New York: Carnegie Corporation of New York and CIRCLE, 2003); David E. Campbell, Meira Levinson, and Frederick M. Hess, eds., *Making Civics Count: Citizenship Education for a New Generation* (Cambridge, MA: Harvard Education Press, 2012).

73. Joseph J. Ellis, *Founding Brothers: The Revolutionary Generation* (New York: Knopf, 2001), 154.

74. Dara Zeehandelaar and Amber M. Winkler, eds., *What Parents Want: Education Preferences and Trade-Offs* (Washington, DC: Thomas B. Fordham Institute, 2013). See also Amy Stuart Wells, Lauren Fox, and Diana Cordova-Cobo, *How Racially Diverse Schools and Classrooms Can Benefit All Students* (New York: Century Foundation, 2016).

75. John J. Heldrich Center for Workforce Development, *Attitudes about Work, Employers, and Government Survey* (New Brunswick, NJ: Rutgers

University, 2000); Rothstein and Jacobsen, "The Goals of Education," 264–272.

76. Camille A. Farrington, Melissa Roderick, Elaine Allensworth, Jenny Nagaoka, Tasha Seneca Keyes, David W. Johnson, and Nicole O. Beechum, *Teaching Adolescents to Become Learners: The Role of Noncognitive Factors in Shaping School Performance—A Critical Literature Review* (Chicago: Consortium on Chicago School Research, 2012), https://consortium .uchicago.edu/sites/default/files/publications/Noncognitive%20Report .pdf; Angela L. Duckworth, Christopher Peterson, Michael D. Matthews, and Dennis R. Kelly, "Grit: Perseverance and Passion for Long-Term Goals," *Journal of Personality and Social Psychology* 92, no. 6 (2007): 1087; Angela L. Duckworth and David Scott Yeager, "Measurement Matters: Assessing Personal Qualities Other Than Cognitive Ability for Educational Purposes," *Educational Researcher* 44, no. 4 (2015): 237–251.

77. Lisa S. Blackwell, Kali H. Trzesniewski, and Carol Sorich Dweck, "Implicit Theories of Intelligence Predict Achievement across an Adolescent Transition: A Longitudinal Study and an Intervention," *Child Development* 78, no. 1 (2007): 246–263; Carol S. Dweck, *Self-Theories: Their Role in Motivation, Personality, and Development* (Philadelphia: Psychology Press, 1999); Carol S. Dweck, "The Perils and Promises of Praise," *Educational Leadership* 65, no. 2 (2007): 34–39; Joshua Aronson, Carrie B. Fried, and Catherine Good, "Reducing the Effects of Stereotype Threat on African American College Students by Shaping Theories of Intelligence," *Journal of Experimental Social Psychology* 38, no. 2 (2002): 113–125; Carol S. Dweck, "Who Will the 21st-Century Learners Be?," *Knowledge Quest* 38, no. 2 (2009): 8.

78. Rothstein and Jacobsen, "The Goals of Education," 264–272.

79. Catterall, "The Arts and Achievement in At-Risk Youth"; E. B. Fiske, ed., *Champions of Change: The Impact of the Arts on Learning* (Washington, DC: Arts Education Partnership and the President's Committee on Arts and Humanities, 1999), http://www.aep-arts.org/files/publications /ChampsReport.pdf; Douglas Israel, *Staying in School: Arts Education and New York City High School Graduation Rates* (New York: Center for Arts Education, 2009); Bill Lucas, Guy Claxton, and Ellen Spencer, "Progression in Student Creativity in School: First Steps towards New Forms of

Formative Assessments," OECD Education Working Paper 86, OECD Publishing, 2013; James C. Kaufman, "Counting the Muses: Development of the Kaufman Domains of Creativity Scale," *Psychology of Aesthetics, Creativity, and the Arts* 6, no. 4 (2012): 298–308; Ronald A. Beghetto, James C. Kaufman, and Juliet Baxter, "Answering the Unexpected Questions: Exploring the Relationship between Students' Creative Self-Efficacy and Teacher Ratings of Creativity," *Psychology of Aesthetics, Creativity, and the Arts* 5, no. 4 (2011): 342.

80. Rothstein and Jacobsen, "The Goals of Education," 264–272.

81. Sonja Lyubomirsky, Laura King, and Ed Diener, "The Benefits of Frequent Positive Affect: Does Happiness Lead to Success?," *Psychological Bulletin* 131, no. 6 (2005): 803–855; Greg J. Duncan, Chantelle J. Dowsett, Amy Claessens, Katherine Magnuson, Aletha C. Huston, Pamela Klebanov, Linda S. Pagani, et al., "School Readiness and Later Achievement," *Developmental Psychology* 43, no. 6 (2007): 1428; Rothstein and Jacobsen, "The Goals of Education," 264–272.

82. James F. Sallis, Thomas L. McKenzie, Bohdan Kolody, Michael Lewis, Simon Marshall, and Paul Rosengard, "Effects of Health-Related Physical Education on Academic Achievement: Project SPARK," *Research Quarterly for Exercise and Sport* 70, no. 2 (1999): 127–134; Roy J. Shephard, "Curricular Physical Activity and Academic Performance," *Pediatric Exercise Science* 9 (1997): 113–126; Roy J. Shephard, M. Volle, H. Lavallee, R. LaBarre, J. C. Jequier, and M. Rajic, "Required Physical Activity and Academic Grades: A Controlled Study," in *Children and Sport* (Berlin: Springer, 1984), 58–63; Cynthia Wolford Symons, Bethann Cinelli, Tammy C. James, and Patti Groff, "Bridging Student Health Risks and Academic Achievement through Comprehensive School Health Programs," *Journal of School Health* 67, no. 6 (1997): 220–227; Duncan et al., "School Readiness and Later Achievement," 1428–1446.

Chapter 4   But How Do We *Get* That Kind of Information?

1. Each of our focus groups lasted for approximately one hour. As a general rule, we tried to limit focus groups to ten people or fewer. There are also financial costs associated with focus groups. Teachers were paid stipends of thirty to forty dollars per focus group.

2. One promising technique for addressing reference bias is the inclusion of anchoring vignettes. For more on this, see Patrick C. Kyllonen and Jonas P. Bertling, "Innovative Questionnaire Assessment Methods to Increase Cross-Country Comparability," in *Handbook of International Large-Scale Assessment: Background, Technical Issues, and Methods of Data Analysis*, ed. Leslie Rutkowski, Matthias von Davier, and David Rutkowski (Boca Raton, FL: Chapman and Hall, 2013); Gary King, Christopher J. L. Murray, Joshua A. Salomon, and Ajay Tandon, "Enhancing the Validity and Cross-Cultural Comparability of Measurement in Survey Research," *American Political Science Review* 98, no. 1 (2004): 191–207. That said, there is evidence from the CORE districts in California that reference bias may be more of an imagined concern than a practical one. These districts have chosen not to use anchoring vignettes, despite having cooperated with ETS to develop and pilot them for use in student perception surveys.

3. To be clear: there are methods for dealing with all of these problems. In this case, creating a "skip pattern" in the survey can create different kinds of questions for different audiences who are taking the same survey.

4. Jon A. Krosnick, "Survey Research," *Annual Review of Psychology* 50, no. 1 (1999): 537–567; Brian S. Connelly and Deniz S. Ones, "An Other Perspective on Personality: Meta-analytic Integration of Observers' Accuracy and Predictive Validity," *Psychological Bulletin* 136, no. 6 (2010): 1092; Joshua J. Jackson, James J. Connolly, S. Mason Garrison, Madeleine M. Leveille, and Seamus L. Connolly, "Your Friends Know How Long You Will Live: A 75-Year Study of Peer-Rated Personality Traits," *Psychological Science* 26, no. 3 (2015): 335–340.

5. Thomas J. Kane and Douglas O. Staiger, "Gathering Feedback for Teaching: Combining High-Quality Observations with Student Surveys and Achievement Gains" (research paper, MET Project, Seattle, WA: Bill & Melinda Gates Foundation, 2012); David J. Wilkerson, Richard P. Manatt, Mary Ann Rogers, and Ron Maughan, "Validation of Student, Principal, and Self-Ratings in 360 Feedback® for Teacher Evaluation," *Journal of Personnel Evaluation in Education* 14, no. 2 (2000): 179–192.

6. Ronald F. Ferguson, "Can Student Surveys Measure Teaching Quality?," *Phi Delta Kappan* 94, no. 3 (2012): 24–28; George G. Bear, Clare Gaskins, Jessica Blank, and Fang Fang Chen, "Delaware School Climate Survey—

Student: Its Factor Structure, Concurrent Validity, and Reliability," *Journal of School Psychology* 49, no. 2 (2011): 157–174.

7. Michael Eid and Ed Diener, eds., *Handbook of Multimethod Measurement in Psychology* (Washington, DC: American Psychological Association, 2006); J. Philippe Rushton, Charles J. Brainerd, and Michael Pressley, "Behavioral Development and Construct Validity: The Principle of Aggregation," *Psychological Bulletin* 94, no. 1 (1983): 18; Angela L. Duckworth and David Scott Yeager, "Measurement Matters Assessing Personal Qualities Other Than Cognitive Ability for Educational Purposes," *Educational Researcher* 44, no. 4 (2015): 237–251.

8. Information about Ron Ferguson's survey assessments for early elementary grades can be requested directly from Tripod Education Partners.

9. Anthony S. Bryk, Penny Bender Sebring, Elaine Allensworth, John Q. Easton, and Stuart Luppescu, *Organizing Schools for Improvement: Lessons from Chicago* (Chicago: University of Chicago Press, 2010); University of Chicago, Chicago Consortium for School Research, "5Essentials," https://uchicagoimpact.org/5essentials, accessed February 11, 2016.

10. For more, see Hunter Gehlbach and Maureen E. Brinkworth, "Measure Twice, Cut Down Error: A Process for Enhancing the Validity of Survey Scales," *Review of General Psychology* 15, no. 4 (2011): 380–387.

11. See, for instance, Gordon B. Willis, *Cognitive Interviewing: A Tool for Improving Questionnaire Design* (Thousand Oaks, CA: Sage, 2005).

12. Chiefly, we wondered if the questions would offer any discriminative power. That is, would we get different results across teachers, or would all teachers issue themselves high ratings? The former turned out to be the case.

13. For more, see Julianne Viola, Joe McIntyre, and Hunter Gehlbach, "Teachers' Interest in Students' Personal Development: The Creation of a New Survey Scale," *SAGE Research Methods Cases*, 2016, http://methods.sagepub.com/case/teachers-interest-students-personal-development-creation-new-survey-scale.

14. Sally M. Weinstein, Robin J. Mermelstein, Benjamin L. Hankin, Donald Hedeker, and Brian R. Flay, "Longitudinal Patterns of Daily Affect and Global Mood during Adolescence," *Journal of Research on*

Adolescence 17, no. 3 (2007): 587–600; Sally M. Weinstein and Robin Mermelstein, "Relations between Daily Activities and Adolescent Mood: The Role of Autonomy," *Journal of Clinical Child and Adolescent Psychology* 36, no. 2 (2007): 182–194; Eddie M. W. Tong, George D. Bishop, Hwee Chong Enkelmann, Yong Peng Why, Siew Maan Diong, Majeed Khader, and Jansen Ang, "The Use of Ecological Momentary Assessment to Test Appraisal Theories of Emotion," *Emotion* 5, no. 4 (2005): 508–512.

15. U.S. Department of Education, Office of Research, "Education Consumer Guide," no. 2, September 1993, https://www2.ed.gov/pubs/OR/Consumer-Guides/perfasse.html.

16. John O'Neil, "Putting Performance Assessment to the Test," *Educational Leadership* 49, no. 8 (1992): 14–19.

17. New York Performance Standards Consortium, *Educating for the 21st Century: Data Report on the New York Performance Standards Consortium,* New York, n.d., http://performanceassessment.org/articles/DataReport_NY_PSC.pdf.

18. U.S. Department of Education, Office of Research, "Education Consumer Guide," no. 2.

19. Ronald A. Berk, "National Trends in Student and Teacher Assessment: Issues in Performance Assessment," in National Evaluation Systems, *Performance Assessment in Teacher Certification Testing* (Amherst, MA: National Evaluation Systems, 1993), 17–33.

20. Desmond L. Nuttall, "Performance Assessment: The Message from England," *Educational Leadership* 49, no. 8 (1992): 54–57.

21. Linda Darling-Hammond and Frank Adamson, *Beyond Basic Skills: The Role of Performance Assessment in Achieving 21st Century Standards of Learning* (Stanford, CA: Stanford Center for Opportunity Policy in Education, 2010).

22. Ibid.

23. For a longer explanation of this, see Jack Schneider, Joe Feldman, and Dan French, "The Best of Both Worlds," *Phi Delta Kappan* 98, no. 3 (2016): 60–67.

24. For more on teacher performance assessment, see Irena Nayfeld, Raymond L. Pecheone, Andrea Whittaker, Ben Shear, and Heather Klesch,

Educative Assessment and Meaningful Support: 2014 edTPA Administrative Report, Stanford Center on Assessment, Learning and Equity, September 2015.

25. New Teacher Project, *The Mirage: Confronting the Hard Truth about Our Quest for Teacher Development* (New York: New Teacher Project, 2015); Allison Gulamhussein, *Teaching the Teachers: Effective Professional Development in an Era of High Stakes Accountability* (Alexandria, VA: Center for Public Education, 2013); Ruth Chung Wei, Linda Darling-Hammond, Alethea Andree, Nikole Richardson, and Stelios Orphanos, *Professional Learning in the Learning Profession: A Status Report on Teacher Development in the U.S. and Abroad* (Washington, DC: National Staff Development Council, 2009).

Chapter 5 An Information Superhighway

1. Thom File and Camille Ryan, "Computer and Internet Use in the United States: 2013," *American Community Survey Reports* (Washington, DC: U.S. Census Bureau, U.S. Department of Commerce, 2014).

2. Susan Cooper Loomis and Mary Lyn Bourque, eds., *National Assessment of Educational Progress Achievement Levels, 1992–1998 for Mathematics* (Washington, DC: National Assessment Governing Board, July 2001).

3. Illinois State Board of Education, "FAQs Illinois 5Essentials Survey," August 2014, http://www.isbe.net/5essentials/pdf/2014–15/faq1408.pdf.

4. Data courtesy of the Massachusetts Department of Elementary and Secondary Education and the *Boston Globe.*

5. For a more detailed account of this experiment, see Jack Schneider, Rebecca Jacobsen, Rachel S. White, and Hunter Gehlbach, "The (Mis) Measure of Schools: How Data Affect Stakeholder Knowledge and Perceptions of Quality," *Teachers College Record* 120, no. 6 (2018).

6. James Fishkin, *When the People Speak: Deliberative Democracy and Public Consultation* (New York: Oxford University Press, 2009); Jane Mansbridge, "Deliberative Polling as the Gold Standard," *The Good Society* 19, no. 1 (2010): 55.

7. For a much more thorough discussion of the experimental poll and its results, see Schneider et al., "The (Mis)Measure of Schools."

8. Baseline rates of "I don't know" responses for randomly assigned schools were 67 percent for control and 69 percent for treatment. For familiar schools, they were 24 percent for control and 23 percent for treatment.

9. Phi Delta Kappan / Gallup, *The 47th Annual PDK / Gallup Poll of the Public's Attitudes toward the Public Schools* (Bloomington, IN: PDK International, 2015).

10. Ibid.

11. Jonathan Sandy and Kevin Duncan, "Examining the Achievement Test Score Gap between Urban and Suburban Students," *Education Economics* 18, no. 3 (2010): 297–315; Suzanne E. Graham and Lauren E. Provost, *Mathematics Achievement Gaps between Suburban Students and Their Rural and Urban Peers Increase over Time,* Issue Brief 52 (Durham, NH: Carsey Institute, 2012); Christy Lleras, "Race, Racial Concentration, and the Dynamics of Educational Inequality across Urban and Suburban Schools," *American Educational Research Journal* 45, no. 4 (2008): 886–912; Selcuk R. Sirin, "Socioeconomic Status and Academic Achievement: A Meta-analytic Review of Research," *Review of Educational Research* 75, no. 3 (2005): 417–453.

Chapter 6 A New Accountability

1. James Vaznis, "After Stagnant MCAS Results, Six More Schools 'Underperforming,'" *Boston Globe,* September 19, 2014, https://www.bostonglobe.com/2014/09/19/mcas/1dq3cKgyvElF7XR6A10vLO/story.html; Will Pinkston, "Failing Schools Demand Board Response," *Tennessean* (Nashville), August 27, 2014, http://www.tennessean.com/story/opinion/contributors/2014/08/27/pinkston-failing-schools-demand-board-response/14680021/; "City to Address Failing Schools," WROC (Rochester, NY), August 4, 2015, http://www.rochesterhomepage.net/story/d/story/city-to-address-failing-schools/20847/eGV1JzYPTUWJKVSB8nRHEw.

2. Lowell C. Rose and Alec M. Gallup, *The 34th Annual PDK / Gallup Poll of the Public's Attitudes toward the Public Schools* (Bloomington, IN: PDK International, 2002); William J. Bushaw and Shane J. Lopez, *The 45th Annual PDK / Gallup Poll of the Public's Attitudes toward the Public Schools* (Bloomington, IN: PDK International, 2013).

3. Also compelling is the fact that while Americans have long rated their own congressional representatives more highly than Congress as a whole, the two ratings move almost in lockstep with each other, with a 0.93 correlation. Ratings of the schools are different in this regard, suggesting that the same mechanism is not at work in both fields. For more on ratings of Congress, see Harry Enten, "Disliking Congress as a Whole, and as Individuals," FiveThirtyEight, July 1, 2014, http:// fivethirtyeight.com/datalab/disliking-congress-as-a-whole-and-as -individuals/.

4. Martin R. West, "Why Do Americans Rate Their Local Public Schools So Favorably?," *Education Next,* October 27, 2014; see also Mark Schneider, Paul Teske, and Melissa Marschall, *Choosing Schools: Consumer Choice and the Quality of American Schools* (Princeton, NJ: Princeton University Press, 2000); Joseph L. Bast and Herbert J. Walberg, "Can Parents Choose the Best Schools for Their Children?," *Economics of Education Review* 23, no. 4 (2004): 431–440.

5. National Center for Education Statistics, *The Nation's Report Card: Trends in Academic Progress, 2012* (Washington, DC: U.S. Department of Education, 2013).

6. For more on the rhetoric of crisis, see Ethan L. Hutt and Jack Schneider, "The Rhetoric of Reform," *Teachers College Record*—Commentary (December 14, 2012).

7. This is not to suggest that the schools are, therefore, models of perfection. Instead, it seems that the schools, over time, are improving slowly, and possibly even at an insufficient pace. The logical policy response to slow improvement, however, is likely quite different from the logical response to precipitous decline.

8. For a more in-depth discussion of accountability and its constituent parts, see Andreas Schedler, "Conceptualizing Accountability," in *The Self-Restraining State: Power and Accountability in New Democracies*, ed. Andreas Schedler, Larry Diamond, and Marc F. Plattner (Boulder, CO: Lynne Rienner, 1999). It is also worth exploring the approach taken by the CORE districts in California, where the state pairs low-performing districts with higher-performing districts; the aim is to build capacity rather than to impose punitive sanctions.

9. For a discussion of local knowledge, see James C. Scott, *Seeing Like a State* (New Haven, CT: Yale University Press, 1999).

10. This does not mean that, even in the long run, all students will achieve at equal levels. It is to suggest, rather, that particular opportunity variables might someday become equal or close to equal, as well as to suggest that levels of student growth on outcomes—when aggregated across the whole school—might be close to equal.

11. The Every Student Succeeds Act, signed into law in December of 2015, does allow for states to determine their own targets, though a number of rules apply to how this is done.

12. For more detail, see Chapter 3.

13. For more, see Andrew Saultz, Kristin M. Murphy, and Brittany Aronson, "What Can We Learn from the Atlanta Cheating Scandal?," *Phi Delta Kappan* 97, no. 6 (2016): 48–52.

14. See, for instance, the resistance to state takeover of the Holyoke Public Schools in Massachusetts, described in "Holyoke: The Schools Our Children Deserve," Massachusetts Teachers Association, 2016, http://www .massteacher.org/issues_and_action/ongoing_issues/holyoke.aspx.

15. U.S. Department of Education, "Teaching American History," archived information, http://www2.ed.gov/programs/teachinghistory/index .html.

16. Rick Shenkman, "OAH 2009: Sam Wineburg Dares to Ask If the Teaching American History Program Is a Boondoggle," History News Network, April 19, 2009, http://historynewsnetwork.org/article/76806; Daniel C. Humphrey, Christopher Chang-Ross, Mary Beth Donnelly, Lauren Hersh, and Heidi Skolnik, *Evaluation of the Teaching American History Program* (Washington, DC: SRI International, 2005).

17. In Massachusetts, an annual PPI is calculated for all student subgroups, and is made up of several indicators. These indicators include proficiency gaps in standardized test scores, test score growth, and dropout / graduation rates.

18. MCAS is the state standardized test for K–12 schools in Massachusetts.

19. Professional development fails for other reasons, too. See Hilda Borko, "Professional Development and Teacher Learning: Mapping the Terrain," *Educational Researcher* 33, no. 8 (2004): 3–15; Suzanne M. Wilson and

Jennifer Berne, "Teacher Learning and the Acquisition of Professional Knowledge: An Examination of Research on Contemporary Professional Development," *Review of Research in Education* 24 (1999): 173–209; New Teacher Project, *The Mirage: Confronting the Hard Truth about Our Quest for Teacher Development* (New York: New Teacher Project, 2015).

20. Thanks to Dan French and members of the Massachusetts Consortium for Innovative Education Assessment governing board for their input on these.

21. It is also important to note here that schools are not like products conducive to free market consumption. Schools, for instance, are quite different from a product such as breakfast cereal, which can be purchased conveniently, tasted quickly, judged easily, and tossed aside with virtually no consequences; consumers can then repeat this process at a very low cost, and in short order, until they find something they like. Schools, by contrast, require great effort to enroll in, take a long time to reveal their strengths and weaknesses, are deeply affected by community turnover, and can be difficult to leave for students who have formed attachments.

22. Elizabeth N. Farley-Ripple, Kelly Sherretz, and Chris Kelly, *School Success Reports, Stakeholder Feedback: Final Report* (Newark: University of Delaware, 2015).

23. Leadership Conference on Civil and Human Rights, "Civil Rights Groups: 'We Oppose Anti-testing Efforts,'" press release, May 5, 2015, http://www.civilrights.org/press/2015/anti-testing-efforts.html.

24. American Federation of Teachers, "AFT's Weingarten on the U.S. Education Department's 'Testing Action Plan,'" press release, October 24, 2014, http://www.aft.org/press-release/afts-weingarten-us-education-departments-testing-action-plan.

25. Students Matter, "About Us," http://studentsmatter.org/about/, accessed February 4, 2016; *Vergara v. California-Tentative Decision,* Superior Court of the State of California, County of Los Angeles, June 10, 2014; California Teachers Association, "*Vergara v. State of California,*" Issues and Action, http://www.cta.org/vergara, accessed February 4, 2016.

26. Joanne W. Golann, "The Paradox of Success at a No-Excuses School," *Sociology of Education* 88, no. 2 (2015): 103–119.

27. "More Than 620,000 Refused Tests in 2015," press release, FairTest, February 3, 2016, http://www.fairtest.org/more-500000-refused-tests -2015; Katie Zahedi, "Those Phony, Misleading Test Scores: A NY Principal Reacts," http://dianeravitch.net/2013/08/08/those-phony -misleading-test-scores-a-ny-principal-reacts/.

Conclusion

1. For a deeper discussion of private versus public goods in education, see David F. Labaree, "Public Goods, Private Goods: The American Struggle over Educational Goals," *American Educational Research Journal* 34, no. 1 (1997): 39–81. See also Denise Clark Pope, *Doing School: How We Are Creating a Generation of Stressed Out, Materialistic, and Miseducated Students* (New Haven, CT: Yale University Press, 2001).

2. For a history of the early American school system, see Carl Kaestle, *Pillars of the Republic: Common Schools and American Society, 1780–1860* (New York: Macmillan, 2011).

3. For more on the examples of police work, medicine, and environmental conservation, see John A. Eterno and Eli B. Silverman, "The New York City Police Department's Compstat: Dream or Nightmare?," *International Journal of Police Science and Management* 8 (2006): 218; Gwyn Bevan and Christopher Hood, "What's Measured Is What Matters: Targets and Gaming in the English Public Health Care System," *Public Administration* 84, no. 3 (2006): 517–538; Anne D. Guerry, Stephen Polasky, Jane Lubchenco, Rebecca Chaplin-Kramer, Gretchen C. Daily, Robert Griffin, Mary Ruckelshaus, et al., "Natural Capital and Ecosystem Services Informing Decisions: From Promise to Practice," *Proceedings of the National Academy of Sciences* 112, no. 24 (2015): 7348–7355.

4. Aldo Leopold, *A Sand County Almanac* (New York: Oxford University Press, 1949), 224–225.

Postscript

1. Jack Schneider and Pat Jehlen, "A Fairer Test Score Measure," *Boston Globe,* May 6, 2014.

2. For more on performance assessment, see Chapter 4.

3. Funding for the consortium was originally vetoed by Governor Charlie Baker. After a legislative override of the veto, the governor called back funds through midyear "9C" budget cuts in December 2016.

Acknowledgments

Several years ago, I was at work on what I believed would become my third book when I was drawn into, and consumed by, a new research project. That project eventually led to a different book—this one.

I was swept up in this work because I found it intellectually stimulating and politically important, particularly as the parent of a child just beginning her journey through the school system. But I was also deeply moved by the community in which this research was conducted—the city of Somerville, Massachusetts. Insofar as that is the case, any acknowledgment must begin with the people who make our 4.2 square miles feel quite a bit larger than it really is. I continue to be grateful to live in a city as diverse, vibrant, and engaged as ours.

I was also drawn into this project by forward-looking civic leaders who were willing to experiment. Mayor Joseph Curtatone, former superintendent Tony Pierantozzi, superintendent Mary Skipper, assistant superintendent Vince McKay, and members of the Somerville school committee have been consistently supportive of this work, as have been the district's principals, teachers, staff, and families. To say that this project would not have been possible without them, though a platitude, is also a fact.

Thanks are also due to a rotating corps of collaborators and assistants whose labors made much of this work possible, and whose insights made all of the work stronger. Among collaborators, particular thanks are due to Rebecca Jacobsen and Hunter Gehlbach—outstanding scholars who are as generous with their wisdom as they are with their friendship. Chapters 4 and 5, particularly, could not have been written without them. Special thanks are also due to Jared Cosulich, who served as the lead web developer on the project, as well as to the staff at the Somerville Family Learning Collaborative, who at every stage helped us include traditionally underrepresented members of the community.

Like the research project in general, this book is also the product of a small-scale solidarity movement. I am grateful to Jennifer Berkshire, Larry Cuban, Elizabeth Farley-Ripple, Scott Gelber, Bob Hampel, Ethan Hutt, Alain Jehlen, David Labaree, and Trey Popp for their careful reading of the manuscript. From my second-rate first drafts through the final edit, they kept me alert as both a scholar and a writer. I am especially grateful to my friend Sivan Zakai, who somehow never tires of offering clear, helpful, and encouraging feedback.

Given the subject of this book, it would be careless not to thank my teachers. From my first day of kindergarten through my last day of graduate school, I have been blessed with compassionate and committed teachers. As both a scholar and a person, I owe them a tremendous debt of thanks. The largest debt, of course, is owed to my first teachers—my mother and father. They taught me to read and write, to love ideas, to seek knowledge, and to work hard. More importantly, though, my parents taught me to laugh and to love, to live with integrity, and to seek justice. The hardest work of all has been showing them my gratitude, which is boundless.

Finally, I want to acknowledge the two loves of my life. My daughter Annabelle, for whom I want school to be a great joy, is the reason I wrote this book. Along with her mother, Katie—who just happens to be the best high school English teacher I know—she is the reason I get up each morning. They are the beginning, the middle, and the end. Everything else is just footnotes.

Index